BY THE SAME AUTHOR

Fiction:

Trespassers Welcome Here
The Diamond Lane
Motherhood Made a Man Out of Me

Nonfiction:

Big Girl in the Middle (coauthor, with Gabrielle Reece)
Generation Ex: Tales from the Second Wives Club

the stuff of life

A DAUGHTER'S MEMOIR

karen karbo

BLOOMSBURY

For Fiona
in whom the spirit of Granddad-in-Nevada lives on

Author's note: The names and identifying characteristics of some of
the people in this story have been changed.

Published by Bloomsbury, New York and London
Distributed to the trade by Holtzbrinck Publishers

All papers used by Bloomsbury Publishing are natural, recyclable
products made from wood grown in sustainable, well-managed forests.
The manufacturing processes conform to the environmental regulations
of the country of origin.

Library of Congress Cataloging-in-Publication Data
has been applied for.

ISBN 1-58234-183-4

First U.S. Edition 2003

1 3 5 7 9 10 8 6 4 2

Typeset by Palimpsest Book Production Limited,
Polmont, Stirlingshire, Scotland
Printed in the United States of America by RR Donnelley & Sons,
Harrisonburg, Virginia

I

The threat of dying ought to make you witty.
—Anatole Broyard

1

The call comes at eight-thirty on Sunday morning. I'm already at my desk in the sunroom, still wrapped in my coffee-stained bathrobe. White had seemed like such a good idea, so clean and spalike. A flock of irate starlings chitters madly in the fig trees outside, battling squirrels for overripe fruit. The figs are deep maroon, rudely testicular. The sunroom opens out from the living room, where Rachel, Danny, and Katherine, still in their pajamas, are lined up on the sofa, flannel thigh to flannel thigh, watching *Animal Planet*, and squabbling over the remote. The television sits on a blond wood trolley meant for kitchen use, on the other side of the French doors, about two feet from my head. The current segment tells the story of a blind Labrador retriever that looks like our own Lab pup. Katherine keeps shrieking, "Mom! Come look! It's Winston on TV!" By the time I push back my chair, pull my robe tighter around me, and take the six steps to the television, I miss it.

"In fifteen minutes I'm going to make banana waffles," I tell them, just as I've told them every fifteen minutes for the last hour, thinking in another fifteen minutes I'll be able to figure out how to rewrite in one month a novel about motherhood that's taken me six years to sell. I'm hoping there's an easy fix, a single, kitchen-sampler-size bit of wisdom that's eluding me. Of course, it's the easy fix that's eluding me. The problem is a common one. The main character, a thirty-five-year-old woman named Brooke, is too, quote unquote, whiny, a charge leveled against every educated female character in contemporary literature who has a good job, a man in her life, all her limbs, and an ax to grind. I don't know how to make Brooke any different: She is the alpha breadwinner in the marriage, has just given birth to baby Stella, and cannot get her adorable husband, Lyle, to stop eating Extra Hot Tamales and playing computer games. (Actually, Brooke doesn't mind much about the Extra Hot Tamales; they give Lyle's breath a nice, cinnamony tang.) Her life is one she chose; still, sleep deprivation is sleep deprivation and a slacker husband makes one feel as if one has another child underfoot. The first chapter is due on the desk of Lydia, my no-nonsense literary agent, tomorrow morning, to be included in a booklet she is taking to the Frankfurt Book Fair. Perhaps the Germans or the French will not find Brooke too whiny. Perhaps they will think she has esprit, or whatever the German word for that is.

From the ratty forest green and maroon brocade couch—a bad purchase; I was so focused on the ability of dark brocade to hide dirt, I forgot all about the two sofa-addicted dogs and their longish, thread-tugging toenails—Danny yells, "Katherine! That was my show." Danny's devotion to *Animal Planet* is complicated, all tied up with his attachment to his mother, my husband Daniel's second ex-wife, who lives in central California and has dedicated her life to raising llamas.

"It's a *commercial*," says Katherine, voice of disdain and reason. At seven she is tall, opinionated, censorious. She wants to be a judge or a horse trainer when she grows up. She already knows commercials are things that try to sell you stuff you don't want. What confuses her is that after she sees a commercial, she *does* want it.

"I like the commercials!"

"Mom, when are you going to make the waffles?" asks Katherine.

4

"I don't care for bananas," says Danny. Where did he pick up this quasi-British locution?

I also have the rewrite of a magazine piece due tomorrow. Two months earlier, I spent several days at the San Francisco School of Circus Arts with a cadre of Silicon Valley software wizards who take time out of their ninety-hour work weeks to learn trapeze flying. The story is for a business magazine, and my gymnastic directives for the rewrite involve strengthening the currently nonexistent connection between the rush/risk/gratification of trapeze flying and the rush/risk/gratification of launching a start-up in your garage.

When the phone rings, I'm startled. No one calls this early. I see my father's Nevada phone number on the Caller ID box and my insides are like dough being rolled flat by a baker who lifts weights.

It can only mean one thing. It can only mean he's dead or she's dead. DadandBev are the kind of people who are polite to a fault, people who feel it's rude to phone on the weekend before noon. They treat long distance as if it were something only to be broken out in an emergency, like the red fire extinguisher bolted to their kitchen wall.

"Kare?" came the voice, breathy, barely there.

Usually my father's voice is deep and hail-fellow-well-met, just this side of FM DJ quality, but he is not a talker, and his telephone voice is like a dinner jacket he puts on for a special occasion. When he makes a phone call, he always identifies himself by saying, "Dick Karbo here!"—a locution that sounds as if it belongs to a superhero receiving a call for help in a phone booth. But the man on the line this time is not "Dick Karbo here!," it's someone in the throes of an asthma attack, someone weak and gasping, calling me from a faulty telephone exchange in an undeveloped country. Someone far away.

I know this voice, even though I've only heard it once, twenty-three years before. The tears squeeze against the inside

5

of me. The afternoon my mother went into a coma, two days before she died, my father called on the house phone of the sorority house where I lived my freshman year at the University of Southern California. It was one phone used by about a hundred girls. I answered it more than most girls, who had their own phones in their rooms. My father was only forty-six then, but it was the same breathlessness, the same helpless mewl. These days, people barely consider forty-six middle-aged.

I say the same thing now that I said then. "Oh Dad, oh my daddy."

Now as then, this is his cue to hand the phone over to someone who could speak. This is one of those elegant matching scenes that would show up in a critically acclaimed movie. My dad, weeping and gasping with the same bad news, handing over the phone to a dry-eyed female. When my mother went into her coma, it was Ennie, her older sister, who had the honor. With Bev, my stepmother, my father's second wife, it was Elsie, the neighbor next door. Ennie and Elsie—even their names are similar.

"Beverly passed away last night," Elsie says. "In her sleep they think. From the looks of it, it was in her sleep. Dick found her this morning. The police and the coroner are here now."

"Oh God," I said. "The coroner? Why?" My poor dad, so private he doesn't even like having someone in to clean the house. The starlings are still out there chittering on the wires. The kids, who now must be told, have switched over to *Power Puff Girls*. Soon they'll want their waffles again. They'll interrupt me on the phone, and I'll have to tell them that unless someone is bleeding from a major artery, it's rude to interrupt. My dad would continue to hold to the rules, even in the face of death.

I try not to get ahead of myself, but already, at the mention of the coroner, I fear that it's not just bad, but also horrible.

You must know this about DadandBev: They were the

perfect Greatest Generation couple. They were neat and thrifty. They planned for the future. When thinking about moving to Boulder City, Nevada, from reasonable Southern California they consulted the *Farmer's Almanac* so they could visit Boulder City during the hottest week of the year. That way, when it was 115 in the shade three months out of the year, they would not be surprised. They didn't make mistakes, or any that I or my stepsiblings could see. They had no friends and few acquaintances, the mess of human relationships being too much for them. They were reliably judgmental. They were monolithic; they never appeared to disagree. They were the only two people I knew who thought President Reagan was too liberal.

They left reasonable Southern California, where they had lived collectively for one hundred years, because a law was passed raising the cigarette tax. As lifelong chain-smokers, they felt discriminated against. They thought it was fascism.

They also thought any form of gun control was fascism. They said things like "An armed society is a polite society." They had enough weapons to outfit the revolutionary army of a small country, but kept them locked in a big safe: shotguns, a rifle or two, a dozen handguns, both revolvers and semiautomatics, my father's collection of things that didn't fire anymore but were a triumph of design, and Bev's tiny revolver from the pre-panty-hose era that a "lady" was supposed to keep tucked in the top of her nylon stockings.

While Elsie talks about her role in the drama as people like to do, I remember when DadandBev were younger and healthy, back in the 1980s, when they still lived in reasonable Southern California and hadn't yet retired to Boulder City, with its two inches of rain a year and sun so fierce it can burn the part in your hair in the time it takes to find your car in the vast Costco parking lot. They sat around the dining room table in their house in San Juan Capistrano, chain-smoking and drinking vodka martinis, his with three cocktail onions—an indulgence. My dad, who has something Clint Eastwood about him, lanky and fit, squint-eyed and calm, suddenly said, apropos of something I hadn't been paying attention to, "If I ever get so I can't take care of myself, just take me out to the desert and shoot me." He was six-two, his weight was 175, his blood pressure 110/70. He could still fit into his Army Air Corps leather jacket. He could say something like this, then. I wondered if it went the same for Bev, and that's why the coroner was there. Bev suffered a number of back surgeries over the years, and a stroke, from which she'd partially recovered. Still, I knew she lived in pain.

But no, no. It's standard procedure, says Elsie. When a death is unexpected, the coroner always shows up. My father had to make a report. The tears find the right way out and tip over the rims of my eyes. My dad, oh my daddy. Women outlive men by nine years and here was my dad burying his second beloved wife.

2

I switch off the phone and stumble to the basement, where my adorable second husband, Daniel, the father of Rachel and Danny Jr., is in his lair playing computer games. Daniel is what one of my friends calls a cuddlebum; he's tall, with comely shoulders and blue-green eyes the color of the Caribbean. He reminds me of the boys I knew growing up in Southern California who tooled around the neighborhood with their bleached blond hair on their Sting-Ray bikes with seats made out of some fancy vinyl that sparkled wickedly in the sun.

This is a typical Sunday morning for us: the kids watching TV, the wife trying to work while within earshot of the kids, the husband hiding in the basement on his computer. It will be the source of considerable friction in the future—why, for example, am I both working and promising to fix the kids banana waffles while he's blissfully absorbed in killing and looting imaginary monsters—but we are newly married and so far I don't mind. When I come downstairs in tears, he hops up from his chair without a thought and wraps his arms around me. They were the first thing I noticed about him, his arms. They looked as if they belonged to a baseball player. This is what Daniel excels at, leaping up at the drop of a hat and wrapping me in his arms. It doesn't sound like much, but he is the first person who ever did this for me, and so I am grateful.

"Bev is dead." It's the first time I've said the words aloud, and

I feel as if I've uttered some spell that should never be uttered, for fear of what it will unleash.

Daniel rocks me back and forth in his baseball-player arms and says, "Shhhh. It's all right. It'll be all right."

"It's Bev. But *still*."

"I know. It doesn't matter."

He means it doesn't matter that I never liked her.

Daniel searches the Internet for the least expensive flight from Portland to Las Vegas, the closest airport to Boulder City, while I attack the laundry, make phone calls, send the kids to clean their rooms, make lists. I'll need to use the money I was saving to pay our quarterly taxes in order to buy two full-price airplane tickets.

I cry throughout the day but I'm not devastated; the relationship between me and Bev had been one of mutual, extra-polite disdain. The pitiless note taker perched in one corner of my heart observes that the sadness is not so overwhelming that it can't be categorized: Part of me is sad for my father, and part of me is sad for myself—self-pity, pure and simple. I weep at the news in part because the death of Bev means the end of DadandBev, an entity I have come to rely on to hold down the far reaches of my life, like the guy wires holding down a circus tent.

I weep because now my father will be a widower and bereft, probably until he dies. I don't want things to change. I don't have *time* for things to change. I don't have the money.

My own mother always kept a few hundred dollars of rainy-day money beneath her tray of lipsticks in her bathroom drawer. We lived in Whittier, however, a suburb of Los Angeles, and in my child's mind it almost never rained. I wondered what rainy day she meant. "In case someone dies," she said. Her parents weren't alive, but she had Ennie and Dudu, her way-older sisters in Detroit. Mom also had Ennie's daughter, Irene, and her husband, Dick Mahoney. Mom called them the

Nutty Mahoneys behind their back. I called them Aunt Irene and Uncle Dick. The Nutty Mahoneys lived not far from us in another sun-bleached Southern California suburb.

In the afternoon I sit the kids down and tell them that Gramma-in-Nevada died. Their reactions are somber, but confused. Gramma-in-Nevada was Katherine's stepgramma, or Not-Real-Gramma, as she insisted on calling her, despite my reminding her that, while Bev was not her biological gramma, she was most certainly "real." For Rachel and Daniel, Bev was their step-step-gramma. (Is there even such a thing?) The kids had met her only once at Daniel's and my wedding—the middle of January, an unprecedented Portland snowstorm, DadandBev stuck here for days, general parental displeasure at my boneheadedness in planning a wedding during such bad weather—but had been privy to plenty of uncharitable humor at Bev's expense.

Daniel and I hosted perhaps too many hysterical episodes at the dinner table during which I regaled them with how Bev used to begin fixing dinner at five o'clock on the dot, but didn't get it on the table until after nine, due to the influence of the martini hour on dinner preparations. When dinner was finally served, it would be something you could toss together in about fifteen minutes: a single roasted chicken wing, a sprig of limp, over-microwaved broccoli, and a freezer-burned sourdough roll. After the ninety seconds it took to polish this off, Bev would ask in her deep Lauren Bacall–with–bronchitis voice, "Has everyone had enough to eat?" I was always afraid to say "Are you kidding? I'm about ready to pass out from hunger," because Bev was actually proud of her cooking. DadandBev were famous noneaters, and if you ever wanted to lose weight, a week at the Palace of the Golden Sofa, as we called their fancy triple-wide, was as good as any spa. Weights and measures are not my strong suit, and at home in Portland, every so often on leftover night, I'd miscalculate and serve up plates with a single piece of sausage and three curls of fusilli and ask, "Has everyone had enough to eat?" It had become a private family joke of such proportions that one risked a milk-shooting-out-of-the-nose episode. And now that the originator of the joke, who would not have found it one bit funny, was dead, the kids didn't quite know what to do.

They sit lined up on the ratty green and maroon brocade sofa. Danny reaffirms, cautiously, "But she wasn't your real mom, was she?"

"She was like a mom," says Rachel, rolling her eyes at Danny's lame remark. Every remark anyone makes is lame. Rachel is fourteen. Surliness oozes from every pore. She is the daughter of Daniel's first ex-wife. "Just like Karen is like our mom. One of our moms."

I say, "I had Bev as a mom longer than I had my own mom."

The looks on their faces are the same ones they got when they were trying to do the times tables in their heads.

"It's still *sad*," says Katherine. "Especially for Grandpa-in-Nevada."

DadandBev, now just Dad, live in a retirement community overlooking Lake Mead. To get there you drive southeast on Boulder Highway from McCarran International Airport in Las Vegas, through Henderson, the fastest growing suburb in the country, past casinos that sit just off the freeway, cheek by jowl with shopping malls and Super Kmarts, past enormous developments of tract homes, all with red-tiled roofs with the same square bald spot, over which the requisite air conditioner is bolted, past Old Las Vegas, a resort that went belly up a few decades ago—the huge sign bleached beyond recognition—up and over Railroad Pass, past the casino of the $4.99 Sunday buffet, with a huge electronic billboard that advertises cheap rooms and loose slots. The Railroad Pass Casino was the closest to Las Vegas DadandBev would venture. It is white stucco, from an era when the casinos looked like Los Angeles apartment buildings and not as if they'd been transported from some European street. Sometimes DadandBev ate at the coffee shop there, where my father ordered liver and onions. Afterward, Bev played the slots with a Ziploc bag full of dimes she kept especially for the occasion. When the Ziploc bag was empty, they went home.

This is the last outpost of gambling before you get to Boulder City, where gambling is prohibited. Boulder City was built by the government in the 1930s to house the workers constructing the Hoover Dam. Even though this is the dead middle of the desert, replete with diamondback rattlers, oily creosote that gives off a diesel smell whenever it rains, and the nose-hair-singeing heat, the city fathers built brick houses and planted elms trees to make the workers feel as if they were still in Kansas. Down the hill from the little brick houses, with their aggressively watered lawns and rose bushes, is a main street with a few exhausted-looking motels that look as if they never hosted anyone but desperate characters on the lam; a curio shop with an extraterrestrial section; and a coffee shop that serves overcooked hamburgers and has written on the wall facing the highway, in green letters bleached by the sun, "BEST FOOD BY A DAM SITE." There are no cafés to speak of. Starbucks has shops in Kuwait, but not in Boulder City. The nearest bookstore is a Borders Books a good twenty miles away in Henderson. There are two supermarkets, across the highway from each other, crowded on the weekends with people camping at Lake Mead, purple with sunburn, buying cases of Bud Lite and toddler-sized bags of Ruffles.

DadandBev loved Nevada because there is no income tax and it was easy to get a concealed weapon permit. They also loved the nose-hair-singeing heat. My father found Southern California too damp, promoting the growth of things like lawns, which he hated to mow. In Nevada it was perfectly acceptable to have a yard of rocks punctuated here and there by cacti, and he did. When they bought the triple-wide, my father marveled at his own decision. "Can you believe I'm living in a trailer?"

There are trailers and there are trailers. The Palace of the Golden Sofa—the living room was dominated by the sofas of my girlhood, an expensive, outdated gold brocade sofa and a loveseat purchased when my mother was in her teak-and-earth-tones phase—sat on a steep hill, up against some red and sand-colored mountains. Out the kitchen window was a million-dollar view of lapis-lazuli blue Lake Mead, and beyond it Fortification Hill, a plateau rising up on the other side of the lake, canted at an eight-degree angle, an extinct volcano whose sides seem to change color as the sun moved through the sky. In the evening, when the colors had gone out of the rocks, it reminded me of the way a hat sat on the head of Frank Sinatra, that jaunty angle.

When Daniel and I finally arrive at the Palace, it's after one A.M. Dad is waiting up for us. He greets us at the back door, the door just off the carport that everyone comes in and out of. He wears beige Lee jeans and a rust-colored golf sweater. He has about the longest legs in the world. When he was in his twenties he wore those pleated pants made famous by Gary Cooper and Cary Grant. Woodrow, the black miniature dachshund, named for Woodrow Call in *Lonesome Dove*, my father's favorite book, is tucked under one arm.

"Thank you, thank you very much for coming," he says, as he might thank someone for attending a business meeting called at the last minute. He looks down at the dog and rubs the top of his knobby head with his middle two fingers. On his pinky, my dad wears a braided gold band that had belonged to his mother. I like the pinky ring; it makes him seem more showy than he is. I stare at the top of Dad's head. It's too tan. There are spots from the sun that look as if they require the attention of a dermatologist.

14

I think perhaps there is something wrong, wronger than the death of Bev, but I am leery of this kind of hindsight. People are too liberal with it when they tell their stories, like so much salt on movie popcorn. *I knew something was wrong. I knew that would happen.* It's an odd human need, like the satisfaction we take in accurately predicting the weather. In the end, the blizzard arrives, the bad things happen, and having known about it ahead of time makes no difference at all. But somehow it comforts us, thinking that we saw it coming. So I've developed the mental-snapshot habit. When something strikes me as strange, I make a point of saying to myself, "Okay, this isn't right. Remember it. You were standing here at X, looking at Y, and thinking Z. Something's going on here. And if something weird eventuates, let the record reflect." Sometimes I write it down. Evidence.

Dad and I saw each other every eighteen months or so. For years on end, he didn't seem to age. He'd had the same hairline since I was a child, a peninsula of coarse, dark, wavy hair with identical coves of bald pate on either side, and had weighed 175 pounds since before I was born. He had cheekbones you could hang a picture from, and an impressive jaw that looked like it had come straight from a natural history display on modern man—features Bev used to called "Baltic," although I never quite knew what that meant. Dad's forebears were from L'vov, a thirteenth-century Eastern European city that has been under the rule of Austria, the Soviet Union, and Germany, off and on, and is now part of the Ukraine. But the Russians and Poles I knew were strapping, round, and blond. My father was olive-complected, bony, and brooding. A Jewish friend, upon meeting my father, was convinced there was, as she put it, "a Hebrew in the woodpile." When I told my father, he looked perplexed. "Could be," he said, neither intrigued nor offended. His personal history held less interest for him than who was who in Hollywood.

15

At that moment, standing in the back door of the triple-wide, his little black dachshund tucked under his arm, he no longer looks like the voice behind "Dick Karbo here!" His age has caught up with him all at once, it seems. The hair he has left has gotten whiter. The lenses of his aviator glasses have gotten thicker. He looks as if something inside him has caved in, in a place no top-notch rescue squad could reach.

Dad leads us into the family room, separated from the kitchen by a wide Formica breakfast bar where he sits most of the time. His battle station. The two chairs attending the breakfast bar are chairs you might find in an office, with oak arms and padded seats of oatmeal tweed. They roll on casters, and beneath the bar is a Plexiglas mat, to ease in the rolling. This is Dad's kind of chair. He is not a lounger. He never owned an easy chair. When he is not in the utility room at his desk, bent over a pocket watch he's restoring for a local jeweler, or down at the train yard restoring a locomotive for the local railroad museum, he sits here. DadandBev ate all their meals here. He drank his second and third cup of coffee here, read here, and chain-smoked Marlboro cigarettes here. At five on the dot, "martoonie hour" would begin, and he and Bev would have their martoonies here; they rolled the chairs around to watch the evening news on the color set in the family room.

My father sits down in his chair, the one closest to the plate-glass window that looks out on to the strip of backyard— all gravel and a few cacti and a shallow circle of concrete my father fills with water from the hose every other day, which attracts desert cottontails, quail, lizards, and coyote—and I sit in what was Bev's chair. Daniel is forced to sit where I used to sit, on the brown-and-beige-plaid love seat, away from the action, but with a better view of the mountains out the big window.

Daniel starts right in with the platitudes, all the worthless things that somebody's got to say. We are sorry, Dick. It must have been such a shock. At least she didn't suffer much. All of that. Daniel is the first one of my friends, boyfriends, or husbands to call my father "Dick." Everyone else has always called him Mr. Karbo, to keep from cracking up. He was also the first one to take kindly to Bev, even though, as with all my friends, boyfriends, and former husband, the reverse was not the case. It was well known that Bev liked almost no one save Dad.

Daniel had only met DadandBev once before we were married, at the wedding of Toni, the youngest daughter of Sadie and Lou, the family friends of my parents who'd stayed in touch with my dad after the death of my mother. The wedding was in September, at a Hilton in the San Fernando Valley. DadandBev drove over from Boulder City, and Daniel and I flew down from Portland.

All of the out-of-town guests were invited to brunch the day after the wedding, before the bride and groom flew off on their Hawaiian honeymoon. Daniel and I were seated near the end of the long table, across from a couple we'd never met. DadandBev had been placed at the very end, next to Daniel.

For some reason Bev was in a wheelchair that weekend. No one ever told me why. I assumed it was because she'd had twenty years worth of terrible back trouble, including a number of harrowing ten-hour surgeries, a few of which involved reaching her spine through the front of her instead of the back. She sometimes walked with a cane. Then she would be feeling better, and the cane would disappear. The wheelchair was a new development, though. Still, pulling Dad aside and stage-whispering, "Oh my God, why is Bev in a wheelchair?" would only reaffirm my reputation as the family hysteric, so I just acted as if it were the most normal thing.

Outside it was warm and smoggy, and everyone suffered mildly from a champagne hangover, and the scrambed eggs placed in front of us were flat, as if they'd been cooked in the manner of hash browns, and the toast was too toasted on one side and not toasted enough on the other. My father wore a beige checked shirt with pearl buttons and a bolo tie. He ate in silence, perfectly happy not to speak at all. It perhaps goes without saying that if my dad wasn't a talker, he was hardly a small talker. He was happy to attend to his eggs. No whiff of social discomfort emanated from him. Daniel and I made some low-grade small talk with the couple across from us until we discovered we were all scuba divers. The relief at knowing we'd arrived at a subject we could milk for the rest of the meal livened us up, like being halfway through a multiple-choice test, glancing down to the end of the page, and seeing you know all the answers. We started in on places where we'd dived and debated whether the Caribbean, with its pretty tropicals, was better than the Pacific, with its enormous manta rays and hammerhead sharks.

Daniel has a voluble nature. If such a thing were measurable, I'd say that Daniel likes to talk to the exact degree to which my father doesn't like to. Daniel starting telling the couple about a trip we'd made to Palau, how on a drift dive at a place called Peleliu Corner, known for its kickass currents, we got pulled out over the reef that lay submerged at the end of Peleliu Island, and out into the Philippine Sea, next stop Manila, about two hundred miles away. Divers love a good getting-pulled-out-to-sea story. Just as the conversation achieved liftoff—with the couple stepping all over each other's words in a rush to tell about a similar incident off the coast of Belize—Daniel made a joke and haw-haw-hawed too loud.

Suddenly, Bev spoke, Lauren Bacall–with–bronchitis deep. "Daniel, would you mind letting someone else get a word in? Not everyone cares what you think, and other people would like to talk too, you know."

That was the thing. We didn't know. Bev hadn't made any of those trying-to-get-a-comment-in gestures that people make during a group discussion, no finger in the air, no sentence poised to leave her mouth, then dying on her lips, nothing. The conversation stopped dead. Daniel's ears turned red with embarrassment. We sat. Bev was a handsome woman, with large chocolate-drop eyes and a slight pug nose, but her natural facial expression was a frowny pout, like you sometimes see on French actresses who were popular in the 1970s, but became more and more disgruntled-looking as they aged. We waited in perfect silence for Bev to get her word in edgewise. Finally, she sighed, as if to say, why does the burden of conversation always rest on me? "Does anyone else find these eggs too dry?"

Daniel had been publicly humiliated, but he was not one to bear a grudge, even the kind of minor ones that are the basis for much family hostility. He'd had no compunction about flying to Boulder City at a moment's notice to do what needed to be done on the occasion of the death of a woman he barely knew, who had never been anything but hostile to him. Sometimes I think Daniel's willingness to dive headfirst into the muck of life without giving it another thought was the reason I married him.

Dad continues to pet the dog. He lights a cigarette, hacks a little. He holds his cigarette in the crotch of his first and second fingers, stares down at the placemat on the breakfast bar. It's one-thirty A.M. I know because over the pantry is a naval clock that chimes twice on the half hour. My father is a clock fanatic; there's an big-faced clock in sync with the atomic clock on the wall at the end of the breakfast bar and a mantel clock on the console table behind the sofa. It has a big brass pendulum that goes *tick-tock*, a sound from a children's song about telling time.

The dead of night in Boulder City is creepy. Three of America's great deserts, the Mojave, the Sonoran, and the Great Basin, all meet here. People come here from all over the globe to experience world-class heatstroke, to marvel at the red canyons and the desolation. Without irrigation and air-conditioning, no modern people could live here. In the middle of the black night, sitting in the Palace of the Golden Sofa, I'm reminded of a sci-fi movie where the tiny human settlement, always filmed in long shot, its few lights twinkling hopefully in the vast barrenness, conveys the message: What in the hell are they doing? Can't they see no one is meant to live there? Their scientific curiosity, or greed, or some fatal tragic flaw, is what got them there, and will assure their demise.

I slouch in Bev's chair, roll around on the casters. I can hear the clock ticking from its spot on the sofa console. I can smell my father's cigarette. I am aware, suddenly, of my bad posture. Is there any daughter on earth who isn't transformed into a sixteen-year-old when she sits down to have a serious discussion with her father? Some British writer, maybe it was Auden, had a theory that a person's mental and emotional age is set at birth; this accounts for all the four-year-olds that seem as if they're forty, and kicky fifty-eight-year-olds who can pass for thirty-five. I'd like to extend this theory: when it comes to our parents, we reach some teen age and there we stay, Peter Pan–like, deep into middle age and beyond.

"And there's something else, babe." I know that tone. Even though it's weary and a little high, not my father's voice at all. I take a quick inventory: What have I done?

"Have you joined the NRA yet?" *Have I joined the NRA?* It's the middle of the night, his second wife has just died, and this is in the forefront of his mind? It's something he's asked me about twice a year for the last fifteen years, ever since I learned to shoot a gun. I have never had the courage to say, When hell freezes over; I always say I've been too busy, and he always says to put it on my list and I always say I will, and that's the end of it.

Then he says, "I don't know how long you're planning on staying now, but I also have a doctor's appointment in two weeks. I seem to have this growth in my chest."

"A growth? What kind of growth?"

"They don't know. It's just an office procedure. But they said I need to bring someone to drive me home. If you're going to be around, of course."

"Where is it, the growth?"

"It's sitting on a nerve that goes up into my head, gives me a headache, but just on the one side. I can't sleep on my left side. It's like sleeping on a golf ball. And it's making my voice like this. They think maybe it's a cyst."

He taps a spot on his chest over his heart.

3

The Palace of the Golden Sofa has a guest room with a too-soft double bed where Daniel and I sleep. An orange halogen streetlight shines through the thin curtains. The bedroom set is cherry, built sometime early in the last century. The set belonged to Bev. One of the interesting things about our family is the way my father's things belonged to DadandBev, and by extension, all the children, but Bev's things belonged to Bev alone. Although no one ever said so, I believe this was my father's idea of chivalry.

Walnut veneer paneling on the walls of every room, including the guest room, is meant to give the place a cozy feeling, and to compensate for the fact that whenever you close the doors, it sounds as if you were slamming the trunk of the car. The wall over the cherry desk is covered with family photographs, documenting DadandBev's brilliant marriage: a black-and-white head shot of my father in his World War II pilot's uniform; a black-and-white of similar vintage of Bev in her stewardess uniform; DadandBev on the deck of the *Ballarat Bay*, one of the powerboats Dad was restoring around the time they began dating—they are in their late forties, thin, happy, kind of gorgeous, with their matching angular bone structures—and one taken during a lifeboat drill aboard a ship during a cruise to the Panama Canal, when they're older, with orange life vests hunched up around their ears.

I warranted one studio baby picture—black and white, a curl

in the middle of my forehead that stuck up like a whipped egg white, a coerced expression of glee—and my college graduation portrait, taken in the late seventies during a phase when I was letting my hair grow out. I used to think this portrait alone shouted to the world that I was motherless; no mother would let her child have an important picture taken with growing-out hair. My stepbrother, Martin, earned a snapshot from his wedding and a formal Christmas picture with him, his wife, Chrissi, and their three girls. There were no pictures of Liz, my stepsister, and only one of Nora, my other stepsister, taken in her early twenties, just before she died.

Once ensconced in the too-soft double bed, Daniel and I lay there shoulder to shoulder.

"You know it's probably lung cancer," I say to Daniel.

"We don't know that," he says. His parents are both healthy photo buffs who ski and kayak and always order the biggest margaritas on the menu.

"Yes, I'd say we do know that. He's been a two-pack-a-day man for eight hundred years. He's had that terrible cough for years. It's a lump in his chest, a lump. What else could it be?"

"The doctors said a cyst. And why would the doctor say a cyst if he didn't think that's what it was? He probably would have said, 'We don't know,' or, 'We can't tell until we take a look at you.'"

"The doctors don't know jack. They try to claim medicine is a science, but it's only scientific principles applied to an art. Half the time they don't know what they're doing."

Our feet hang off the edge, and we try to decide whether to turn on the electric blanket, which is as thin as something issued by a penitentiary suffering from budget cuts. In the same way oatmeal is merely a vehicle for butter and brown sugar, this pathetic blanket is merely a conduit for heating wires, wires that I am sure will cause a fire or alter our brain waves in their electromagnetic field, or whatever the hell it is people who are good enough to be concerned about these sorts of things are always on about. Naturally DadandBev *would* have electric blankets. They smoked their heads off, ate red meat, butter, and whole milk, glanced at a green vegetable about once a month, and were in all ways against everything conventional wisdom said was good for you.

We decide against turning on the blanket, and opt for snuggling. At six feet, Daniel is the first man I've slept with who's considerably taller than me. I fit against his front, spoon-style, just right.

Once the sun inches over the hills, around six A.M. this time of year, the metal sides of the triple-wide start creaking, expanding in the heat. I lie in bed for a while, listening. *Tick-tick-tick.* Daniel hugs the other side of the mattress, his back turned to me, sound asleep despite the heat and examination-room brightness.

Outside, some desert bird is screeching. I get out of bed, pull on some shorts and a T-shirt. It's too hot for a bathrobe. I sometimes thought DadandBev were like a pair of industrious rodents in a fairy tale, he in a blue jacket, she in a pink straw hat, having made a sweet, nicely furnished mouse house in a tin can. Other times, this being one of them, I have felt as if we were refugees from an early Sam Shepard play, a family of malcontents bumping into each other in a trailer in the middle of the desert. The difference between us and the Shepard play, however, is that no one hollered or held forth or waved a knife around out of sheer boredom.

My dad is already sitting at the breakfast bar in his gold velour robe, reading the newspaper and drinking the world's weakest coffee, as if it were a regular day, and not the first day of the rest of his life without Bev. He has set another place, with a teacup and saucer, and a teaspoon on a folded white napkin. It is for Bev. It is for whoever wakes up first. It is force of habit. I pour myself a cup of coffee, reach over the breakfast bar, and refill his cup without asking if he wants more. My father never says no to coffee. DadandBev always made a fresh pot of Folger's every morning in their old Bunn-O-Matic, then ran water through the coffeemaker over the same exhausted grounds all day long. By the third or fourth time, what came out was a hot cup of roasted desert water, rusty-pipe brown. My father liked a cup of this in the afternoon, after a stint at the rail yard, or a walk with the dog up on the hill behind the Palace.

Before, when I came to visit DadandBev, my father and I would spend an hour or two of an afternoon hiking in the ocher-colored hills that rose up behind the Palace, on the other side of the cement wash that flooded once a summer, gushing with fresh thunderstorm rain. We scrabbled around, looking for priceless gold nuggets or rare Indian artifacts that were going to allow us to retire. The fact that my father was already retired was immaterial; "retired" for us meant never having to worry about anything ever again. He used to say to me, "Stick with me, babe, you'll be wearing onions as big as diamonds." We thought that was hilarious. Up in the hills we occasionally found a rock with a thread of glinty mica in it. It looked like gold, but it was always either crapite or leaverite, as in "leave 'er right there." This private joke was between me and him. But I wouldn't. I wouldn't leave the crapite there, or the leaverite. I'd fill my fists with rocks, then leave them outside on DadandBev's old redwood picnic table. The next time I would come to visit, I'd find them lined up in a row on the edge of the patio. He never got rid of them; he called it my "collection." When we'd come in from our hike, parched and dusty in the heat, my father refreshed himself with a cup of the world's weakest coffee.

It occurs to me, sitting with my dad in Bev's spot, that now it is just him and me. Me and my dad, my dad and me. It's the childhood fantasy of every Daddy's girl. I imagine that once he is able to recover a bit, we'll have more hikes into the hills in search of crapite, we'll guzzle gallons of weak coffee. We'll share books. I'll get him on the Internet and we'll e-mail daily. I'll visit as often as I can. I'll drag him into Las Vegas. Yes, I know he claims to hate it, but with me as tour guide, he'll love it. I begin to see that one could view this in a positive light, without applying any phony positive spin. Bev died in her sleep, a very lucky death. She also died first. It could have easily gone the other way, should have gone the other way, women routinely living nine years longer than men.

I ask my dad what needs to be done today. Anything? Anything at all? I try to think of the most odious task, the one my father would want to do least. Does anyone need to be called and given the news? "No, not anyone I can think of," he says. We are not only a small family, we are an isolated one: DadandBev had almost no friends.

"I do have some errands. Beverly had some library books out." At this he drops his head, rests his chin on his chest. He takes a few big gulps of air, trying to compose himself, trying not to sob. I stare at a mole beside his ear, at the earpiece of his eyeglasses, hooked over his ear. I think about the growth in his chest, what feels like a golf ball to him, in there.

I say, "Dad, please. Please cry. It's okay. This is *me* here."

What in the hell am I talking about? Crying in front of me is the last thing my father wants to do. Next to the right to bear arms, my father's most cherished value is bucking up. He trained me to be a trouper from an earlier age. That I later got myself a little psychotherapy and became someone who was able to fall apart and weep into a shredded Kleenex in a restaurant or on an airplane is a another story, one my father did not know. In his head, I was still the four-year-old who jumped out of a tree house and snagged a nostril on a nail, nearly tearing off her entire nose. My mother fainted, like they do in the movies, while I remained as dry-eyed as a paid assassin. Nor did I cry when the various childhood vaccinations came my way, choosing instead to stare down the syringe as the doctor plunged it into my arm. Nor when one of the boys who lived in our apartment building on Hazeltine Avenue in the San Fernando Valley burned my arm with his mother's iron, revenge for my having slugged his little brother in the stomach, making him cry in public out by the swimming pool. There were no girls living in this apartment building, except a few teenagers who occasionally appeared in their two-pieces to tan by the pool. There were lots of wild boys, though, boys who would tease Stevie Director, my beloved, who was the best colorer in kindergarten, and whose mother, an observant Jew, put up with my request for salami and butter sandwiches. I loved him and thus was forced to defend him. He was small, and had a lisp. His mother told him that Jewish people "fight with our words, not with our fists." We were Episcopalian, so I felt free to pop anyone with impunity. Boys slugged by me were already being instructed by their fathers not to hit girls, which must have left them puzzled, since I was twice their size and already knew that a good punch meant leaning into it with your shoulder. I got my hair pulled, usually in retaliation. I got my instep stomped on. There was the famous iron burn.

I was so well known for my stoicism that someone wrote on the cinder-block wall that ran behind the parking lot of our apartment building: YOU CAN SLUG KAREN KARBO AND SHE DON'T EVEN CRY! He wrote it with green sticks of ice plant, whose flowers bloomed like pink sea anenomes all over the hills in the San Fernando Valley. I hear that now the ice plant is considered invasive, single-handedly taking over the sandy soils of the subtropical world. We used it like sidewalk chalk; the juice inside stained the cement. This was my father's favorite story about me, how he came home one evening from work and found this graffiti on the wall behind the parking lot. He pulled his white Falcon into one of the spots, and there it was right over the hood of his car. He told this story to Katherine when she was five and liked to weep loudly and passionately, like a girl who's got some Slavic blood in her should; she was nonplussed. Also, I don't think she believed it. She's seen me cry plenty.

No way is my dad about to have a sob-a-thon. No way. He lifts his head, sighs deeply, returns to his newspaper. When he turns the page, he flattens the new page by swatting the paper against the top of his bald head. I watch him do this. I watch him sip his coffee. I watch him light a cigarette. In the other room, the clock on the sofa console tick-tocks. The last time I saw him he had been trying to quit; he chewed Nicorette and kept his Marlboros stashed in a cupboard. Now it was the crack of dawn on the day after his wife's death and he was on his fourth cigarette. The only other time he'd tried to quit was before my mother died. The day she died he started back up. Now, I'm sure, it's What the hell!

Just behind him, out the double-paned plate-glass window with its gray sunshade, I see a ground squirrel drinking from the pond. His little tail curls back up over his back, revealing a thick white furred stripe. It looks insufferable out there, already, bright and hot. It's October 11, and the people at the dry cleaners are still reminding customers not to leave their clean clothes in the car, or the plastic bag will melt and glue itself to your best dress. In the grassy parks, of which Boulder City has many, the slides aren't metal but brown plastic. Otherwise children would burn the back of their legs sliding down. The pond sits nestled among some rocks, in the shade of a small creosote bush, a miniature oasis.

On the parking strip that runs parallel to the playground of the small parochial school attended by Danny and Katherine there is a tight row of ornamental cherry trees that put out loads of Pepto-Bismol pink blossoms every year. There is one tree in the row that, for whatever reason, suffers; it is shorter than the others, has fewer branches, and half of them bloom white. I'm no horticultural expert, but offhand I'd say the graft did not take, that one side of the tree couldn't be made to bloom pink.

This one is the literal metaphor for my family tree, blooming along with the rest, but stunted and funky. Two years after my mother died in the spring of 1975, my Dad married Bev, his old college sweetheart. They'd dated at USC until she dropped out during her senior year to become a stewardess with Western Airlines. How they got together, why she dropped out, whether my dad's placid heart was stomped to bits all remain a mystery (mystery and obfuscation being the norm in this family as in many others).

I do know he took Bev into the Mojave Desert and taught her to shoot a pistol, one of my father's favorite courtship rituals. I have an odd collection of curling black-and-white snapshots of DadandBev out in the Mojave looking dusty and in love, both with the unexpected, crazy-eyed look of someone who's just shot a tin can off a post, and of my father and my mother at the same spot with, for all I know, the same pistols. Joan is not looking dusty and in love and crazy-eyed, but long-suffering. She was copper-haired, freckled within an inch of being part of an alien race. In one picture, she's looking desperate for some roadhouse where she can have a Coors 102, find a pay phone, and call a friend. She's looking desperate to zip on over to Vegas and set up camp at the craps table at the Tropicana. She's looking like, *Get me out of here.* My father loved my mother, her charm, her ease with people, her laugh so loud it could scare birds off a wire, but these sets of pictures remind me of the famous lobster scene in *Annie Hall*, only my mother is the subsequent humorless girlfriend, the one with whom Woody Allen tries to duplicate the same good time he had trying to boil lobsters one afternoon with Diane Keaton, the one in the short shorts who says, "What are you making such a big deal about? They're only lobsters." The difference is, my mother was the one who liked what other people would consider a good time (partying, drinking, card playing, dancing, gossiping, cooking, eating) and DadandBev, two peas in a pod, were perfectly happy out there in the desert, with their weapons, the silence, and the heat.

On the wall of the guest room in the Palace of the Golden Sofa is another black-and-white photograph of Bev in her stewardess uniform, posed before a DC-3. She was so handsome at nineteen that Western Airlines hired her to appear in their print advertising. She wore red lipstick that reads black in the picture, her cap at a clever angle that bespeaks sass, which in real life she either had never possessed or had had stomped out of her by life, like sparks that leap out of the fireplace and are mashed out by the zealous homeowner. Bev met her first husband, Mr. Barry, on a night flight full of drunken revelers traveling from Los Angeles to Las Vegas. He wooed her by rescuing her from the tush-pinching of the other male passengers. He was also a drinker with schemes that never panned out, but he was charming. The family claim to fame was his father's stint as the dentist of FDR. After they were married, the Barrys moved to Haddonfield, New Jersey, and had three children, *boom boom boom*: Martin, Nora, and Liz. When the children were eleven, nine, and seven, Mr. Barry, age thirty-seven, dropped dead of a brain aneurysm one morning while shaving before the bathroom mirror.

Meanwhile, on the other side of the country, in reasonable Southern California, lived the Karbos, Dick and Joan and their daughter, Karen, a small family that was about to get smaller. Neither one of my parents had their parents, who'd all met early deaths in ways that seem appropriate to their time. The grandfathers both were dashing ne'er-do-wells, one Polish, one Irish. The Pole, Viktor Karbowski, a formally trained structural engineer from Warsaw, with dreams of being a prospector, unceremoniously dropped Emilia, his convent-educated wife—petit point, Chopin études on the viola, five languages, training

30

in managing the help with kind firmness or firm kindness—and young son in Chicago, before taking off for Mongolia, where, presumably, he was going to find gold. Viktor sent his struggling family pictures of him posed beside a derailed Chinese train tipped over on its side. He was never heard from again. George Sharkey, the Irish grandfather, from whom my mother allegedly inherited her copper-colored hair and Irish gift of gab, was coming home from a bar one night in Ypsilanti, Michigan, where his wife, Maude Edna, ran a boardinghouse, stumbled on a train track, blacked out, and was run over.

As for the grandmothers, they never met, and the only thing they had in common was their refusal to have anything to do with doctors, and their subsequent deaths of treatable cancers. Maude Edna, who in pictures resembles Gertrude Stein, was hardworking, chapped of hand, and dull of spirit. She succumbed to a melanoma. Emilia, my father's mother (who rechristened herself "Luna of California" after she moved to Hollywood with my father and made a career for herself as a dress designer for the wives of directors, doctors, and financiers), was exotic, passionate, self-dramatizing, and tough tough tough. She died of uterine cancer, after refusing a hysterectomy. She was reputed to have bellowed, in her heavy Polish accent, "No man is messing with my parts!"

When my mother was diagnosed with brain cancer, she behaved in the modern way. There was no untoward bellowing, no resistance to the possible cures offered by modern medicine. She subjected herself to the disfiguring surgery, the slow fry of radiation and nauseating chemo, only to succumb as well.

My mother had two sisters, Julia and Lorraine, nicknamed Dudu and Ennie. Both were old enough to be her mother, and when my father remarried, so quickly after the early death of their baby sister, and did not spend every Sunday for the rest of his life weeping over her granite headstone, they stopped speaking to him. And because he had secretly found them hysterical and tedious, he happily allowed himself to stop being spoken to.

Thus, the new nuclear and extended family of DadandBev, formed in the summer of 1977, consisted of the newlyweds and their children. DadandBev were both only children. There were no aunties or uncles, no cousins twice removed. No daughters– or sons-in-law, not yet. Not many hands on deck, not enough people, really, to launch the production. As sports commentators often observe when analyzing the problems of a basketball team with strong starters and a losing record, the bench, sadly, was not deep.

Who came to my dad's aid the day his second wife died? Me, his only child, his last blood left in the world besides Katherine, my seven-year-old daughter. My husband, Daniel. Bev's eldest son, Martin. His wife, Chrissi. Bev's youngest daughter, Liz. Not even enough people to warrant putting the leaf in the dining room table.

4

At a quarter to eleven, the bell on the back door goes *trrring trring!* It sounds like a bell that belongs on the handlebars of a child's bike. Woodrow barks and tears around the living room and up and down the long hallway. It's Martin and Chrissi, huddled together on the metal platform—three steps up on one side, three steps down the other—that serves as the Palace's back porch. The back porch is just off the utility room. On one side are the washer and dryer, on the other, the desk where my father works on his watches. Above the desk, on a shelf about ten inches wide, my father built a model train. There's a miniature station, trees, a water tower, and even a tiny outhouse with a small man caught with the door open and his pants around his toothpick ankles. The shelf wasn't wide enough for a track that went round and round, so my father improvised. It's a switching yard, with six parallel tracks. An existentialist would have a field day with this arrangement. The perfectly painted rail cars don't go anywhere but forward and backward, forward and backward.

Martin shakes my dad's hand, grieving man to grieving man. At fifty he still looks like an Irish altar boy crossed with Bob Dylan in his prime, with dark hair that curls over his ears and forehead, and heavy-lidded, unreadable eyes, a pugilist's flat nose. Martin is the family's quiet genius. He has a brain for both music and science, but instead of going on to be the one to discover the cure for cancer (he has a researcher's temperament), he started a bluegrass band. He plays the mandolin, the pedal steel, the banjo, the guitar, and some other instruments I can never remember. For a living he manages a laboratory where they perform experiments on rhesus monkeys. There was some consternation around Martin and his gargantuan gifts. Like a lot of talented people of the Woodstock generation, he'd gotten a little sidetracked, and found that he liked it there, off on the sidetrack.

Since I'd heard about Bev's death, I'd worried about this moment, the meeting of Martin and my dad, the one's mother gone, the other's wife gone. Would they hang on each other's necks like the more volatile characters in a *Godfather* movie? I wanted them to. I wanted them to set a tone that involved less bucking up.

Chrissi and I stand to one side with our hands folded, the daughter-in-law and stepdaughter. Chrissi is tall and green eyed, a long-legged marathon-runner-type woman. A woman who cans and weaves and wins prizes for her preserves and tapestries at various California county fairs. I admire such industriousness. Every time I bake a loaf of banana bread, plant a petunia, or fold a fitted sheet I feel so taxed, I must take to the sofa with a novel. Not that I don't try. In my attic I have several baskets full of half-knitted sweaters. I have a half-abandoned cross-stitch sampler project up there too, the white canvas still stretched on the pale pine frame. It was a quote from French writer and nutcase Colette: "You will do foolish things, but do them with enthusiasm." I only got as far as "You will do foolish" . . . before I had to take to the sofa with a novel.

Chrissi and I don't look at each other. We stand around like funeral directors, trying to emanate concern. Daniel is at that moment in the kitchen grinding coffee beans for a fresh pot. He is unsure where he stands in the pecking order, so absenting himself to make more coffee seems perfectly useful and sensible. It appeals to Daniel's inner Boy Scout. I hear the grinder whirr and stop, whirr and stop. I think: The world is changing already. Fresh coffee grounds in the middle of the day. My father is too shattered with grief to put up a fuss. Martin is a French roast man. We have in common our mutual disdain for our parents' weak coffee.

I hug Martin in that full-bodied way meant to display genuine compassion, meant to show I am not afraid of the sadness of this situation, of the muck of life. This is a misleading message, to say the least. Martin is just my size, five-nine, and he gives me a full-bodied hug back. He is of the Woodstock generation, and I am of the generation that is old enough to know about Woodstock, but still had a bedtime, but we also have this in common: We are huggers, while our parents were not. Our parents were of a generation who felt the only people who hugged were the drunken Irish and the Italians.

We try to figure out how long it's been since we've seen each other. My daughter hadn't been born yet. His eldest daughter, now contemplating law school, was still raising lop-eared rabbits for 4-H.

Martin and Chrissi had visited DadandBev enough to know the drill. We all troop into the family room, single file. Woodrow tears up and down the hall a few more times for good measure. Before sitting down, Martin gazes out the plate-glass window to see if there are any critters perched on the edge of the pond for a drink. Martin is also herpetologist, a specialist on the California garter snake. No. No snakes or birds out there. It's midday now. All the desert creatures are hiding from the heat.

Everyone sits. Dad is at his post at the Formica breakfast bar. Me in Bev's spot, in the rolling office-type chair, also at the breakfast bar. Martin and Chrissi, thigh by thigh, on the plaid foldout love seat (too small for comfort, but just slightly, so that when you sit on it, you feel there is something wrong with *you*, and not the chintzy piece of furniture). Daniel sits by the window, beside the large television, in a rocking chair with a gold corduroy seat cushion.

Everyone is here now except Liz, the baby of the family, who currently works for a temp agency in Las Vegas. Perhaps because she already lives in Las Vegas, thirty miles away, she doesn't feel there is a point to taking a day off work just to come sit around. That's what we're doing, sitting. Sitting and staring at the dog. The dog's bed sits against the wood-paneled wall, between the television set and the too-small love seat. He curls up into a ball on his bed, and that's the cue to have someone drop an old bath towel over him. The towel, which looks perfectly good to me, has RAG printed with a permanent marker on the border. I feel a pinch of pure despair. DadandBev's rags are so unraglike, they must be identified. Shouldn't you be able to look at a towel and know whether it was a rag or not? I leap up and make a big production of dropping the rag/bath towel on the dog. Then he scoots around in a tight circle beneath it, twisting it around him as if he were a piece of salt water taffy.

My father smokes his head off, pops a steady stream of generic-brand ibuprofen. It's stuffy in the Palace, cigarette smoke drifts around. I pine for some air-conditioning, but because it's October—technically, autumn—the thermostat is set to kick off automatically only if the temperature inside reaches eighty-five degrees.

I often have a hankering to be Jewish, and this is one of those times. If we were Jewish, all this sitting around would have a name, then we would be sitting Shiva, at which time we wouldn't go to work or leave the house. The outside world would come to us. But DadandBev were lapsed Catholics, bordering on atheists, and Martin *is* an atheist. As mentioned earlier, I am Episcopalian, like my mother. This means I must scurry away from my father's devastation and my own guilt at not feeling sadder—Bev had been my stepmother for twenty-two years, after all—by going to the grocery store to make sure there is food in the house. This is a necessity not because, as some people seem to feel, you need a lot of food to keep up your strength for all that mourning and gnashing of teeth, but because Martin and Chrissi and even Daniel and I constitute my father "having guests," and when you have guests, you have to be able to offer them an assortment of delicious things to eat. It is only polite.

Chrissi and I get into my dad's Ford Explorer and drive to Albertsons. Daniel, who unlike me actually enjoys grocery shopping, begs off, thinking he should stay behind with the guys. Until today, Dad has always walked me to his car when I ask to borrow it, wanting to make sure I buckle my seat belt. I have a little daughter; I'm the mad seat belt buckler at home. Here, however, borrowing my father's car, I'm sixteen and not to be trusted. But today, for the first time ever, he stays inside. He tells me where the keys are, but doesn't move from his seat, from where he is smoking his head off and drinking his fresh cup of dark roast coffee, coffee he's not used to. He drinks it anyway. With cream and sugar, as always.

Having something to do is a great relief. I back the Explorer out of the driveway, zoom up the hill, with black Fortification Hill and lapis-lazuli blue Lake Mead in the rearview mirror. Chrissi has just gotten braces on her teeth. In addition to buying groceries for the sitting-Shiva-that-is-not-sitting-Shiva, Chrissi needs soft food for her teeth: yogurt, ice cream, canned pears.

Word has not yet reached this part of southern Nevada that sun is hell on your skin. Even though it's nearly Halloween—with Buick-sized displays of red delicious apples set up in produce, accompanied by bins of caramels for the making of caramel apples—just about everyone in the enormous overly air-conditioned place, every matron leaning over the handle of her shopping cart in her khaki shorts and sandals, is the color of bacon. Some of these women are no more than thirty, with small children swarming around their carts, having moved to

Boulder City from somewhere in California because in Boulder City they could afford to buy a house.

The deeply alarming southern Nevada suntan is not the golden-brown glow attained at balmy coastal spots the world over, where the breeze wafts in off the ocean and where on summer mornings there might be fog, sometimes drizzle; it's the tan you see on people who show up in the news, people who've attempted Everest, been lost for weeks in the wilderness, or participated in an ultramarathon in a hot clime. It advertises nothing save the mercilessness of the sun.

Chrissi and I are albinistic by comparison. We are brunettes from northern cities, our arms sticking out of our T-shirts as white as frozen cod fillets. We are united in our paleness. We pass the monumental apple-and-caramel display and wonder if people here have missed the fact that they are not living in a Norman Rockwell painting somewhere in Illinois, but in the middle of one of the world's fiercest deserts, a place in which no one could survive, were it not for the miracle of modern technology which brings water and meat-locker-cold air conditioning.

"They should do something with cactus instead," I say. "There's got to be something Halloweeny you can do with tumbleweeds."

Chrissi is pushing the cart. She stops in her tracks, a bag of romaine lettuce in her hand, and laughs out loud, *ha ha ha*, with her mouth open, her new braces showing. She's maybe forty, with new braces, laughing out loud with no self-consciousness at all.

In addition to our lack of desert suntan, Chrissi and I have something else in common, something we've never spoken of: We were both disliked by Bev. I imagine that Chrissi's tragic flaw was marrying Bev's son, a common story. Over the years I'd heard complaints about Chrissi whenever I visited DadandBev. They were never large complaints—Chrissi didn't

38

like to swim; Chrissi was afraid of big dogs (maybe it was the other way around)—but were delivered in such a loaded fashion that I was meant to understand that what I was hearing was only the tip of the iceberg, that the fear of water and dislike of large dogs were markers for larger, more insufferable and inexcusable personality problems, problems that Bev would have liked to elaborate upon, except that she also liked to imagine herself as someone who did not spread gossip. She was too well bred for gossip, but she was not above innuendo.

When I would ask after Martin and Chrissi's three daughters, Bev would say, "We did have a letter from Chrissi." Then she would roll her big brown eyes in my father's direction. It was impossible to read my father's expression. It is always impossible to read my father's expression. "She spent all those years in school, and never learned to spell." Chrissi had her doctorate in botany; DadandBev disapproved. They approved of higher education—they both had master's degrees—but not too high. Too high, and you were putting on airs.

Still, DadandBev visited Martin and Chrissi every Christmas, driving up through godforsaken central Nevada, home of lonely towns passed over by even McDonald's, and Area 51, the top-secret air base beloved by alien-abduction aficionados. I've lived in Portland nearly fifteen years, and DadandBev've never visited me, about which my feelings are mixed. On the one hand, I am my father's only child, and gave birth to his only grandchild. He *should* visit me. On the other hand, if DadandBev had come to visit, they would have seen my house, a nice 1920s Portland craftsman-style bungalow, with a lot of deferred maintenance: gutters that need to be replaced, a half-painted kitchen, a big crack in the driveway. They would have been witness to my scrubbing out the bathtub, then having to take to the sofa with a novel. They would have been subjected to rain, most likely, about which they would have had nothing good to say.

On yet a third hand, there is something to be said for the

cozy, self-righteous feeling of being neglected. As my mother used to say, a grudge is a warm thing.

Chrissi and I push the cart up and down the wide aisles, tossing in packages of cold cuts and rye bread, salsa and chips, Diet Pepsi and cookies. Sara Lee pound cake for my dad. My dad only likes sweets that are yellow: pound cake, Lorna Doons, Nilla Wafers, French vanilla ice cream. We seem to have lost track of the occasion; our basket looks as if we are off to a picnic.

"Here's something I've always been meaning to ask you," I say. (Meaning to ask her as of fifteen minutes ago, when she stopped and chortled there in produce, and I saw that she was okay, that her fear of water or dogs or whatever meant nothing, that my stepsister-in-law could be someone I might know and like.)

"How did you manage to get Dad and Bev to come up to visit you guys? I couldn't blast them out of Boulder City. I asked them to come up for years, but my dad would say they didn't like to travel much, that it was hard on Bev's back. Then they took that three-week cruise through the Panama Canal. I thought, Well, okay, they had to fly from Las Vegas to L.A., then they were on a ship. Lots of room on a ship. Bev's back was probably fine on a ship. The flight from Las Vegas to L.A. is less than an hour, and it's a two-hour flight from Las Vegas to Portland. I thought, Well, maybe that's too long to sit. Then they took that three-week Alaskan cruise, and they had to fly to Vancouver, B.C. I thought, Wait, that's a way longer flight than the flight to Portland."

I stop rambling. I don't tell her that once I'd asked my father to come up, sometime after he could no longer in good conscience give me the we-don't-like-to-travel-much excuse, and my father said, "We'd come up, babe, but what's up there?" *Well, I am,* I thought to say, but didn't. *Your granddaughter is here.* I didn't want to sound too hysterical.

"Did you ever write Beverly a letter? She wouldn't respond

unless you wrote her a letter. And it had to come from me," Chrissi says. "Lady of the house to lady of the house. Once Marty wrote the letter inviting her to come, but we never heard back."

In respect for the dead, I do not shriek, "You mean, she needed a fucking *written invitation*?" Instead, I say, "How did you know to do this?"

"Marty suggested it. It was the only thing that worked."

It was pointless to wonder why my father didn't tell me after, say, a dozen years had passed, and I'd invited him and Bev to visit me about forty-seven times, that Bev would have liked me to write a letter. I would have written the letter on proper stationery (not the usual twenty-pound copier paper I sometimes use for notes), purchased a seasonally appropriate postage stamp, no Madonna and child Christmas stamps or I Love You hearts; perhaps a simple American flag, which would have spoken to Bev's right-wing tendencies. I would have double-checked my *they're*, *their*, and *theres*. I would have written a letter beyond reproach. I would not, as Chrissi did, allow misspellings.

"Christ, you think someone could have TOLD me!" I say. I feel a Dramatic moment coming on, pushing itself from the inside out, like an air bubble seeking the surface of an otherwise still pond.

This is along the lines of my dad telling me two years ago that Bev didn't like to be called Bev, she preferred Beverly. *Two years ago. TWO*. Dad and Bev started seeing each other in, what, 1975? Since 1975 I've been calling her Bev. *Hi Bev! How are you? Bev! This is sure good clam linguini! Bev, I'd love another cup of coffee while you're up. Wow, Bev, that sure is a pretty turquoise necklace!* For twenty-two years it was Bev this and Bev that. Then, one night I'm on the phone with my dad, and before we hang up, I ask him to give Bev my best, and he says, "Oh, by the way, I've been meaning to tell you, she likes to be called Beverly."

I can't stand this. I cannot stand this. No wonder Bev didn't like me. I can't control myself. "DAD! You're telling me this NOW? I've been calling her Bev for over twenty years and you're only just telling me this NOW? Don't you think we might have gotten along better if I had called her the right *name*. Jesus Christ on a green raft!"

"Aw, babe, there's no need for that," he said.

As usual, I couldn't figure out what that meant, and I didn't ask. There was no need for what? No need to get upset? No need to take the Lord's name in vain? No need to respond? No need to have a heart, a soul, a pulse? What?

5

Woodrow the dog weighs eleven pounds. He is black, with brown eyebrows and paws, two quarter-size brown dots on his chest. DadandBev outfitted him in a black harness, as if he were a rottweiler or pit bull, some fierce beast that cannot be restrained by a normal collar. As evening descends upon the desert, my father insists that Woodrow be taken out on a leash, lest a coyote steal down from the ocher-colored hills on the other side of the wash and snatch him up while he pees on a weed. I don't mind standing out there in the twilight while Woodrow sniffs around the gravel. Venus is the lone pinprick of light in the sky, hanging over Lake Mead, no longer vitreous blue, but gray and flat in the dusk. I have a terrific headache, either from a lack of water or all the cigarette smoke. Since we've been here, my father has smoked nonstop. I try not to imagine what'll happen to the dog after my father dies. Little dogs live forever, and Woodrow is only six. My father, however, has a golf ball in his chest.

When I walk the dog back inside, my stepsister Liz is there, sitting in the rocker with a bottle of beer balanced on her knee. Liz is short and wiry, with a dark blond braid hanging down the middle of her back and bangs she cuts herself. She's had this hairstyle since she was about eleven. We do not try to figure out how long it's been since we've seen each other. Unlike Martin, she's not a hugger or a talker or an enjoyer of French roast. She's unfriendly, or maybe just shy. Who knows? The last time I saw her was on Christmas Eve a decade ago, when

DadandBev still lived in reasonable Southern California, and she gave me a poster of a pair of kittens in matching straw hats, snuggled together in an artfully rusted wheelbarrow, still in the long white paper sack from the poster shop.

Liz has never quite found a place for herself in this world.

Martin is a zoologist and I am a writer—neither one a secure profession, but professions nonetheless, with proper labels you can put on your income tax return—and Liz is a temp. She has neither husband nor child, nor friends that I know of. Once, when she was in her early twenties, she was riding along a Southern California city block and was so thin, the wind threw her off her bike and into a plate-glass window. Since I last saw her she's had her brown front tooth capped. She looks good.

Liz is talking about *Star Trek*, of which she is a huge fan. "'Trekkie' is old school. No Trekker wants to be called a Trekkie anymore."

Meanwhile, the television is on the five o'clock news. Martin is in the kitchen, browning sausage for his world-famous rigatoni. While Chrissi and I were at Albertsons, the outside world had come to us in the form of two Tupperware vats of potato salad from different neighbors, and a ham that could feed a family with fifty-one cousins. More picnic food we don't want.

It's always best to humor Liz, so I say, "Ah. I see the difference." Like I care.

"There *is* a difference. I'm a Trekker, not a Trekkie. You know the joke, right?"

Daniel and Chrissi lean against the kitchen counters drinking beer and having a lively discussion about pesticides. Chrissi works for the state of California, something in agriculture (using her degree, a miracle of which any parent would be proud) and Daniel used to be an exterminator. They know pesticide lingo, share pesticide humor. There are a lot of jokes about dioxin, apparently. It's good to have Martin in the kitchen making his sausage rigatoni, and me there too, washing radishes for the salad. We bump into each other as we cook. We laugh insanely at the dog. In the past, Friday nights were butter-wrapper night, when DadandBev kicked up their heels and indulged Woodrow with a wrapper from a new cube. It is Monday, but the butter-wrapper routine cracks me up, so I unwrap a new cube, stick it on a saucer, put it back in the fridge, and give the wrapper to Woodrow. He licks at it in a frenzy, his pink tongue darting in and out. The harder he licks, the further he pushes the wrapper away from himself, until he finally figures out that he can hold it flat with his paw. Dad is unhappy about this. Friday night is butter-wrapper night.

"You know the joke, right?" says Liz. She's getting irritated.

"I'm afraid I don't."

"A Trekker wears a Starfleet uniform to a convention because it's a gas. A Trekkie wears a Starfleet uniform to a convention because he's heard it's what all the dudes are wearing at the academy."

She offers some more distinctions, but I stop listening. All this mad laughter, this cooking and goofing as if we were any family, is meant to disguise the horrible fact that it's martoonie hour, the Number One shared ritual of DadandBev's married life. Bev was the expert martoonie maker, it was her own Japanese Tea Ceremony. Even when she was recovering from one of her back surgeries and was full of prescription drugs— the kind with a sticker on the side of the bottle featuring a dozy eye and a warning against mixing with alcohol—she would still make my father a martoonie. Now, it's five o'clock, the saddest time of day on a good day, and my father is left to make his own martoonie.

I cannot stand the sight of him staring down into his glass. He says, "I'm going to be so lonesome now."

Oh oh oh. What to say to this, what to say?

Liz says, "Get it? The difference is that a Trekker is a fan, and a Trekkie thinks he's like part of the *Star Trek* world. Get it?"

No one answers.

After dinner, which my father barely touches, Daniel and I do the dishes. Chrissi sits outside on the front porch, at the old round redwood picnic table from my childhood, and enjoys the evening. The evening is lovely in Boulder City, balmy, with planets rising over the lake and the festive lights belonging to jets coming in for their final approach to McCarran Airport in Las Vegas gliding by overhead. It is not yet middle-of-the-night creepy, where you feel as if you are living in a tiny human settlement on another planet.

Martin, Liz, and my father have a powwow on the other side of the breakfast bar, to talk about the distribution of Bev's stuff. By stuff, I mean both her things, and her money. They murmur, and I cannot figure out whether they are murmuring because they are all murmurers by nature, or because their business is private, and they don't want me to hear. But if their business is private, why don't they go into the living room, where they can have true privacy? Or do they feel that their business is not private—I was not Bev's daughter, and therefore it's only natural that she should have excluded me from her will—but still, it's a bit awkward.

I inherited from my stepmother of twenty-two years not one chipped teacup or funky, beloved brooch. I never expected to inherit anything, our relationship being as fraught with low-grade loathing as it was, but now that it has come to pass I am on the verge of pitching a self-righteous fit. Then I realize I am somewhat relieved. I think it is only fitting, refreshing even. In death, Bev understood that she was through being civil to me for my father's sake. As a result, I am freed from having to feel guilty for not feeling worse that she was gone. Suddenly, I like her better.

Still, there's the weird matter of the money. Two trusts have been set up, one for the three of us, one for the two of them. My father's money, and the money he and Bev accrued when they were married, form the Karbo Family Trust; the money Bev inherited from her mother, which she invested until the end of her life, was in a separate trust for her children. This is what they are discussing. It's not a lot of money, but it is a lot for our family, somewhere in the high six figures.

Even though my father's back is turned to me, I do the dishes the way he likes. If I don't do them the way he likes, he will know. As in all things, my dad is fastidious. All pots and pans and any knife with a wooden handle are washed by hand. The Tupperware is also washed by hand. Daniel washes and I dry. We bump each other's hips as we move around the kitchen, trying to inject some zaniness into the proceedings. At home, we are always roughhousing in the kitchen. Here, of course, no one roughhouses anywhere. I suddenly feel as if we are the kindly couple brought in to help out. Liz has done nothing but sit since she arrived. I hear her ask if she can have the sofa console table.

I hear snippets of their conversation as I dry the pans and knives, the Tupperware that is so old, it's sticky, the polymers that make up the miracle plastic giving up the molecular ghost. Liz, who lives in a studio apartment, wants the bed frame from the matching cherry bedroom set, but not the rest. My father wants to keep it all together.

"Let me have it until the time comes when I won't need it," says my father.

"I want the bed frame," says Liz. "I need a bed frame. It was Mother's set."

"When I have guests, they'll need a place to sleep," says my father.

Guests. When does my father ever have guests? By guests, he means me. He means Martin. No one else ever comes to stay.

I dry a piece of Tupperware long past the point of its being

47

dry, run the towel around inside of it, around and around. I feel myself getting Dramatic. I want to lean over the breakfast bar and say, *Liz, my father was married to your insufferable mother for twenty-two years, let him keep the goddamn bed. He's seventy-four years old, he's bereaved, and he's got a fucking golf ball in his chest which is probably lung cancer.*

It's a good sixteen-year-old feeling. I stomp around a little. Of course, Liz and Martin don't know about the golf ball, because my father has told only me. For all they know, he has another twenty years. For all *I* know, he has another twenty years.

Except, I know he doesn't.

I open the cupboard to put away the Tupperware, and have a minor moment. In the cupboard, there must be a hundred containers. Some are Tupperware, some are Tupperware knockoffs, some are margarine containers, the kind with posies dancing along the side, which my father uses to store bolts and finishing nails. There is every piece of Tupperware DadandBev accrued since their marriage, and every piece of Tupperware my mother owned as well. I recognized Tupperware that I stored Play-Doh in, Tupperware that I used to keep squares of cantaloupe in when I really was sixteen and on some cockamamie diet. I suddenly think about all the stuff in the Palace, not just the matching cherry bedroom set, that is worth having a powwow over, not just the money in the trusts, but the real stuff, the stuff they used and the stuff they saved. Not just the stuff they'd accumulated during their marriage, but stuff from each of their previous marriages, as well as stuff they inherited from their respective parents. A lot of stuff, like the Tupperware, that was essentially worthless.

Years before, I'd read *Patrimony*, Philip Roth's story about his father's death. Mr. Roth's father, Herman Roth, died of a brain tumor, as did my mother, so I was interested, under the misery-loves-company rubric, to read about his father's horrific, heart-cracking decline. There is a scene that stirred some controversy among people of a literary bent who consider such things, in which Mr. Roth's father, after having suffered a bout of constipation, shits all over the bathroom, a shockingly voluminous amount. Mr. Roth describes it as if it were a crime scene and he is the forensic's expert (even how he promises his father he will never tell anyone—this is the part people take issue with: he *promised*, and here is his book published by a major American publisher sparing no lurid detail). The part I remember that evening in Boulder City, staring into the cabinet full of Tupperware and pseudo-Tupperware, is the part where he talks about how cleaning up his father's mess was his patrimony, not the money coming to him, not the stuff coming to him, but cleaning up his father's shit.

My patrimony would not be so primal, so dramatic. Martin and Liz would bicker over their trust and their mother's antiques. My patrimony would be all this stuff that no one else would want, stuff that was not good enough to keep, but too good to throw away.

Suddenly, Liz is up in arms about something. I stand up from where I was crouched in front of the Tupperware cabinet in time to see her stomping down the hall and out the back door. Martin rubs his forehead, then after a minute goes after her. My dad folds his hands in his lap and examines his thumbnails. This sort of display is uncharacteristic of anyone in our family.

"What was that about?" It is rude of me to ask. When it comes to my dad, it is always rude to ask. The simplest question always seems like an invasion of privacy, unless you are trying to purchase a large appliance and need to understand the fine print on the warranty, or to engage in anything automotive. Then you are required to interrogate the seventeen-year-old salesperson or non-English-speaking mechanic as if you are an investigative journalist angling for a Pultizer.

Hinting around never works with Dad. As I learned from my

first husband, a documentary filmmaker, never ask questions that can be answered with a simple yes or no.

So I say again, "What's with her?"

"Aw, she's got her panties in a twist."

"She's got her *panties in a twist*?" At that moment I adore Dad for using this locution. It opens up new vistas. "What's she have her *panties in a twist* about? Her mother just died, and doesn't that kind of trump everything else?" I worry about having mentioned this; but I can't possibly pretend it isn't in the forefront of everyone's mind, can I? Even if ignoring reality is part of the Karbo Family Credo?

"She's riled up about the terms of the trust. She was under the impression that she could just show up and half of Beverly's money would be hers." I swear I hear a smidgen of pique in his voice.

"But half of that money *is* hers, isn't it?" Dad starts to cough, then. He coughs for so long I worry we'll lose the thread of the most substantive conversation we've had in years. When he straightens back up in his chair, I bring him a glass of water with ice, the way he likes it. "But half of that money is hers, isn't it?"

"She was expecting the principal, which isn't to be disbursed until Martin and Liz are sixty-two."

"Sixty-*two*?" Liz is in her late forties, Martin is fifty. What did their mother imagine they were going to do with the money? Fly all their friends to Puerto Vallarta on a private jet for a drunken week of tequila, parasailing, and Mexican whores? Initiate a middle-aged cocaine addiction? Invest in junk bonds? What? And what if they did? No wonder Liz has her panties in a twist; she was expecting to return to her Las Vegas studio apartment a half-millionaire or thereabouts. Instead she gets another dose of her mother's controlling nature and the knowledge she'll be receiving nothing more than quarterly interest checks for the next fifteen years.

I can't help myself, though. I say, "Dad, they're already middle-aged, for God's sake. What did she think they were going to do with it?"

But the conversation is over; he flips on the TV.

6

Three days after Bev's death, Daniel and I fly home with the logical-sounding idea that I will get things in order so I can return to Boulder City in two weeks for my father's biopsy. Martin and Chrissi assume Daniel and I are flying home early because there's no point in hanging around the Palace, staring at the dog and waiting for the heartbreak of martoonie hour to come and go. I am in the loop for once, but only because DadandBev is now just Dad. Suddenly, I am not just *in* the loop, I *am* the loop. It goes straight from my dad to me and back, something we both find alarming.

My dad is a somnambular wreck, inching through his daily routines as expressionless as Mr. Spock during a preoccupied moment. Like so many guys of the Greatest Generation, this lack of affect signals distress in him more surely than keening and carrying on. I ask him hourly if there is anything I can do before we leave. Does he want me to stay? Does he want me to go? What does he need? I am desperate for him to help me know what I can do for him. But it is always the same noncommital answer: *Whatever's good for you, babe.*

What my father needs, of course, is to believe that despite the loss of his wife and his impending biopsy, he still doesn't need anyone. To need me would be the beginning of the end, even if it were only company he needed, another heart in the room, cracking with empathy for his loss. Every martoonie hour, his chin falls to his chest and he sucks in enormous breaths, his

way of stemming tears. It is terrifying to behold, the end of
the known world. Women claim they want men to express
their feelings, but when they do, it's unendurable. Out of sheer
cowardice I made my decision: He would need me more before
and after his biopsy. Then, at least, there would be driving him
to the hospital, shopping and cooking, cleaning house, laundry,
consulting with doctors. All stuff I wasn't wild about doing, it
must be said, but things women have done to make themselves
useful since God was a boy, as my mother used to say.

Returning to Portland I travel back to the future, where it's the
final year of the final decade of the century. At the Palace of the
Golden Sofa the march of progress had paused in about 1985
and decided that was as good a place as any to set up camp.
Rotary dial phones, Kaypro computer with 64K of memory
and no hard drive, hi-fi stereo with turntable, eight-track player,
Louis L'Amour paperbacks with crisp edges, as dry and yellow as
autumn leaves in a place known for brush fires, and the Palace's
most recent title, *Lonesome Dove*.

Back home there is the cacophonous world of cell phones,
Nintendo, GameBoys, and Furbys, with their snapping eyes and
beaks, their insane mechanical yatter—Katherine has not one,
but two, given to her by my childless friends—which were
routinely buried in a closet to shut them up. There were
people of the world, namely the kids, who, unlike my father
have managed to see a movie in a theater since *Star Wars*,
and know that *Survivor* is a reality-based television show and
not a person's lot in life, and pay attention, lame as it is,
to how Madonna is wearing her hair these days. It's the life
I've made, this fly-by-night world of smoke alarms with the
batteries removed to keep them from going off when Rachel
burns pancakes on Saturday morning, of misplaced car insurance
bills, of slow-draining bathtubs so determindedly unresponsive
to Drāno, you suspect they might be characters from Stephen

King, a world inhabited by three children and a man with chaotic tendencies, not an organized soul among them, all slobs who make it up as they go. We have one bathroom and have been known to go through a roll of toilet paper in forty-five minutes.

Before Bev's death, and the news of the tumor in my father's chest *(It's just a cyst; the doctors said it was just a cyst. Are you a doctor? Are you trained at all in these matters? You were a liberal arts major. Yes, there was that one biology class, but a biology class does not an oncologist make. If they say it's a cyst, it's a cyst. Would it kill you to be optimistic?)*, the disorder drove me mad. I was the daughter of Dick Karbo, the Man Who Alphabeticizes Take-Out Menus, living in a house where the dogs really did eat the homework.

Now, I am unaccountably grateful for the bedlam. The kids have already begun their yearly tradition of asking me what I want for Christmas, and I give them my standard reply: "World peace . . . and quiet." This year I don't mean it, though. I want them raucous and needy, bugging me to make them scrambled eggs and admire their Lego forts, untying their triple-knotted shoelaces that are soaked through from the rain, lacing up their soccer cleats, listening to their book reports, and busting up arguments over who broke the leg of Katherine's favorite Breyer horse (they are all her favorite). The kids signify the messy reality of life with their endless needs, and I would rather have that than the opposite: my elegant father slowly fading in the deep desert silence of the Palace. In a larger sense, of course, that's what all the noise of living is about, staving off quiescence that is the hallmark of our mortality.

In Portland the phone rings a dozen times a day, usually for fourteen-year-old Rachel. I have married into a family of mild hysterics, a family of people who can't think of anything better to do in excitable moments than pick up the phone. It's not uncommon for the phone to ring five, six, seven times after nine o'clock at night. Messages are left first by Betty, Daniel's mother, at fifteen-minute intervals, then by his father, Jim. "Call us! We need to talk to you!" It's always an idea for a family vacation eight months down the road, or a cute craft project for the kids to do over winter break. The calls are diametric to the ones I receive; they are always urgent and they are always about trivial matters that can wait. They irritate and please me. I complain about them, but don't want them to end.

I call my father at four-fifty every evening, hoping to get a jump on martoonie hour, thinking if I do I'll somehow be able to outwit his misery, or at least distract him from it. This is not altruistic. The days I crawl into bed believing that he's a little less devastated are better days for me too. I collect all the lunatic events of the day—Danny got sent home from school for spitting rocks! Katherine fell off her horse at riding lessons (and of course, being half Karbo, got right back on!). Rachel just tried out for *The Trojan Women* at school and was cast as a Roman soldier—to give to my father my gift of life, of all the clutter and nonsense he's better off missing out on. I try to be upbeat, like he taught me, the offspring of Dick Karbo here!

He makes a dutiful accounting of his time. He spends an hour or so each day sorting through Bev's stuff. He works at this until he comes upon something that wrecks him, and that's it for the day. He tells me that when he was going through her clothes he kept finding pairs of soiled underwear stashed in odd places—in a shoebox, behind her paperback books on the bedside table, in a cosmetic case in the bathroom. "She'd obviously been unable to control herself for sometime before she died," he says. "And she didn't even tell me." This makes him sob.

Bev's back had been bad for decades and she'd acquired a collection of pillows and supports and a special whirlpool gizmo for the tub. She had a wooden cane, and a walker I never saw her use. She had a "reacher," an aluminum stick with rubber-tipped pincers on one end and the kind of handle you'd find on a squirt gun on the other. Dad spends one morning trying to find a convalescent home that would accept these things as a donation. On one of the better of the bad days he meets a physical therapist called Ray who says that he will put together an exercise program for him.

"Ray said a little strength-training might help my mood, help me get back in the saddle," he says. On this day he sounds genuinely optimistic, which makes me feel as if perhaps everything will be all right after all.

Sometimes when I call he's already eaten his Stouffer's macaroni and cheese; he loves its cheddary uniformity, the same reliable bite from first to last, no surprises. The day before I left, Daniel and I went to Albertsons and stocked up on all the orange boxes they had in the freezer case, more than would fit in my father's freezer. My father gave me cash from some of the envelopes Bev had stashed around, tens and fives tucked into her shoes, in the pockets of sweaters hanging in the back of her closet.

It was the end of 1999 in a state with more than its share of survivalist types, so no one stared at our cart. The suntanned checker had dyed white hair that looked like cotton batting and silver fingernails curving over her fingertips. She looked very old, but was probably only fifty. She had the look of someone who had lived her whole life in southern Nevada, basking in the sun and smoking her head off. "Y2K got you worried?" she asked as she passed an orange box over the scanner.

"Actually, my stepmother just died and my dad isn't much of a cook."

"They never are." She glanced at Daniel.

"Don't look at me," he said. "I can cook Top Ramen like no one's business."

"It's part of the trouble with men," she continued "They not only imagine they'll live forever, they also imagine the person who's there to cook for them will live forever too."

My dad may not cook, but he is a religious dish doer. When I call, sometimes I catch him at the sink.

"How ya doing, Dad?"

"Hi, babe, how are you." He says this every time. His voice always goes down on the "you" instead of up—his own special brand of asking. It sounds as phony as can be.

"I'm okay, how are *you*." This is my special and slightly smarmy inflection, meant to convey that this isn't just a pleasantry, that I'm genuinely interested.

"Sad sad sad."

"I know. It'll be okay." I neither know, nor believe it will be okay. I am so full of platitudinous shit, I want to hang up. I can only live with myself because I have never yet uttered the phrase, *Don't worry, she's in a better place.*

One evening his project was making an emergency card for his wallet with important phone numbers on it.

"Dad, what other numbers ya got on there?"

"Well, yours. All of your numbers."

"How about Liz? She's just over in Las Vegas. She could come in an emergency."

"Liz doesn't have a car."

"Well, okay. That's good. You call me if you ever need anything. I'll call every night, but you can call me anytime for anything else, okay? And I'll see you in less than two weeks."

"Every minute seems like an hour," he says.

"I know, Dad. It'll be okay. Does it help to know that Bev is in a better place?"

"Well . . ." I can tell he's really thinking about this. Bless his heart, bless his *heart*. "Not really."

I once read that the oldest English phrase still in everyday usage from its coinage to the present is "Woe is me."

Every day, lately, the wind blows the rain sideways and rattles the storm windows in their frames. Up on Mount Hood it's already blizzarding; from certain streets in Portland the mountain is a white equilateral triangle stuck on the horizon, the sky behind it eternally bruised with threatening storms. Rachel has thought about her Halloween costume for months; she's an introspective girl with an impulse toward the theatrical. Her friends are all going to be dead scientists, dead businesswomen, dead doctors. She wants to be a dead singer, but acknowledges that the problem with being a dead singer is that the type of headbanger she wants to be already looks dead, so how will anyone know the difference? She understands certain nuances of trick-or-treating that escape so many others: you're only on someone's front porch for thirty seconds. If your costume is too complicated they'll have to ask what you're supposed to be, which defeats the purpose. We debate while folding laundry. She is also considering a vampire princess, but that's a little cliché. I suggest wearing a sign around her neck that says IRS in writing that looks like drippy blood. "Yes!" she says, dropping her end of the sheet and clapping her hands. I am not her mother, therefore she's not obligated to roll her eyes. I love her for this.

Danny hasn't decided because he is awaiting the arrival of an alien costume from his grandmother. He had been promised that it would come with real green alien blood, pumped via a small, handheld bulb through the see-through veins in the big green head. Nonnie is notorious for her good intentions and lack of follow-through, so, as Halloween gets closer, Daniel and I encourage Danny to consider something else. Danny humors us but he doesn't trust us. He's nine, and the year before, we talked him into being dead Snow White, and he's still in recovery from wearing the gold and blue satin costume, complete with puffed sleeves and a full ankle-length skirt, a hand-me-up from seven-year-old Katherine, who looks like the real Snow White, and wore the costume the year before. We are anxious for him not to be disappointed. After he goes to bed, Daniel leaves messages on Nonnie's answering machine: Where is the costume? She doesn't return the calls, but the costume eventually shows up on Halloween day.

Katherine has an image in her mind she can't articulate. She is determinded to be "a dancing cat," but can't elaborate on what a dancing cat might look like. Not the Cat in the Hat, with one of those tall red-and-white-striped hats, not that. She is contrary, even at seven. She only knows what she doesn't want. After several evenings of trying to figure out how to put the "dancing" in the costume—we can figure out how to make her look like a cat—she decides that maybe she'll just stick with being a witch. We buy the last children's size Large at the Halloween Superstore, but it's too small. I was five-nine at age twelve, when I abruptly stopped growing, and my daughter is following in my footsteps. She weeps. I refrain from telling her that one day she will appreciate her height; it's what my mother said to me, and I hated it. Of course, my mother was right.

All this helps me forget what my father is facing, is about to face. The dutiful Oregon rain lets up for an afternoon or two, but the mornings are dark and wind-whipped. I come home after walking the puppy, Winston, and he is soaked. I try to towel him off in the basement, but he squirms out of my hands and races upstairs to leap on our bed, where he joins smelly old Anubis —named by Daniel's ex after the jackal-headed Eygptian god who conducts the dead to judgment—already deep in the middle of his morning nap. Our pillows smell perennially of wet dog. I always ask what turns out to be a rhetorical question: Why am I the only one to take the dog out? Because, no one else in the house needs to run to the point of dry heaves just to get through the day.

7

On the topic of his impending biopsy my dad and I have unproductive conversations. I want to know about the plans. I want to know what his doctor said. And what kind of doctor is be seeing? Is it Swifton, his regular family doctor, or some specialist? I sound nosy, even to myself.

"It's just some office business. They'll pop this cyst out and be done with it."

"I'll come down the day before then."

"What was that?" He engages in his infamous selective hearing, something he claims was part of his flight training in the Army Air Corps, in which he served at the end of World War II. He was trained to block out unwanted sounds, which sometimes means the words coming out of my mouth.

"Or I can come the evening before. I'll get a rental car so you won't have to pick me up at the airport."

"I can pick you up at the airport, babe. There's no reason for you to go to all the expense of getting a rental car. It's just a cyst. Just some office business."

He hasn't returned to his projects, which surprises me, since he's found solace in them all his life. Before he retired to become an arch tinker, his true calling, he was an industrial designer involved in the creation of some neat stuff of the twentieth century, about which he never speaks. He doesn't like to talk about designing the hood ornament for the Lincoln Continental, a version of which is still in use today, or the early packaging for

McDonald's hamburgers (he keeps the clear plastic prototype on his desk. It looks like a flying saucer). He has nothing to say about working for Wham-O in 1964, when he was involved in the final design of the first professional Frisbee. His true love is machinery. From the large to the little, he can and does fix it all. He has restored airplane engines for the Howard W. Cannon Aviation Museum, located at McCarran International Airport—so huge they barely fit in his garage, world headquarters for all his major tinkering—and fixed slim ladies' pocket watches for a local jewel smith. The small tools he needed to work on the watches didn't exist, so he machined his own; he later made a set for his dentist, who still uses them in his practice. He's rebuilt race cars, powerboats, a Japanese clock from the thirteenth century—which required him to learn a smattering of Japanese—and a narrow-gauge railroad engine for the Nevada State Railway Museum. He is a perfectionist, but in the any-job-worth-doing-is-worth-doing-well sense, not in the modern type A neurotic sense.

But now he isn't doing any tinkering at all.

Then one night, two days before I leave for Boulder City, he has real news. There has been a change in plans. The biopsy has been rescheduled. It is now no longer office business, but day surgery. It means going in the hospital. My father plays it off.

"It's just their excuse. The only way they can get me to sit still for more tests is to hospitalize me." Over the course of his lifetime, my father has refused to involve himself with doctors. He feels that doctors are only good for one thing: If you have nothing better to do, the bad news that they always have will at least focus your attention on something. As a result, he hasn't had a physical in decades.

"So . . . it's no longer an office procedure but a full-fledged surgery?"

"It's a chance for them to gouge the insurance company."

"How long will you be in?"

"Not any longer than I can help it."

"How long, Dad?"

"I don't know. Overnight. A day or two. I forgot what they said."

I switch the phone off and set it on its battery-charging cradle. The kids are playing Bust-A-Move on the PlayStation in the living room. An incessant *ding-ding-ding-ding-ding-ding-ding* issues from the game. Daniel is playing on the computer in the basement. Anubis is asleep beside our bed on his dog bed. I can hear him snoring. Winston, the Lab, is asleep in his kennel, which sits like a piece of furniture in the dining room. It's time for dinner and I'm tempted to call Domino's. I suddenly feel the need to take to the sofa with a novel. I'm tempted to call Domino's for every dinner in the foreseeable future.

Until that moment I'd been able to be more or less optimistic about my father's condition. I thought about all the cancer survivors I knew. There were a lot! My ex-father-in-law who beat colon cancer with the aid of a vegetarian diet, an experimental course of chemotherapy, outrageous optimism, and working every day in his garden. The two women I know who suffered breast cancer but lived to see their hair grow back thicker than before and published a book apiece. I knew we were still saying it was only a "cyst," but my own optimism couldn't stretch that far: He had smoked two packs a day for sixty years. After I remembered those people, I further tried to remind myself that it was 1999, not 1975, the year my mother died. If back then we didn't even have VCRs and now we have laparoscopic surgery, wireless networking, and Dolly the cloned sheep, just imagine how much more technologically sophisticated cancer treatment is? (Not much, it turns out: They can diagnosis it with greater accuracy, but it's still the same old poison-and-burn song and dance).

We Karbos have a peculiar relationship with the medical profession; the only time we ever saw a doctor was to receive the news that we're dying. We suffered not from diabetes, hypertension, rheumatism, depression, or obesity. We didn't have allergies or moles that needed to be removed. We didn't get many colds, and never had the flu. Prescription medications were exotic to us. Our medicine cabinets held mouthwash and Band-Aids, no tobacco-colored plastic pill containers anywhere. Growing up, I have no memory of my mother or father ever seeing a doctor; I went to my pediatrician only to have my wrists and ankles x-rayed for miscellaneous sprains and breaks. Nothing ran in our family but terminal disease.

8

When my mother was diagnosed with brain cancer, we were all young. My parents were in their early forties, the age I am now. Then, I was sixteen and surly. A wisenheimer according to my mother. Her headaches began in the summer after my senior year. If she suffered other symptoms, I never knew. Her doctors wrote them off as menopause, hypoglycemia, a thyroid problem. In three months I would enter USC. I had a close circle of best girlfriends, random boys in the picture, and Linda Ronstadt warbling "You're No Good" on my stereo. There was Huntington Beach, twenty miles down Beach Boulevard, past miles of car lots and fast-food restaurants and Knott's Berry Farm, to which I would ride on my ten-speed bike with Diane Urban, the only girl in my circle up for such an arduous ride during a third-stage Southern California smog alert. I attempted to read some nineteenth-century writers in preparation for what I thought would be on the reading list of my first English class. I know I did this, because I kept a sporadic diary, which I still have.

But my only active memory of that time is of going to various doctors with my mother, where I would sit in the hushed, windowless waiting rooms in stucco buildings in the old part of Whittier, where, apparently, all the brain specialists kept their offices. She went in. I did the hidden-picture puzzles in *Highlights* magazine. She came out patting her hair. She wore a pixie-ish bubble do that needed to be teased out in the morning.

She never said a thing about what went on in there. I didn't wonder, really, because I was sixteen years old.

My mother's appointments always seemed to be at ten-thirty in the morning. Afterward, we went out to lunch at the Jolly Roger at the Whittwood Shopping Center, where we would then go to Broadway to shop for my new college wardrobe. We would each order a club sandwich, a prelude to the Mauna Loa, the chocolate sundae my mother would allow me to order if I wasn't currently on a diet. I was always on a diet that summer and also ate a lot of Mauna Loas. Perhaps my mother already knew that she was dying and thought there was no harm in indulging me. Or, less poignantly, she didn't see any reason for me to be on a diet—at five-nine I weighed 130 pounds, which seemed a lot to me, since all the girls in my circle of friends were five-three or thereabouts and weighed a whole lot less. The Mauna Loa was shaped like a volcano, the chocolate sauce cascading down a cone of vanilla ice cream, a flaming square of melba toast stuck in the center. To give you a clue how not-grown-up I was: I ordered the Mauna Loa not only for the ice cream, but for the magical sight of the waitress walking toward me in the dark restaurant with a flaming dessert made just for me.

Over our club sandwiches, my mother and I discussed the items still left on my college wardrobe list. She was not unlike a general discussing battle plans with his immediate subordinate. We never talked about her health. We discussed what they were showing in the new issue of *Seventeen* magazine. At that time, in our part of suburban Southern California, the polyester high-waisted bell-bottoms John Travolta would later immortalize in *Saturday Night Fever* had come into vogue, as had platform shoes. My mother worried.

"At your height you cannot possibly wear platforms, even the shorter ones, those cute wedgy sandals with the corky heels we saw at Bullocks. But those pants, which suit you well enough, need platforms of some kind."

"But what about those sandals we saw at Thom McAnn? Those were cute."

"They made your feet look too big. And those pants demand platforms, or else they make your legs look too short. And, God, you really don't want *that*. Unfortunately for you, you inherited the worst of both worlds—the length of my legs, but the shape of your father's. Though God knows I'm grateful you didn't inherit the *length* of his legs too. Then you'd be easily six feet tall."

These conversations with my mother were incomprehensible: With the platforms I would be too tall; without the platforms, my legs would be too short. I also sensed there was always something beneath her chipper analyses of my fashion woes— subtext, in a word, which I thought was something that only showed up in *Ethan Frome* and *The Great Gatsby*, and not in regular conversation—having to do with the alarming nature of my body, which was poised at every turn to betray me, unless we kept a strict eye on it, dressing it in clever ways meant to minimize the width of my shoulders and hips, the length of my arms, maximize the length of my legs, my flat chest, accentuate my smallish waist and nice "prom area," her term for the part of your chest above your breasts and beneath your clavicle. Once she said, "You do have nice skin. I will give you that."

I know for a fact that other people in 1975 worried about the fall of Saigon, the implications of *Roe vs. Wade*, and the rise of a sexually transmitted disease called herpes, but my mother was only concerned about preparing me for college. She hadn't had her consciousness raised, had no real opinions about Vietnam, had never been to a key party or smoked a joint. Even though every once in a while she worried that I would up and run off to Haight-Ashbury and become a hippie flower child, her biggest concern was that I would go off to college and fail to land a man. My high school dating career had been a bust. I graduated in the top 5 percent of my class, but without a date to the prom. USC was my chance to find a guy who would vault me into a higher socioeconomic class. My mother's great achievement in life had been to marry up—she was the first one in her family to finish high school and avoid marriage to a factory worker or garbageman; my father had a bachelor's degree from USC and a master's degree in design from the Art Center School of Design in Pasadena—and her goal for me was marrying further up, into the stratosphere of the professional classes. Her greatest hope for me was that I would one day be "Dr. and Mrs."

When my mother and I would return from shopping, she would make me model what we bought. She would even make me model new underwear and bras under the new clothes. She sat at the breakfast bar with a Coors 102 Brew and a ciggie perched on the corner of a huge glass ashtray that could double as a murder weapon, waiting for me to appear from my bedroom. If something was wrong with the ensemble, we needed to know now, so there would still be time to fix it, as if I were going off to the Peace Corps in some far-flung developing country, where they might not have the proper gold Monet accessories. Once, I complained about this. I said, "Mom, it doesn't have to be perfect."

"But it does! Honey, it does! You never get another chance to make a first impression. Remember that!" She was endlessly frustrated with me. Once she said, "I wouldn't want to be you for the world, but I wouldn't mind being myself at your age, with your advantages."

I moved into my dorm in late August in order to participate in sorority rush, which was part of my mother's plan for my dazzling college career. During the sixties and seventies, sororities and fraternites were in decline on college campuses around the nation: They were sexist, racist, and elitist. But for some reason it was still 1952 at USC. Fraternity "men" wore sweaters tied around their necks and dutifully trained to participate in the Greek Week tug-of-war, and sorority girls still got pinned in candlelit ceremonies on the green front lawns of their sorority houses, their arms entwined around each other's waists.

I was invited to pledge Delta Gamma—I got down on my knees and thanked God, because I didn't think my mother would survive the disappointment had I been dropped by every house, as had my roommate—even though I had all the wrong clothes. These girls wore prep clothes: pink and mint green Lacoste polo shirts and pleated khakis, Pappagallo espadrilles and Tiffany jewelry. They had swingy hair, which they wore in ponytails tied with thick grosgrain ribbon. My mother didn't mind; she also had a ready lecture about being myself and establishing my own personal style. Which, of course, was her style. She didn't know what to do about my huge head of curly/wavy hair.

The second Monday of every month was the "mothers' luncheon," in which our mothers drove into gang-infested, smog-ridden central Los Angeles in their shiny cars to eat chicken salad with us and hear an edifying lecture. My mother attended exactly one, before she learned that most likely her headaches and, now, loss of strength in her left hand, were due to a brain tumor.

The call came late one night in my dorm room. It was past eleven. I was listening to Elton John on my stereo and studying for an oceanography exam. The police helicopter that patrolled the USC campus had already *thwap-thwap-thwapped* by overhead. Somewhere in the dorm someone was burning incense. My roommate was out. My roommate was always out. My father spoke of exploratory surgery, brain tumor, they don't know. He delivered the information as if he were giving me instructions on how to make sure I didn't get ripped off when I took my car in for a tune-up. I went into the hallway to sit against the wall with my legs pulled to my chest to weep, like a girl in a TV show. I don't know why I did this, why I didn't just weep inside my room. I was frightened, but also intrigued by the drama of something Big in my little life. It was like in a movie.

I got over it.

My mother went into surgery the morning of December 7. It was a brilliant day, clear of smog and warm. I waited in the waiting room with my father and Ennie, one of my mother's way-older sisters, who'd come from Detroit to take care of my mother in her convalescence. Ennie was twenty-two years older than my mother, four-eleven, round as a wren, with curly black hair, pale blue eyes, and a large nose. She was weency and old. She looked nothing like my mother, who had auburn hair and green eyes, so many freckles that when she spent any time in the sun, more freckles cropped up between the freckles and she called that a suntan.

The Nutty Mahoneys were not there. Even though we spent every blessed holiday with them, including the minor ones like Labor Day, and even though my mother talked to Aunt Irene on the phone just about every day, and even though Aunt Irene and Uncle Dick frequently got into marital brawls which culminated with one of them showing up on our front porch at midnight, asking my mother for solace and advice, and perhaps a Coors 102, they couldn't be there. Aunt Irene worked dispatching school buses for the district, and Uncle Dick drove a truck for some soft drink company. They could not get the time off. Aunt Irene told Ennie that not everyone could just get time off in the middle of the week like Dad could, as if waiting for someone to get out of brain surgery was some fun thing only the professional classes enjoyed, like country club golf.

My mother's relationship with the Nutty Mahoneys was complicated. She was the only one of her sisters who hadn't married a guy who worked the assembly line at Ford Motor Company. Ennie and Dudu married guys off the line, and Aunt Irene married a truck driver. My mother didn't marry a guy of Irish descent with a drinking problem, but a Pole with an advanced degree and a job in Ford's design department. She married a guy who wore a tie to work and didn't come home smelling of machinist's oil. Aunt Irene lived in a stew of envy and my mother lived in a stew of guilt. And just as Aunt Irene got a kick out of making my mother feel guilty, my mother got a kick out of making Aunt Irene jealous. They were like two bloodied, exhausted boxers in the twelfth round of the match hanging on each other so they wouldn't fall over, while at the same time wanting to knock the other one out.

They competed in the categories of Cooking and Children. My mother didn't have to dispatch school buses every day, so she could experiment with recipes. She could afford fine ingredients. She had the party giver's gift of timing, of preparing the food in such a way that it all was ready at the same time. Aunt Irene made the fatal mistake of hitting the cheap white wine before she started cooking. Then, a little sloshed, she'd fight with Uncle Dick. They were incredible fighters, those two. They were the exact same size and Aunt Irene had a temper and punch that could rival his. By their mid-thirties they both had false teeth and had suffered a broken nose or two. One Easter we arrived with a baking dish full of rumaki—the one who wasn't hosting the holiday would bring the hors d'oeuvres—and found the ham in the middle of the living room. Aunt Irene was weeping in the bathroom and Uncle Dick was in the backyard passed out in a lounge chair. My mother felt terrible, picked up the ham off the shag carpet, and took it in the kitchen. Aunt Irene was at first grateful for my mother's help, then she drank a little more and felt resentful and accused my mother of being a shanty Irish putting on airs.

Aunt Irene scared me. She wore her blond hair in a beehive and had a wicked laugh. Her false teeth clicked when she chewed and she liked to pull my hair when I was staying there for the weekend and my parents weren't around. But

I loved Uncle Dick. He liked to dance in the living room, and let me and my cousins eat potato chips and drink RC Cola in front of the TV. Sometimes, when he got depressed, he pulled me on his knee and said, "You're lucky you're nice and tall." I felt bad for Uncle Dick. Since Dad's name was also Dick they were known by the women as Big Dick and Little Dick. How could a man possibly overcome a nickname like that?

It was a toss-up whether my mother won in the Children category. For one thing, Aunt Irene had two to my mother's one. My cousin Cindi Su and I were exactly two weeks apart in age, and spent the whole of our lives in twin holiday outfits. She wore the pink whatever-it-was and I wore the blue, since I was long-armed and hulking, with enough snarly hair on my head for sixteen people, and Cindi Su was a petite strawberry blonde. My mother was tortured by Cindi Su. She scoffed at Cindi Su's meekness and diffidence, but she also thought if you were a girl in these United States, being agreeable and dithering probably got you further than being a hulking wisenheimer who skipped grades in school and aspired to be a race car driver. Plus, Cindi Su had long legs that looked perfect poking out of a miniskirt.

My mother, Aunt Irene, and Ennie all wanted Cindi Su and me to be like sisters, since neither of us had one of our own. The problem was, Cindi Su was gullible and I had a mean streak. Once, when we were six or seven, we made a bet. Cindi Su was born on Easter, and she bet me fifty cents that her birthday was always on Easter. I knew Easter rotated each year. We went to ask the parents, who were out by the pool playing pinochle and drinking Coors 102, and sure enough, I was right. Cindi Su wept. Cindi Su said she didn't understand exactly what we were betting on. She didn't even *have* fifty cents. My mother, feeling guilty because she was winning at cards, and had married the educated Pole from the design department who didn't knock her teeth out, and had the wisenheimer daughter who started this mess, gave each of us a quarter from her purse. I hated her for that.

My mother's neurosurgeon was as tall as Dad and wore green scrubs. In those days the trend for euphemism hadn't yet settled in; spinning the truth as part of a patient's treatment plan was unknown. It was still thought that the best thing to do was to hear the worst, accept it, and do your best. Or hear the worst, then repress it and behave insufferably. But hearing the worst was always a component of the experience. The neurosurgeon appeared, the corners of his mouth turned down, stricken. I've often wondered whether this stricken look is practiced, a readable warning, the nonverbal equivalent of "you'd better sit down."

He looked at me and asked how old I was. He said, "It was malignant. I couldn't get it all. She's already asked all the hard questions."

My father sat down on the edge of the nearest chair. Ennie cried out, "Mother of God, let's go to the chapel, let's go to the chapel."

I said, "The chapel? What the fuck for? You think God's going to suddenly listen because we're in some stupid hospital chapel?"

"*Ahhnnnn!*" Ennie's hand went up to her little pruney mouth.

"No fucking way." I was a college girl now, and I could say "fuck." I could say it loudly, in the hospital where my mother learned she was going to die and where, three months and one day later, she would. It was one thing that my mother hadn't counted on. That I would learn to swear.

This was the only information I ever received about my mother's illness, that it was malignant and that the surgeon had not gotten it all. Only after my father died, and I opened his safety deposit box and found, among other things, her death certificate, did I learn she died of an astrocytoma, grade III, left parietal and frontal lobes. Grade I is the least malignant, grade IV, the most. Grade III is considered midgrade, like the lead content in gasoline. If a tumor invades the frontal lobe, it changes your personality and causes paralysis. A tumor in the parietal lobe affects your writing and hand-eye coordination. Astrocytoma is cancer of the astrocytes, the cells in the nervous system that are shaped like stars. I knew none of this, then.

Instead, I knew this: My mother went into surgery one woman and came out someone different. The woman who went in had a laugh loud enough to startle birds; could beat every man she knew at craps and poker; could cook a meal for eight hundred and still stand with one hand on her hip, a cigarette on her lip, getting off good one-liners; loved nothing more than a party; drank beer to the exclusion of all other beverages; liked spaghetti with carbonara sauce and beef Stroganoff— anything with noodles—bread, cheddar cheese, baked squash— this woman was no more. The woman who had been known to read a novel a day, but would prefer to gossip on the phone with her friends. The woman who loved intrigue. The woman whose great gift was finding the one interesting thing about anyone (she spent hours talking to my friends, dumb teenage girls, about their personal dramas. Even I thought what most of them had to say was lame). The woman who eschewed her native Catholicism for Episcopalianism, because she liked the sleekness of their churches and their belief. If there was anything unique about her, it was her wit and her persuasive abilities—my father said she would have made a good trial lawyer—but mostly, she was just a lively, optimistic suburban mom of that era, who believed that sewing a new sundress could improve a mood. She wore orange-peel lipstick and Jean Naté. At the time of the operation she had not begun menopause. She had pale, well-toned legs that I often caught other dads checking out at the A&P.

This woman was gone gone gone. The mother who emerged with the wound on the side of her head, which resembled a rusty croquet wicket, was remote, moody, suspicious. Whether this was the result of the surgery, the meds, the radiation, the chemotherapy, or the progression of the disease, I never knew. In fairness to her, and to my father, who withheld everything they possibly could from me, I don't think they knew either.

The day she was to be released from the hospital, I planned a surprise, something I was sure would make her feel better. My sorority's Christmas formal was two weeks away and I'd bought a dress I was sure would meet with her approval: a white, floor-length halter dress made of Qiana. She herself had proclaimed Qiana to be a flattering fabric, and white to be one of my colors. The cut of the dress was similar to a pink gingham number she'd sewn for me that spring. I knew I'd done well. And I found it all by myself!

I drove from USC to the hospital on fumes, empty Tab cans clattering around the backseat of my red Volkswagen bug as I careened around the corners. The dress was in a paper bag in the backseat. I had not seen my mother since the operation, over a week before. I had never known anyone to stay in the hospital that long; when I got my tonsils out at age four, they kept me overnight. My father thought it was best for me to wait until she was up and at 'em. It was one of those world famous Southern Califonia winter days, eighty degrees and clear from the San Bernardino Mountains all the way to Catalina.

At the hospital I changed into my dress in the bathroom. I felt I was being very dramatic. My mother loved dressing up and threw a costume party every year. I tended to be shy, like my father. I thought my sashaying down the hospital corridor in a long, white, backless formal, earning the stares of the nurses and orderlies, would delight her.

I hadn't remembered I would need shoes with the dress— something for which she would berate me—and squeaked down the hall in the white Qiana halter dress and my Mexican huaraches, the thick rubber soles made from Goodyear tires. I knew she'd have a white bandage around her head, like a turban. She wore an orange turban sometimes down at our beach house in Laguna, when her hair got dirty and she couldn't get to her regular Whittier hairdresser. I thought it would be like that.

She was dozing when I came in. The white bandages were wrapped tightly around her head. Her head looked small, without her teased-out pixie haircut. She didn't have black eyes, which is sometimes the result of brain surgery, but her face was swollen, her cheeks flushed and scaly. Her lips were dry and chapped. When she opened her eyes I knew she was on the other side of something. She had hazel eyes that snapped, that always looked as if she were up to something, as if she knew something no one else did. This was her natural expression, one of impudence. She was a flirt. They were paisley shaped, olive green flecked with gold. These new eyes were just ordinary, without curiosity or intelligence behind them. She stared at me like she didn't know who in the hell I was.

"Surprise! This is my dress for the winter formal. What do you think? Good, huh? Not the shoes. I still have to get some shoes. What should I get? Maybe when you get home we can go to Whittwood."

She just stared.

"I didn't wear this here. I changed in the bathroom. To model it for you. I'm even wearing a strapless bra. It works okay, don't you think? That's the one thing about halters, they make your boobs look sorta flat."

"Is your father here?"

No, my father was not there. No one was there but me.

After she got home from the hospital her interest in food and cooking abandoned her utterly. A woman who had never had any interest in sweets or dessert—once, I'd given her a box of See's candy for some occasion. She put it away in a cupboard and my father found it after her death; the chocolate was white, like ash—now lived on glazed donuts. On Friday I had no classes and would drive back to Whittier to take her to chemotherapy. On the way home she demanded in her new, slurred, and unnaturally low voice that we stop at Winchell's donuts. I'd buy her a dozen glazed; that winter, for some reason, they were baking them in the shape of a foot. When we got home she plopped down at the breakfast bar, hunkering over the box, eating one donut after the other, flecks of glaze trickling down her blouse. She looked at me slyly, as if she were getting away with something. "Get that look off your face," she'd say. No matter how I was looking, she always wanted that look off my face.

When she was done with the box of donuts, she smoked a cigarette. To do this, she needed to rubber-band the tops of her fingers closed around the filter.

Occasionally, my mother forgot who I was. She didn't know where we were going on the Fridays I came home from college to drive her to chemo. Naturally, the chemo made her sick. Once, she was throwing up and somehow the toilet seat fell on her nose and broke it. She howled and when I came to help, to do the only thing I knew to do for a bloody nose, hold her head back with a tissue clamped to her nostrils, she shoved me out of the bathroom. She locked the door and hollered "Get thee behind me, Satan!" through the door.

She cried a lot, for no reasons I could tell. A small bottle of holy water appeared by her bedside. For a while she kissed it every morning when she woke up; then one day she stomped into my room, threw the vial on my bed, and said, "What's this supposed to mean!" Once, she took me aside and, gripping my arm, whispered into my face, "You know I'm dying, don't you?" Her breath was bad from the medicine, and from not brushing her teeth. I believed her. She was my mother, and I was a young sixteen; I thought she still knew everything. Days later, when I would say something about what she'd told me, that she was dying, she'd shriek: "What are you talking about?" Then she'd moan to Ennie that her own child wished she were dead.

No one took me aside and tried to explain why these things were happening, not Ennie nor my father, who—I understood this only a good decade later—were both staggering beneath the weight of caring for her, and the anticipation of their impending grief. No one explained that she didn't know what she was saying, or that she didn't mean what she said, or even that the chemo made her nauseated. They thought the less said, the better. I like to imagine it would have mattered, to know. The theory behind keeping me in the dark was that it would allow me to Live My Life, meaning the life of an average spoiled, middle-class college girl who should concern herself with boys and dances and dates and clothes and hopefully, considering the tuition, an exam or two. What no one considered was that it was now and forever impossible for me to be an average, spoiled, middle-class college girl, that knowing nothing concrete about her illness only isolated me; it didn't minimize her illness one whit.

My mother was dying. This knowledge radiated from me like heat from a bad sunburn. It was not unlike the vibe given off by people desperate to get married. I tried to act giddy, I tried to act as if I were always up for a good time, but it was all an act. Mostly, I felt imprisoned behind a sheet of Plexiglas no one else could see. I tried to act exactly like Sarah, my best friend—sandy-blond hair, freckles, from exclusive Rancho Santa Fe. She had a breathy voice, just this side of Marilyn Monroe, and endeared herself to boys by siddling up and instantly granting them a flattering nickname. She was beloved; I imitated her and merely wound up sounding demented. My sad vibe accompanied me everywhere, when I went on set-up dates to fraternity mixers, where I dutifully drank too much rum punch and danced like a maniac to "Brown Sugar"; during sorority chapter meetings where we planned lunches and dances and special inspirational events for our pledge class; on Thursday nights, the official beginning of the weekend, when we were expected to show up at the 901 Club and get cutely hammered. There was something in my mien, something that was the opposite of light and flirtatious, it was anti–joie de vivre.

My mother was dying. It didn't help matters that at USC I was out of my league, socially. I was younger than everyone else; I'd skipped half of kindergarten and all of first grade. Our Whittier neighborhood was populated by three-bedroom ranch houses; in the tract you could choose from one of four floor plans. A few houses, like ours, even had a kidney-shaped swimming pool. The fathers in the neighborhood were middle managers. My father, the industrial designer, had the most interesting job, especially during the years he worked at Mattel and brought home free Barbie clothes. The chief of police lived two doors down. On Whittier Boulevard, the nearest big street, there was a Burger King, a putt-putt golf course, and several used-car lots. We shopped at department stores at the Whittwood. I'd never heard of Rodeo Drive or Melrose, of Gucci or Fiorucci or Tiffany's.

One girl in my sorority lived on Roxbury Drive in Beverly Hills, across the street from Lucille Ball. Another girl lived in Hancock Park in a house so grand, there was a bowling alley in her basement. On Saturday nights, my sorority sisters cleared out and went home, roaring off in their Porsches and BMWs to Hancock Park, Beverly Hills, Pasadena, and Newport Beach, their Gucci luggage filled with their Lacoste polo shirts. The homes they roared off to seemed filled to the gills with siblings and stepsiblings, with mothers who were going to go to the club with their daughters to play tennis, or to take the sailboat out. Many of the girls in the house were "legacies"; their mothers, aunts, or sisters were also Delta Gammas. There were over one hundred girls in my sorority and I was the only one with a terminally ill mother. Then I was the only one with a dead mother. Statistically, that seems impossible, but it was so. Stepmothers abounded, but no one was motherless.

Only now that I'm a mother myself can I imagine how my mother's own heart must have been breaking. Last summer Katherine went to sleepaway camp for the first time. I missed her, wandered into her god-awful messy room a dozen times a day, pretending to myself I was checking on Mojo, her dwarf hamster. Sometimes I took a nap on her bed, just to smell her on her pillow. I try to envision what it'll be like to ship her off to college—I've already determined it won't be at sixteen—and cannot. I'll immerse myself in a million writing projects and paraliterary events—committees, teaching, panels, and readings. I'll travel, ski, send myself to exotic parts of the ocean to scuba dive. My mother had none of these things with which to fill her empty days. She had her housework, her books, her beer and ciggies, her vast network of friends. Then, not three months after her only child was gone, she was diagnosed with a terminal disease.

Perhaps part of the reason they kept me out of the loop was that it was simply too tragic to deal with. I not only left for college, I left my mother for good.

In case the fates had not impressed this upon us sufficiently, the last time I saw her alive was the day I turned seventeen. She'd spent a week, with Ennie's help, trying to put together my favorite birthday dinner of prime rib, mashed potatoes, glazed carrots, and a devil's food cake. I dutifully drove home from school and ate my meal. My mother could hardly steer the fork to her mouth. She kept stabbing her chin. I was impatient. I was supposed to meet a boy I liked and his roommate back in L.A. for drinks at the 901 Club at nine P.M. I excused myself as soon after the cake as I could. Dad asked what did I think I was doing? My mother had worked all week on that meal. I lied and said the drinks were a real date. My mother put her hand on Dad's. I can still see her freckled hand, pink and scaly from the chemo, a piece of white paper tape protecting the bruised veins where the doctors had put the needle. My mother said, "Oh Dick, ler her go, she's got a date." That was the last thing I'd ever hear her say. I would never be back, because she was going away too; she would not be there for me to come back to.

9

The day before Dad's biopsy, Daniel and I take him to lunch at his favorite hamburger joint in Boulder City. It's no place you'd notice, stuck in a small strip mall across the parking lot from Sav-On Drugs, where only hours before, there's been a holdup. Yellow crime-scene tape stretches across the front of the store. Three booths are jammed with checkout clerks drinking chocolate milk shakes and giggling like kids unexpectedly released from school due to some unseen calamity, a freak snowstorm, burst pipes. The hamburger joint is one of those places usually empty enough to make you wonder how they stay in business, but the dashing proximity of the holdup gives it a festive air. A skinny waitress tosses a half dozen red plastic lattice-work baskets brimming with fries on her arm and delivers them to the tables of chattering clerks.

My father, the politest flirt imaginable, asks the waitress, What's all the hubbub? He grins up at her from behind his photosensitive aviator glasses, always tinted gray in the high desert glare, even indoors. He tells her he used to volunteer at the Boulder City police department answering 911 calls and remembers one call that came in on a cell phone. "There was a mountain goat standing in the middle of Boulder Highway and it wouldn't move. That was the emergency!" The waitress is politely uninterested.

My father was let go from the police department because he had trouble hearing; he wasn't getting all the information down right and sent squad cars meandering off to the wrong house to check out imaginary bumps in the night reported by lonely widows marooned in the desert after having retired here with their now-deceased spouses. He scoffed, said his hearing was fine. He probably needed a hearing aid; he most certainly needed a hearing aid, but that would mean a visit to the doctor, an acknowledgment of need.

The waitress brings bacon cheeseburgers for Daniel and me, and the same almost-inedible meal Dad's ordered since before I was born: a plain hamburger with nothing on it save a big slice of raw onion, the patty cooked extra well-done, the bun toasted just this side of burned to a crisp. The food Dad likes best tends toward the austere. A big, juicy burger is an alien concept. There is never any comfort in Dad's comfort food.

Daniel is as chipper as one of the checkout clerks, repeatedly offering Dad fries from his red plastic basket and asking him about the type of planes he flew in the Army Air Corps. Daniel was in the air force for a brief time, and he and Dad share a love of aircraft. Daniel's what the short-story writer Lorrie Moore calls a "dunk"—half dork, half hunk. He's mostly Norwegian, nearly as tall as Dad. I listen while they yatter on about B-50-this and B-50-that. They're being men, in the finest meaning of the word, playing poker for matchsticks in the foxhole while shots whiz by overhead. They're like the gentlemen smoking their cigars at the railing of the *Titanic* as it slid into the Atlantic. This is men at their best. They take so much flak for being out of touch with their feelings, repressed, nonintuitive, and generally boneheaded, but there is a place for these characteristics in the world. I admire them.

I eat one french fry after another, taking care to dip no more than one-half inch of the fry into the pool of ketchup, as if each fry were a paintbrush and I were painting some tricky trim that demanded the most care I could muster. My father taught me the right way to paint. Taught me how to hammer a nail straight, how to pull one out, how to draw a box in perspective, how to pull a weed and plant a cactus, how to wax a car, clean the whitewall tires, and check the oil.

I do not want him to have this biopsy. I would rather not know.

A depressing realization is born inside me. I try to smother it, as if it were an interesting beetle you might glance at briefly before dropping it into a jar with no air holes in the lid. Perhaps Dad and Daniel aren't being heroic at all, but merely clueless. Perhaps neither of them realizes the significance of the biopsy. Perhaps Dad is swaddled in grief so thick he doesn't know or care, and Daniel imagines the surgery, which is scheduled to take a scant two hours, is nothing more serious than an appendectomy. For, unlike me, my husband, with his two strapping parents, the manic phone callers who ski, kayak, and hike the Pacific Crest trail whenever the spirit moves them, has every reason to hope.

My father's surgery has a name, and it is not "some damn thing." It's called "a left chamberlain with biopsy and possible post thoracacotomy." This time around I did my research. I was not going to be standing there like some stupid kid, not knowing what anyone was talking about. The problem is this: Look up *chamberlain* in the dictionary and you discover it means "an officer who manages the household of a sovereign or a noble." I looked up *thoracacotomy* and saw, there on the first line, on a Web site called "yoursurgery.com," that the most common reason for opening the chest is to remove a cancer of the lung. But my father's surgery had "possible" in the title, which gave me a tiny gasp of hope.

When Daniel and I check him into the hospital, a large rose-pink stucco box in Henderson, I ask the admitting nurse what a chamberlain is, confessing I'd had no luck looking it up in the dictionary. Was it perhaps named after the some surgeon who pioneered the procedure? The nurse is the type whose immense lap you want to crawl into.

"Or maybe Richard Chamberlain," she says. "You know, Dr Kildare." *Please God, let her be joking.*

The surgery is scheduled for nine A.M, but he doesn't get rolled away until close to noon. I sit beside his bed in the Same Day Surgery staging area. I watch him doze off and on. He sleeps with his mouth wide open, his thin lips slack against his large teeth, his hands curled against his chest. I try not to get carried away, tell myself that we don't know anything yet, but he doesn't look well. He doesn't look like a person with a cyst. When the nurse weighed him upon check-in, he was 138 pounds, fully clothed. My weight exactly, buck naked. He was six-two.

In the bed on the opposite side of the narrow room there's a young woman in her late twenties, tall, blond, and several months pregnant, who's there for a breast biopsy. Despite the horror she and her people must be feeling, there's a celebratory air over on that side of the room. Her surgeon bounced in moments after she arrived, pressed his clean-handed self against the side of her bed, leaned over, and clasped her hand. "Hey," he said, in the voice a lover might use, "I bet you're ready to get this over with." Her husband is there, with his thick brown hair like the pelt of some animal and a wedding ring a size or so too small for his finger, her parents too, all hovering solicitiously, as well they should be. Still, I feel a wee bit disgruntled. No one is checking on Dad; indeed, I'm having a tough time getting him a cup of water, or information on why his surgery is being delayed.

My shaky optimism is eroding by the second. I get the feeling that because Dad isn't young, blond, and pregnant, his case is less compelling and therefore less important, that just because he's a seventy-four-year-old two-pack-a-day man with lung cancer—*Who said this? No one said this. You don't*

KNOW. *Sure you feel in your bones that this won't go well, but what do you know really?*—there's somehow less suffering, that somehow his predicament is, quote unquote, just part of life. Here's a heads-up, something I'm sure most of us would prefer not to think about: Just because it's part of life, it's not any less agonzing. Knowing that we all die, and that Dad has lived a, quote unquote, full life, blah blah blah, does nothing to stop the sensation that my own chest is undergoing its own do-it-yourself thoracacotomy, like something out of a sci-fi movie, my ribs being pried apart by unseen hands, my heart eager to leap out and flee its own breaking.

Where is his goddamned surgeon?

Long after the blonde is wheeled away, and Dad is the only one left in the room, an attendant in dark blue scrubs bounces in and prepares to wheel him off. His name tag says JORGE. "Mr Karbo! How are you today!" At least Jorge has the false jocularity thing down. Despite its falseness, I want to embrace Jorge. I impute to him all sorts of marvelous qualities I'm sure he doesn't possess. Jorge is suddenly the only caring, empathic human being in the entire hospital. Despite his lack of training, I wish Jorge, he of the girlish lashes, brown eyes, and Eeyore wristwatch, were performing the chamberlain on my dad. What he lacked in surgical skills he would make up for in good karma. He kneels down and pops the brakes on the wheels of the gurney, giving my dad a solid pat on the shoulder on the way. Dad's gray eyes flutter closed.

I encircle Dad's bony wrist with my hand, the way I'd grab the wrist of one of my kids who was crossing the street without looking. I'd planned to lean down for a hug, then realize how awkward it is to hug someone in a hospital bed. Dad isn't hooked up to any tubes or wires, the jostling of which might set off an alarm that would summon a displeased nurse, so what is it that gives me pause? The damn gown. Here I am in my uniform: hip-hugger jeans, black Doc Martens, and black

T-shirt, my attitude square, my identity on straight, while my poor father is imprisoned in that too-soft, oft-washed blue and white cotton gown—skimpy, bum-revealing, persona-stripping, joie de vivre–eradicating—and that simple sartorial difference puts him at the mercy of people who care about him because they are paid to. I can't stand it. I suspect it is the first step toward him becoming unrecognizable to me.

Even if I were set on giving my father a hug of support, he would never lean forward to help receive the hug, so there would be nowhere to put my arms once I got down near his face. I'm not sure whether I should try to tuck my hands behind his shoulders, or put them on his chest—a tad intimate—or what. And even if the hug were to happen, then what? Hollywood air kisses. I think about patting my dad's hand, but that seems too patronizing, too belittling. I am not ready for my father to become someone whose hand I pat.

I do not know what to do.

In this moment I forsee long months of neither of us knowing what to do.

I say the only words of consolation we have for one another: "Hey! Don't worry, we're tough old Polacks, me and you."

He releases a smile, relieved. He won't be required to field anything more emotional from me than this. "That we are, babe, that we are."

The surgical waiting room is also the maternity waiting room. Daniel and I sit thigh by thigh in two small chairs—hard, overpadded, with too-low backs—lined against walls so aggressively textured that leaning your head back against one means the risk of scratching your scalp. On the maternity side, the waiting is less punishing. There are comfy-looking barrel chairs, a love seat, magazines that are the print equivalent of the sluttiest chick in high school, handled by many but appreciated by none. There are no magazines on the surgical side. There are, however, a series of somnambulistic reproductions of pigtailed Indians dozing in serapes in desert southwestern colors.

Is this some kind of joke? Or was the architect going for some kind of Circle of Life motif, with disfigurement and possible death on one end of the room and happily laboring soon-to-be moms, squalling babies, and bouquets of Mylar balloons on the other? I laugh out loud, *ha ha*, fish around in my purse, a brown leather Coach handbag that belonged to Bev, given to me by my father when he was cleaning out her things, and find a tube of lip gloss. I roll it on, then lick it off my lips.

My husband has been unlucky with marriage, but has had the good fortune to live thirty-seven years without one bad waiting room experience. This makes him the voice of reason. I'd always been under the impression that experience makes you wise. Turns out, it only makes you a self-doubting, ambivalent wreck. Daniel is ready to sit down and wait politely, whereas I want to *mock*. If Daniel and my father were the ones in the foxhole playing cards, I was the one quipping madly, "Aside from that, Mrs. Lincoln, how was the play?" I want Daniel to get in on the gallows humor, so I don't feel so alone.

"For ten points and a chance to go for the dinette set, how is this like when my mother was buried?" I ask him. He squeezes my knee, sweet and concerned. He has no idea what I'm talking about.

It's the only image I remember clearly from my mother's funeral. Graveside. Rose Hills Cemetery, located in the spacious crotch of several Southern Californian freeways, the largest cemetery in the world. Rolling lawns bisected by real streets, a Disneyland-style map required to get around. Early March, and therefore warm enough for me to be wearing a sleeveless calico print dress that can only be called Western-inspired—fashionable for forty-eight hours sometime in the late seventies—with a tight-fitting bodice trimmed with lace, a cinched waist and a full skirt, a flounce around the ankle-length hem. It was maroon and green, me having staunchly refused to wear anything that was, you know, too much of a *drag*, not realizing that the memory of my mother's funeral with me squeezed into that hideous dress (it was purchased before I went to college and gained the requisite freshman fifteen) would be branded in my memory for all time. I sat slouched in a folding chair next to my father, my arms folded across my stomach, the international teenage girl sign for self-loathing, glaring and surly. My mother's coffin was lowered into the ground with the aid of a some special hydraulic machine, and the guy who pressed the button, who a century ago would be the one lowering the coffin by rope with the aid of a toothless cohort, was dressed in his Sunday best. He knelt down in front of me to fuss with something, and there at eye level was his pink tie (Rose Hills had a color, like a sports team; the hearse that picked us up to take us to the funeral was nipple pink. I refused to get in and for a moment it seemed as if I would have a full-on, eye-rolling teenage fit). The tie was held in place by a tack in the shape of . . . could it be? . . . a small gold shovel. I sputtered, rolled my lips inside my mouth to keep from giggling. My father was oblivious, but other people stared. I'd sat dry-eyed throughout the funeral service but now here I was laughing. I was seventeen years old and away at college, almost an adult and therefore not worthy of the pity that would have surrounded me had I been seven, or ten, or even twelve. I should be behaving myself.

My mother's funeral was attended by a few hundred people, amazing, since she wasn't a professional woman and our family was tiny. In addition to Ennie and her husband, George, and the Nutty Mahoneys—Aunt Irene and Uncle Dick, their children, my cousins, John and Cindi Su—there were our neighbors in Whittier; several friends; some of the checkers at the A&P where my mother drove every day for her six-pack and ciggies; her hairdresser; the head writer for *The Dating Game*, who lived next door to our beach house in Laguna; some friends of mine from high school and their mothers; and some of the girls from my sorority and their mothers. Some of them must have known that in addition to suffering the loss of my mother, I was too young to be subjected to the alarming truth that dying and death are still part of the topography in the land of the living and are thus subject to the same emotional weather. My mother was dead and I was not simply sad, but also enraged, resentful, frightened, relieved, and now, entertained. That tie tack was unbelievable. It was hilarious. I put my hands over my face and laughed into my palms. I was swooning with guilt and amusement. There was nothing resembling a Hallmark sentiment in any of this. Wasn't then, isn't now.

Back at the hospital, on the maternity side, at a white laminate sofa console table pushed against the back of a floral love seat, two heavyset women wearing plaid blouses and reading glasses dangling from silver chains vigorously scrapbook, their glasses bouncing on what can only be called their bosoms as they reach across one another for scissors or glue. You can see how the act of assembling a scrapbook has been mistaken for a verb; splayed across the table are envelopes of photographs, colored paper of varying sizes and thickness, translucent squares of vellum, glue sticks, silver metallic thread, tubes of sequins, and pages of baby-related clip art, replicas of Victorian paper dolls. The women snip and paste and wonder loudly whether they should add cards, poems, and quotes. From what I gather, a niece is having a baby.

Two teenage girls and a boy stumble in, their hair tousled, just in from Barstow, across the Mojave Desert. One of the aunties shows them a page to be dedicated to the display of the baby's soon-to-be belly button. One of the tousled-haired girls, in a blue sweater and hip-huggers, strides through the double doors into Labor and Delivery and, moments later, strides back out. "I can hear her screaming in there!"

"She's been in labor for nine hours," crows an auntie.

"Heh, that's nothing," says the other one. "I was in labor for thirty-six with Loreen. That girl damn near tore me in half. You should have seen how swollen my you-know-what was. Now, they'd give you a Cesarean for that. You got the glue stick over there?"

Somerset Maugham once wrote that the only people you can truly love are those you will never meet, and this is true of the scrapbooking family. I love them for behaving as if no one else were in the room, as if Daniel and I and one other wraithlike gentlemen at the far end of the room—legs crossed, arms crossed, dozing—aren't even there, the way people who are used to renting videos behave in movie theaters these days. Waiting for this baby to come is an excuse for time off school and work, for a party in the waiting room. One of the auntie's sons— tall, scraggly blond beard, tight black T-shirt through which you can see his own belly button straining—arrives with white paper bags from McDonald's. The smell of french fries masks the vaguely sour odor of Betadine and disinfectant. Three more women show up, examine the scrapbook, wonder how dilated the mother is, reminisce about their own children who nearly tore them in half, plunk their big bums down, and commence to eat tuna sandwiches out of a vending machine. (A tuna sandwich in southern Nevada! Out of a vending machine!) At that end of the room life is chaotic but benign, rich in love and attachment. I am envious.

I'd brought my laptop along in order to pretend to myself that what was happening here was routine. Just waiting for my dad to have a little procedure, a little cut-and-paste that would take no more than two hours. I thought I'd get a little work done. Getting work done was not something I did the last time with my mother. The last time I waited, like the room said. I slouched in the uncomfortable chairs, put out by the inconvenience and terrified.

For a while, I play the game in my head that's supposed

to generate optimism. I try to visualize a positive outcome. I mentally travel into the operating room with my father, into my father's open chest, where I become the tissues that appear red, healthy, and cancer-free, and all those other alternative New Age strategies for coping that we natives of the West Coast are supposed to have a natural aptitude for. When this fails to generate anything more than gut-twisting anxiety, I switch to the meditating-on-the-march-of-history technique. There weren't laptops last time. "Scrapbook" was still a noun.

Suddenly I'm overcome by the need to bolt. I come up with all kinds of reasons why I simply can't do this: I have a family a thousand miles away! I have a career that's been taxiing down the runway ready to take off for the last ten years! I have a dog! I have a new lawn! I'm running on the fumes of maturity. I am still and always the long-suffering sixteen-year-old. Frank Zappa once said, "The older you get, the more you realize that life is like high school." He should have elaborated and said that the reason for this is that we frequently *behave* as if we're still in high school. Only hours ago I was jealous of the lovely pregnant blonde here for a breast biopsy, the Homecoming Queen of the Same Day Surgery staging area.

I think about where I might race off to and still save face. The ladies' room? The cafeteria? The car? What would happen if I just got in the car and disappeared into the vast desert that fanned out from this stupid hospital for hundreds of miles in every direction? For if I, my father's only living blood relative aside from my seven-year-old daughter, wasn't here to receive the bad news, perhaps there wouldn't be any bad news to receive, like the tree-falling-in-the-forest thing.

Just about the time I wish my chair had a locking seatbelt, so Daniel can lock me in, my wish is granted. We hear a noise that makes the scrapbooking ladies and their brood and the wraithlike man and Daniel and me startle in unison, cartoon-character-like. *Aaaaannnt! Aaaaannnt! Aaaaannnt!* A fire alarm. The same kind we had in high school. *Aaaaannnt! Aaaaannnt! Aaaaannnt!* Daniel has borrowed the laptop and booted up some submarine game. At the sound of the alarm, he glances up, shoulders still relaxed, tennis-shoed feet crossed at the ankles, calm as pudding.

I leap up, ready to run. *Aaaaannnt! Aaaaannnt! Aaaaannnt!* The milky-glass window between the waiting room and the maternity reception desk scrapes open and a black-haired nurse in a blue smock sticks her head out. "You'd better go," she says loudly, pointing up at the red EXIT sign over the hallway leading to the elevators. *Aaaaannnt! Aaaaannnt! Aaaaannnt!* The scrapbookers abandon their scrapbooks and mosey toward the door. The wraithlike man walks down the hall, expressionless. Hurrah for American public schools. We were all trained so well. We are courteous, calm, and obedient. I pass the double doors that lead to the operating rooms, with their unfriendly sign, MEDICAL PERSONNEL ONLY BEYOND THIS POINT! and stop.

What am I thinking? I can't leave. How can I *leave?* Are these people insane? Is this the kind of daughter they think I am? My dad is cut open in there, a tube taped to his face, a stupid paper cap covering his tender bald head. I will go down with the ship. If my dad is going to perish in a hospital fire, then so am I. Relief rolls in like the tide. I won't have to soldier through the next four, six, eight, ten, fifteen months at all. I'll die with Dad in a fire. The thought is only beginning to occur to me that dying in a fire is supposed to be a terrible way to go, when the alarm stops. The milky window rattles open again and the nurse says, "Just a fire in the kitchen. No biggie."

"I thought kitchen fires were the worst kind," I say, too loudly. I'm pissed off that my fantasy was interrupted just as it was beginning to offer me some comfort. We file back to our places, and the waiting resumes.

One of the main appalling shocks of being fortyish and no longer sixteen is that the doctor is suddenly your peer, which makes you realize that had you pursued that med school dream for longer than seventy-two hours, you too might be operating on your dad's chest. Dr. Lagstone shows up a half hour after the false alarm. Short, curly-haired, round wire-framed glasses. I didn't see him approach but feel as if he just dropped in front of us, *Star Trek*–style. He doesn't introduce himself, shake our hands, or give us a consoling clap on our arms. I am suddenly looking at his feet, in their expensive black Rockports. Small shoes on small feet, the heels worn down further on the outside than the inside. Lagstone is a supinator, with smaller feet than mine, who refuses to make eye contact.

Surgeons are world famous for their lack of bedside manner, which we excuse by saying we'd rather have a good surgeon who's rude than a polite surgeon who does sloppy work. Why these two traits can't coexist in the same person is one of the mysteries of modern medicine. I suspect surgeons are friendlier to people they have a chance of curing. A patient who'll never recover despite all their wizardry stands as a reproach to the surgeon's skill and power.

Lagstone is a mutterer. He stares at my collarbone like a kid forced to muster the energy to come up with an explanation for something he shouldn't have done. "You're the Karbo family murzha murzha the mass murzha cancerous murzha murzha not sure where it originated murzha not the original mass murzha a metastasis originated perhaps in the lung murzha murzha didn't even touch it, the lung murzha was all in there murzha candidate for radiation."

The moment Lagstone turns his back I collapse over my lap as if someone has hit a lever, tears falling straight from my eyes to the carpeted floor. It's a mark of how much I've changed since last time that I'm able to carry on in public this way. I am glad Dad is sedated and isn't able to witness me betraying the tough old Polack credo. I inhale in that hiccupy way kids do. I lose track of everyone in the room. The wraithlike man at the other end of the row of chairs vanishes, as does the scrapbooking family. The bad news has arrived, as I knew it would, like a force-five hurricane sweeping in off the Gulf, tearing sheets of protective plywood from over plate-glass windows, forcing people who didn't evacuate to huddle atop the roof of their pickups, which is now high ground. Did Lagstone say they got most of it? Did he say the mass *is* cancerous, or *was* cancerous? Did he sew up my dad without doing anything but taking a quick peek? If not, why not?

Daniel has his arm around me, leading me out of that place, past the double doors that lead into the surgery, past the maternity ward and the scrapbooking family. I press my hands to my cheeks. When I pull them away I see my fingertips coated in black as if they took my fingerprints down at police headquarters. Oh God, what is *this*? My heart feels like a big dog straining at a small leash. My tears are black, like those of some crumbling Spanish statue of the Virgin Mary that attracts pilgrims seeking miracles.

"It's your mascara, hon," says one of the scrapbookers. At the end of her arm is a hand waving a pink tissue. I say, Oh, oh thank you. I want to be in this family, where there are alert and compassionate ladies with large bosoms and a devotion to archiving family history, tissues at the ready.

Daniel and I have two hours until my father is out of recovery. There's nothing to do but drive fifteen minutes to the Las Vegas strip, where despite all the swanky faux-European hotels with their $285-a-night room fees, Wolfgang Puck–ish restaurant menus and wholesome amusements for the entire family, it's still the hard-luck capital of the West. Sleazy guys still lurk on the hot, wide sidewalks outside each casino pressing handbills for escort services on everyone who makes eye contact, and inside you can still get drunk and weep at the bar in the middle of a casino without drawing attention to yourself. In Las Vegas a weeping woman who wipes her nose on the back of a hand, glistening with so much snot that it looks like a snail freeway, doesn't even warrant a glance.

Daniel, tears, and me are not a happy trio. Crying makes Daniel feel ineffectual, since as both a man and my husband, he feels he should be able to do something to stop them, which means fixing what caused them. That he does not feel similarly about fixing things related to other forms of water leakage in our house—the bathtub drain that leaks into the basement into a gray plastic bucket used for bringing snacks to Danny's once-a-month Cub Scout meetings, the rusting chrome elbow pipe beneath the bathroom sink that leaks into the cabinet where the toilet paper is stored, things he had a chance of fixing once and for all—is an occasional sore spot, but right now his stream of reassurances is welcome. Not reassuring, exactly, but much better than some of the male alternatives, such as stiff-lipped silence, or changing the subject to sports in an attempt to pretend that nothing is happening.

Paris Las Vegas, with its cobblestone pathways and wrought-iron streetlamps, the main casino floor huddled beneath a replica of the legs of the Eiffel Tower, has the worst acoustics in the city. The whirring, ringing, clanging, and electronic beeps and buzzes from the floor bounce off the cobblestones and reverberate off the pale blue ceilings painted with clouds. Still, Paris is my favorite world city, and I feel fortunate having phony Paris a few miles away. The strange thing is, the place is crawling with French people, who seem as content with the Las Vegas version as they are with the real thing. Perhaps they're just glad to be able to touch base with something that seems vaguely familiar in this part of the American Southwest, with its acres of pale sky and sandy flat desert floor, nothing like what they must have imagined: sand dunes punctuated by the occasional oasis dotted with date palms.

I order a Glenlivet on the rocks, sniffle, and eat the ice. It's so loud in here that Daniel has to lean over so his lips are touching my ear in order to be heard. He's wearing a blue-green T-shirt that complements his tropical-ocean-colored eyes. Nobody has a more beautiful eye color than Daniel, unless it's Rachel, his daughter, whose eyes are paler still, like beach glass.

"He didn't say the tumor was inoperable, did he? I didn't hear the word 'inoperable' used. And anyway, even if it was inoperable, even if it is the thing that's going to end his life, he could live for ten years. You don't know. We don't know."

"I *know*," I say. "There's no way he's going to live another ten years. Ten months, maybe. Six of which will be sheer hell." I start to cry again.

"You've got to be more positive, Peach." We have a pair of silly nicknames for each other. We said they were the names we'd have for each other if we were in a motorcycle gang. He is "Buck" and I am "Peach," so named because the hair on my arms is like peach fuzz. I inherited this smoothness from my dad, who has a smooth chest and shaves his angular jaw only every few days. I was an adult when I realized that lots of guys had hair on their backs and that lots of them worried about it.

I crunch on my ice. "Excuse me, but I don't have to do *anything*."

"We all die, though, you're going to die, I'm going to die—"

"—I get the picture—"

"—but he's not dead today. He's still alive today, and you have a lot of good days left with him."

I pat Daniel's knee, felt his bony kneecap through his Levi's. At the tiny table beside ours, a quartet of Parisians are exclaiming over the quality of a baguette they've just purchased at the casino's large *boulangerie*. Poor Daniel, what can he say? This is all bullshit, but it's enough of a boost to get me up and out of the chair and away from the cocktail waitress, who's headed our way with her tiny tray. We trudge around. While I'm in the fancy WC daubing my eyes with toilet paper, Daniel wins fifty bucks on the dollar slot. "See," he says, wrapping his arms around me. "Things are looking up."

Back at the hospital we find Dad in his room on the second floor, his long arms brown against the pale gray blankets. The Levelors are closed against the merciless sun, and the room smells of the war between disinfectant and sickness. I hold onto the handrails of his bed and make myself look at him. He's blinking up at the ceiling. I can count on one hand the number of times in my life I'd ever seen my Dad *lying down*, much less groggy, wan, and helpless. The clear plastic prongs of the oxygen tubes disappear into his aristocratic Baltic nose. An IV is stuck in his arm and pouffy, flesh-colored anklets that look like a cross between Cheerios and blood pressure cuffs inhale and exhale around his ankles, like some kind of weird animal that lives in the sea.

The director of a local museum that specializes in displaying mining equipment, ancient train parts, and other machinery from Nevada's silver-rush youth used to say that when Dad restored an item for them, the piece was entering the Karbo Zone, where something that looked ready for the junk heap was not simply restored to its original luster, but worked better than when it was brand-new, a hundred-odd years ago. On this day, the Karbo Zone is temporarily out of service, and I can't help feeling that the vast machine world of gears that turned smoothly, bushings that slid without seizing up, valves that opened and closed without protest, felt unnerved. One more person who truly understood them is down for the count.

I tuck the Ziploc bag with Dad's toothbrush, mouthwash, hair brush, and Old Spice into the cupboard beneath the television. He insisted I bring these things, though I doubted he'd get to use them. The plaid cowboy shirt, the tobacco-colored knit sweater, and the beige Lee jeans he wore to the hospital were already hanging up.

"What happened?" His voice bubbles up low and gurgling, the way a swamp might sound if given the power of speech.

A young nurse, with wavy waist-length auburn hair and freckles, and wearing one of those new-style nurse's tops that comes in a fabric you might use to make a quilt for a five-year-old—this one a red, blue, and green print of Labrador retrievers—bustles in and checks the monitors. Linda is Australian, and like all people in the western United States with Britishy-sounding accents, immediately attractive. She checks the cuffs on his ankles and makes sure he knows where the buttons are to turn on the TV or summon a nurse.

"You are looking good, Richard!" she says, "considering what you've just been through. Good indeed. My name is Linda."

"What's going on?" says Dad. "What did he find in there?"

During my sob-a-thon in Paris Las Vegas, it hadn't crossed my mind that my dad would be more in the dark than Daniel and I were. I imagined that by the time we got to the hospital Dad and Lagstone would have had The Talk. The last time, with my mother, when the surgeon came out in his green scrubs to deliver the bad news, he said, "She's awake now, and has asked all the hard questions."

"Hasn't Dr. Lag . . . hasn't he . . . hasn't . . . haven't they talked? My dad and the surgeon?"

"Dr. Lagstone has already been in to see him," says Linda.

"I didn't see him," gurgles Dad. He tries without success to clear his throat.

"You were just coming out of the anesthesia, Richard," says Linda.

"Is he going to come back?" I can hear the panic in my own voice. I see the next moments loom like a metal guardrail in the headlights, seconds before the car plummets over the bridge. I will have to be the one to tell my dad he has lung cancer. My feelings of loathing for the cowardly Lagstone sprout like June dandelions. That little schmuck cut my dad open, glimpsed the ropey tumor sprouting from my dad's black lung, realized there was nothing he could do, and then fled the scene of the crime. Is there no law, no fine print of the Hippocratic oath that obligates the surgeon to advise the patient of his condition?

Linda sees the look on my face, makes three phone calls, and is able to chase down Lagstone's nurse. Dad is still blinking away the grogginess, trying to lift his head from his pillow. He plucks at the blankets, trying to reach the cuffs around his ankles. I want him to talk to Lagstone's nurse, but he's in no position to talk to Lagstone's nurse. It would always be this way now, I saw, me gauging whether the self-assured, competent dad I knew was up to the task at hand. Minute by minute, stuff was changing.

I take the receiver and swallow a knot of reluctance. *Shit.* It's an old-fashioned phone with heft. I put on my Party Suit, the personality I adopt when I have to speak in public. The Party Suit is a special invisible suit that I slip into like a superhero, which makes me self-possessed and witty, a real adult moving in a world populated with other real adults. I explain that my husband and I are here in my dad's room, that my dad is awake and lucid and is eager to know the outcome of the surgery.

"Mr. Karbo will have to speak to Dr. Lagstone about that," says Lagstone's nurse.

"Wonderful. When will Dr. Lagstone be in, do you think?"

"Tomorrow morning sometime."

"But he still hasn't spoken with my dad about what he found in the surgery."

I hear the telltale sound of computer keys. Is she checking on my dad's case, or writing an e-mail to her sister? "He's already been in to see him, after he got out of recovery."

"But my dad was just waking up."

"I'm sure the doctor will be happy to talk to your father tomorrow."

"But my dad wants to know today. And I know Dr. Lagstone

is a busy guy, but frankly, he didn't tell us too much. Afterward, I mean. We don't have any real information either."

"I can't tell you anything until Dr. Lagstone talks to your father."

"I understand that. I get that. But my dad is wide awake now, and he'd really like to talk to the doctor about what he found."

She sighs. "All right. Hold on." I am clearly being a pain. There is the sound of her chair scraping, then silence, then more computer keys clicking. My armpits are clammy, the room is cold with too much air-conditioning. Doesn't the creepy dude Lagstone know I am not fortyish, but sixteen, and should not have to be doing this? Doesn't he get that I am wrecked, bereft, grief-stricken, and not a tough Polack at all?

My dad asks Daniel, "Who's she talking to?"

Daniel looks at me. What should he say?

"Your surgeon's nurse, Dad."

"What's going on?" My dad's big brown hands reach down and tug at the blanket around his feet.

"Those things buggin' ya, Dick?" Daniel pulls the sheet back, revealing Dad's large pale feet. They are like something you might find in loamy soil beneath a large rock. Dad tells him the cuffs are too tight, and Daniel wrestles with them a bit, seeing if he can loosen them; Linda says, No, they are supposed to be that way, to encourage circulation, to prevent edema. Daniel removes his hands from the cuffs, pats my dad's shins in what looks like an attempt at a reassuring gesture. This is what I love about Daniel: He's not afraid to touch a man who is dying but doesn't know it.

"It says here 'metastatic disease,'" says Lagstone's nurse.

Metastatic disease?

"But the blood work was clean," I say. Am I going to argue with the diagnosis like some lamebrain in a TV movie? Apparently, I am. "If the tumor had already metasized, wouldn't there have been cancerous cells in the blood? Isn't the circulatory system the body's highway or something?"

"I don't know about that."

I don't know if she means she doesn't know about the blood work being clean, or that the circulatory system is the body's highway.

I am polite. I am so polite. I thank her very much. I thank her so very much. I am insipid and sincere in trying mask my urge to shriek at her in a way that would summon a large orderly bearing a straitjacket. *Metastatic disease*. A euphemism coined for the use of medical professionals who need to pass on information but don't want to say anything that could be interpreted as dire. *Metastatic disease*. In other words—and I am rapidly learning the lesson that when you are dealing with doctors, there are always other words, real words, that aren't being said—the lung cancer has already spread. Aren't they supposed to at least preface that with, "I'm so sorry, the news isn't good, I'm afraid . . ." Isn't this supposed to be the second bit of bad news you get after the first bit of bad news?—the second punch of the proverbial one-two punch? You have cancer, and it's spread? Metastatic disease is a basketball game that starts in the fourth quarter with no time-outs; a movie that begins in the third act when the hero's buddy on the beat is shot and bleeding to death in the hero's arms. It's not manageable like, say, heart disease, or diabetes. It's not alcoholism, or anorexia, not something a nurse should read from a chart to the terminally ill man's daughter in a voice a bank teller uses to tell you your balance. I put the receiver down and think, What the fuck?

I look at Daniel, then down at Dad, and Daniel, without saying anything more, performs the service for which I will feel grateful to him the rest of my days.

"Well, Dick, they said sure enough, it's cancer you've got there. Lung cancer."

"Ah." My dad nods.

"We'll know more later," I say. "That was his nurse and she said he'll talk to you more about it tomorrow."

"The hell with that," he says. "When do I get out of here?"

He got out of there the next day—as it turned out, without ever speaking to Lagstone, not then or ever again.

10

That night, for the first time in family history, Daniel and I sleep alone in the Palace of the Golden Sofa. You'd think we'd take the opportunity to raid the liquor cabinet, have loud sex on the living room floor, leave dirty glasses on the kitchen counter, and fail to pick up wet towels. But we are chastened by the creepy middle-of-the-night Boulder City silence, afraid of waking the dead. Even Dad, who doesn't believe in anything he can't see, who can't even get into the spirit of movie special effects (I took him to see the original *Star Wars* at Grauman's Chinese Theater on Hollywood Boulevard, thinking he'd enjoy the design of the spaceships and blasters; his first words when we emerged into the sun were "You know, babe, there's no sound in space"), was spooked the first night he spent alone in the Palace after Bev died. His phone had rung at three A.M. on the dot and when he'd answered, no one was there. The next day he reported this to me over the phone. He said, "I think it was Beverly, letting me know she got there all right."

When the naval clock over the pantry chimes eleven o'clock, Daniel takes Woodrow out on his leash to pee and I take the hottest shower I can stand. Earlier in the evening I called the kids and told them Grandpa had done well in his surgery. They were glad to hear this, since they'd spent the evening, under the tutelege of Betty, Daniel's mother, drawing get-well cards. Daniel got on the phone with her and said, Yes, lung cancer, to which she said, We *knew* it! Humans are odd that way—we are so happy to have suspected something that turns out to be true, even if it's disastrous.

I turn off the furnace so it won't kick on during the night and wake us up. We crawl under the electric blanket and permit ourselves to roll toward each other for a chaste peck on the cheek. We don't want Bev showing up in any form to express her disapproval.

It doesn't matter that the furnace isn't on or that I am exhausted from my sob-a-thon at the casino bar in Paris Las Vegas. Three o'clock A.M. and my eyes click open, the same time the ghost of Bev had called. Three A.M. is the most famous dead-of-night hour because it's the most desperate, too late to be called night and too early to be called morning. Song lyrics always equate loneliness with this hour, and "three A.M. code" is the name for a software code written in such a funky manner that it could only have come out of someone's head when they were slightly loony with fatigue. I always wake up exactly at three A.M. according to whatever clock is in the room. In Portland our bedroom clock runs ten minutes fast, whereas the clock on the nightstand in the guest room at the Palace is in perfect sync with the kitchen clock which, via radio waves or some such thing—Dad once explained it to me—is in sync with the United States Naval Observatory's atomic clock. It doesn't matter. Somehow my body obeys the clock and not itself.

The floor plan of the Palace is L-shaped. Standing at the doorway of the guest room, which sits at the L's right angle, you see the long hallway stretching past the guest bath, the living room, the laundry room, and the dining area, ending in the dark kitchen/family room. Off to the right the shorter leg of the L leads to DadandBev's study, the master bedroom, and bath. I get up and go to the bathroom, then instead of going back to bed, wander in my T-shirt and underpants into DadandBev's study. Even from there I can hear the clock on the sofa console ticking away. It always reminds me of the clock tick-ticking on *Chiller*, the Saturday afternoon monster movie I used to watch when I was small, and which always scared me to death. One time I watched *Chiller* on the day of the night my parents had a cocktail party, and when it came time to take my bath, my dad had to excuse himself from the party to sit in the bathroom and keep me company so I wouldn't be scared. He brought in his old-fashioned and the recent issue of *Car & Driver*, and was happy to sit on the little vanity seat while I played with my bath toys.

Before his surgery, Dad and I had a discussion, just after we'd returned to the Palace from the hamburger joint. This is what Dad always said when it was serious business, that we needed to "have a discussion," which always made me feel as if I was in the doghouse for something, even though I never was. (When I was in the doghouse for something, he said, "Babe, I have a bone to pick with you.") He led me back to the study, to the big safe that sat against the wall, next to Bev's old treadle sewing machine. The sewing machine was covered in plastic to protect it from dust—as if there was ever any serious dust in that place.

As I mentioned before, DadandBev were a little insane on the topic of the Second Amendment. They were a little insane when it came to the number of firearms a person might truly need for protection. They feared that some afternoon, while they were out doing their weekly shopping at Albertsons, or up at Railroad Pass Casino taking advantage of the $4.99 buffet, a posse of deranged thugs on PCP would break into their house and steal their weapons, before going on to perpetuate unspeakable crimes for which DadandBev would then be held responsible. It was well known that law-abiding citizens like DadandBev routinely took the fall for deranged, tattooed thugs on PCP, since the thumb-sucking, liberal-minded media, in cahoots with sleazy, over-paid lawyers and the nation's Democrats, secretly supported the thugs and had no sympathy for the likes of DadandBev. Still, they were conscientious. You had to give them that. The gun safe was serious, taller than a man, with an oily black sheen and jumbo lock that spun with a loud *click-click-click*.

This discussion Dad wanted covered two topics: giving me the combination to the safe, "in the event something happened," meaning, in the event he died on the operating table, and asking me whether I wanted Bev's Walther PPK.

I was confused and stared at the back of his dark blue denim shirt as he spun the lock. With the exception of Bev's cherry bedroom set in the guest room and a few other pieces of furniture, all of her stuff had already been distributed to Martin and Liz.

"What about Martin, doesn't he want it? Or is it one of those things where he can't have it in California?" California gun laws were far stricter than Nevada's, and there was a rifle belonging to Bev that Martin couldn't take back with him to Davis because it was illegal. "Or what about Liz?"

"Liz can't have it," he said.

"Martin didn't want her to have it?"

"No, she can't have it, can't have a weapon."

Liz can't have a weapon? Why can't Liz have a weapon? Were there medical reasons why Liz couldn't have a weapon? Was she prone to some exotic and rare neurological disorder that might trigger—you'll forgive the pun—a seizure at the first crack of gunfire? Or was the reason religious? Maybe she belonged to some pacifist cult that demanded their members never own a weapon, never *hold* a weapon, never be in the same *room* as a weapon. Maybe her strained relationship with DadandBev—we all had our own variety, like ice cream flavors—had to do with their badgering *her* about joining the NRA, whereupon she preached to them from the pacifist guru she followed, slavelike to his teachings. (Except I couldn't see Liz following anyone slavelike—okay, maybe the Prime Directive, or whatever it was Trekkers worshipped.) Maybe maybe maybe. This was the problem with being a person with a narrative flair in a repressed family that operated on a need-to-know basis. What I could imagine was probably infinitely worse than the reality. I stared at my dad's bony back as he rearranged some things on the upper shelves, which were covered with leftover remnants of the orange shag our living room in Whittier had been carpeted in.

"But why?" There was no point in asking this, but it was part of our routine. I'd learned long ago that my being a nosey parker just helped move the conversation along.

"My bank information and the title to the Explorer are up here on the left-hand side, next to the safe-deposit box," he said. He wouldn't think of saying "None of your business."

I would never know about Liz and the gun, why it was she couldn't have it. Even after all the other stuff I would find out, that one thing would remain a mystery.

The orange halogen streetlight shines through the thin curtains of my dad's bedroom. It's bright enough that I can see plainly the numbers on the lock. The clicking is loud enough to wake Daniel, and certainly loud enough to inspire Bev to call on the phone and wonder what in the hell I'm up to. Until the end of her days, Bev always seemed to creep around her own house on cat paws. Her favorite thing to do was creep up on me while I was hanging on the open refrigerator door, ostensibly looking for something to eat, but sometimes just looking. I had the same relationship with DadandBev's refrigerator as I did with my mother and Dad's; it was like a friend you just had to check in with every few hours. Bev didn't like this. She didn't like me snooping around her cold cuts, or letting all the cold air out. I'd be hanging on the door and she'd suddenly be at my shoulder saying, "Can I *help* you?" as if she were a sales lady and I was a known shoplifter.

Inside the safe are the two orange shag-carpeted shelves, on which rest my dad's pistols. There are some envelopes stuffed with bills, the aforementioned financial documents, and the blue safe–deposit box. My dad had given me the combination to this too, but I'm not yet at a place where I can snoop so thoroughly. My dad's collection of gold pocket watches hangs from small pegs affixed to a carpeted board on the left wall. (He'd restored each and every watch with his own hands, at the small desk in the laundry room he keeps for such purposes.) A black automatic rifle leans up against the back wall, an AK–47. I don't know what I am looking for. Maybe I am just practicing at poking around in my dad's life where I formerly had no business. Suddenly, I'm bone-tired by the thought of all the stuff in the safe. Forget all the Tupperware, what am I going to do with an AK–47?

While Dad is in the hospital, we never glimpse a single doctor. They're the grown-up equivalent of Santa Claus or the Easter Bunny. They only check in on Dad when he's conveniently asleep—strange, since during the hours Daniel and I spend with him he's wide awake and agitated. According to the metal chart that hangs from a hook at the foot of Dad's bed, the doctors think he'll be able to go home two days after the surgery, but the next morning at nine, when Daniel and I show up to visit, he's sitting up in bed in his beige Lee jeans, tugging at the white paper tape on his forearm, trying to get the IV out. This is just like Dad, who has been known to stitch himself up and glue loose dental appliances back into his own mouth. Someone has already been by to remove the dressing from the incision on his pale chest; it's only about two and a half inches long and is the usual rusty-looking thing. I try not to look straight at the incision, try not to think about what's under there, the rope of tumor that Lagstone didn't touch, the one that wasn't the original tumor. It's a secondary tumor, imported from somewhere else. The throat, perhaps. Or I'd say melanoma, looking at all the odd-shaped, discolored moles and whatnot on Dad's pasty chest and teak-brown arms. My father has had a devastating farmer's tan his whole life.

I scurry over to him. "Dad, what are you doing, do they want you to do that? Shouldn't we call the nurse?"

"I'm all done here."

"Maybe we should get someone in here, Dick," says Daniel.

"I don't see any reason I should spend another second here."

I jog off to find Linda, or someone, momentarily relieved to flee the situation and find someone, anyone, who could claim to be in charge. At the nurses' station there is one nurse with fluffy, shoulder-length yellow hair, playing solitaire on the computer. She has long fake nails with tiny gold charms glued to the tips. I pine for a brief moment to care enough about my appearance to desire such an elaborate manicure. I ask her about my dad and she doesn't even need to look up. She knows all about him. She says he needs to have someone come by and make sure his incision is draining properly before he can be released. She doesn't know when that would be. She doesn't know when, roughly, and cannot even give me an estimate. Sometime soon.

Back in the room, Dad is complaining to Daniel about the breakfast. It was leather pancakes and rubber sausages, just what you'd expect. The IV needle is now out of his arm. He's looped the clear plastic tube around the bracket that holds the bag of fluids—carefully, the way he'd treat any other cable, cord, or hose.

"Dad, you need to wait."

"I don't need to do any such thing," he says. "Hand me my shirt." But before Daniel or I can make a move, he's on his feet, tottering toward the cabinet. This is the cowboy in my dad, the part that says things like, Never drop your gun to hug a grizzly. In this case, the grizzly is the hospital bureaucracy and the gun is his own sense of self-determination.

"I'm never coming back to this place again."

"But what if they need to give you instructions? Or what if, what if, the insurance won't pay if they don't formally discharge you?" These were the types of issues he himself had taught me to consider. Still, this wasn't grammar school, where rushing out the door would earn him a week on the fence during recess and perhaps an essay on following rules and respecting others.

He clamps his hand around my wrist—we're doing that a lot lately, hanging on to the other guy's wrist—and looks me square in the eyes. (His eyes are light gray, an unusual color that you never notice unless he is staring you down.) "Promise me you will never let me come back here again."

"I promise, Dad. Of course I promise."

And so we collected his things and walked out the door, down the hall, past the nurses' station, and out into the white high-desert light, and no one said a word. In the coming months I would do many things I would not be proud of, but I never did break that promise.

II

Inside every seriously ill person there's a Kafka trying to get out.

—*Anonymous*

11

Even though I don't know anyone less temperamentally suited to play nurse than me, I vow to be there for Dad. I vow to be different with Dad than I was with my mother. Growing up I suffered from what is now called ADHD and am still plagued by foot-wagging restlessness. I have little patience with the necessary routines of caregiving. I trust doctors about as much as I trust mechanics or the retail associate at Nordstrom who tells me I look fabulous in a pair of $1,200 Calvin Klein capri pants, and am a barf-o-phobe to boot. (There's actually a word for the fear of throwing up: emetophobia.)

God, who doles out his mercy at random, appreciates this about me. When I was pregnant with Katherine I experienced not a jot of morning sickness; likewise, she's only thrown up twice in her life, both times in the company of her dad. The first time, she was old enough to announce, "Look! The Cocoa Puffs that were on the inside are now on the outside." Once, I wrote a story about fear for *Sports Illustrated for Women* in which I freely admitted that I would literally rather swim with sharks than ride a roller coaster where I might experience motion sickness. I never set foot on a boat without Bonine, not even a fishing boat tied up at a dock on a glassy lake.

Still, I will be there for my dad.

Even though, in high school, after I took one of those career aptitude tests, I was advised to become a test pilot or an architect, and none of the so-called helping professions even made the list.

Even though, for a time in college I wanted to be a physical therapist (secretly harboring grandiose dreams of manipulating the limbs of professional athletes in distress), but when I had a summer internship between my junior and senior years at a small, tragically ill-lit nursing home, where my duties included playing catch three times a week with lobotomy patients who smelled bad and shrieked to themselves, I fled the major the first day of registration my senior year and decided to go to film school.

Even though Dad has the same aptitude for being sick that I have for caregiving, and for this reason we're not a well-matched patient-nurse couple (it's of note that as a young man he *was* a test pilot), I'm all he has and am madly determined to get in there, roll up my sleeves, and do this right. By "do this" I mean, be on the front lines of his care, in the trenches—apply all the war metaphors you can think of—in his upcoming battle.

I am going to be with Dad through sickness and more sickness, cook him calorie-laden meals he won't eat, sit with folded arms on the little uncomfortable chair in the examination room, grilling his doctors as if I were Christiane Amanpour during a particularly persistent moment, fluff his pillows, and hold his hand while he sleeps. I am going to be good, selfless, competent, like a movie heroine.

I view this as a do-over, like they have in hippie baseball, where the concept of striking out doesn't exist, where you get to swing at the ball until you make contact, and send it flying triumphantly into the air. It's a chance to do for Dad that which I did not do for my mother, part of the poignant blessing of having two parents to tend at the end of their lives.

I am fortunate to be self-employed, and have a husband willing to care for the kids while I fly back and forth between Portland and Boulder City for months on end. At the time of Dad's diagnosis Daniel worked one day a week, delivering packages for UPS. The rest of the time he was supposed to get the kids to school, keep the house clean, grocery-shop, and cook. Yes, we were engaged in that popular modern-day domestic experiment that nearly always fails: I was the bread-winner and he was the househusband. (The problem with this arrangement is that your average househusband is uppity; unlike the average housewife, he has things he simply won't do. For example, he'll run the vacuum cleaner and the dishwasher but he won't scrub the toilet. If you do manage to coerce him into scrubbing the toilet, he will never do the part behind the toilet, where the really nasty things reside—invisible splotches of pee, unidentifiable blobs that may be desiccated vomit, dog hair, dust, you name it.) But it was an excellent arrangement, considering the circumstances. About forty million people lose a parent every year and I'd wager most of them aren't so lucky. They have jobs they desperately need that won't allow them time off; or they have a spouse with a job he or she desperately needs that won't allow time off, or there are no grandparents around to help out, or money is so horrifically tight that flying back and forth to anywhere for months on end isn't even an option.

The problem with being the self-employed breadwinner at a time like this is that you've got to keep a lid on the sob-a-thons, on the dissolute hours spent in casino bars drinking Glenlivet in the middle of the afternoon. You've got to keep working, even though your heart feels as if it's been caught beneath a tank rolling through a city under siege. And if you're me, you have to travel. Travel on top of the flying back and forth, for months on end.

For about six years I'd been making my living as a freelance magazine writer with a weird subspeciality in the guinea pig story, where I subjected myself to terrifying and humiliating experiences for the enjoyment of smarter readers everywhere. One of my first stories, for an in-flight rag, involved traveling to Puerto Rico to earn my scuba-diving certification, which required overcoming a hefty case of claustrophobia. Once I was a diver, I landed stories in Hawaii and Micronesia, where I dove the World War II shipwrecks of Truk Lagoon. I wrote a story about becoming a certified shark handler in the Bahamas, for which I had to wear a thirty-two-pound chain-mail suit, descend to a sixty-foot-deep sandy flat on the edge of the mile-deep Tongue of the Ocean, and feed a dozen Caribbean reef sharks from a plastic bucket full of red snapper. I covered a national cheerleading competition at Walt Disney World.

I muscled through several ski camps, one in Sugarloaf, Maine, one in Whistler, British Columbia, where I tore the medial collateral ligament in my left knee on the first day, coming off a run called Choker, but stayed to finish the story after a generous Canadian ER doctor wrote me a double prescription of Percocet. I enrolled in a women's-only sailing school in the Florida Keys and a whitewater rafting school in Utah; flew to Dallas to do a story on something called White Collar Boxing—a cross between kickboxing and karate; spent a week at a place called the International Performance Institute in Bradenton, Florida, training with the Boston Red Sox, and another week with a bunch of sixteen-year-old boys and a few intrepid girls at Paskowitz Surf Camp in San Clemente, California, where I earned the surfing nickname Grown Woman. (The story: Old Man Paskowitz, the patriarch of the operation, spied me on a wave one day and said, "My God, that's no boy, that's a grown woman working that curl."). I learned to street luge on the winding Southern California streets of Turnbull Canyon, not far from where I grew up.

I loved the work and complained about it in equal measure. I claimed I only did this stuff to support my family, but I also liked the kick-ass rush of putting myself in these amusing predicaments. There was always a fun back story. I hadn't skied in twenty years when I agreed to go to Whistler. Before I went to Florida, the last time I'd sailed had been in a Laser dinghy in Balboa Harbor when I was in college. It was December: I was run down by a large sailboat, got tossed in the drink, and suffered hypothermia. There doesn't need to be any back story to appreciate the lunacy of diving with sharks.

The strangest assignment was the one that got my guinea pig subsubspecialty started: a week-long intensive handgun training camp out in the middle of the Arizona high desert for *Outside*. The instructors were no-nonsense brutes who'd spent a lifetime breaking stuff and hurting people: an ex–Army Ranger, a Navy SEAL nearly deaf from his days as an underwater demolitions expert, a retired SWAT team trainer for the Chicago police department—seriously deadly guys who put us through military-style drills on the firing line for eight hours a day, under the blistering sun. We had our names written on masking tape and stuck to the back of our baseball caps so they could personalize our humiliation. In a week's time, we put a thousand rounds through our weapons. We went through hundreds of paper targets. We learned such maneuvers as the "El Presidente," where you begin with your back to the target, then spin around and get off two shots to the chest and one to the head in as few seconds as possible. During water breaks, which they were forced to give us so we wouldn't collapse in the dust and accidentally discharge our weapon, the instructors and the students—eighteen men, three women—liked to curse loudly about the government and the "boneheaded, bed-wetting, cock-sucking liberal media" of which I was a part. Fortunately, I was there for *Outside*, which mercifully wasn't one of those suspicious publications with "new" in the title—*The New York Times*, *The New Yorker*, *The New Republic*—and so I wasn't lynched in my sleep.

The idea for this story came from DadandBev, who'd been to this particular place not once, but twice, during the high point of their survivalist years, when their love of weapons was one of the interests they shared as a newly married couple. Gun camp was their idea of a fine time, which cracked me up. They'd recounted stories about it for years over endless martoonie hours, thinking I'd be interested because I seem to have inherited Dad's aptitude for shooting.

You must know this: The business with DadandBev and me and shooting guns is complicated. Once, just after DadandBev were married, at the beginning of their love affair with the semi-automatic, they took a one-day class at the Huntington Beach police department. Without asking me—very uncharacteristic—Dad signed me up for the next session. I was twenty-two. I had not yet met the two friends who would be murdered by sociopaths bearing handguns (one, a friend from film school, who would be shot in the head coming out of work at an animation house on Hollywood Boulevard, the other, the actress Rebecca Schaeffer, who in 1989 would be shot on her front step by a lunatic claiming to love her). I'd grown up with guns around—Dad kept a World War I submachine gun propped in the corner of the guest bathroom when I was a teenager, claiming he wanted to see the reaction of my dates—and had no real feeling about them one way or the other. But I knew I wanted to please Dad. That, I always knew.

Until then, Bev and I had a courteous relationship, even though she was already permanently peeved at me for having wept at her wedding to Dad. I tried to apologize, explained it had nothing to do with *her*, but that she wasn't my mother, and that made me sad. I told her she shouldn't take it personally. To which she said, "What would you know about taking things personally?" To this day I feel like hosting a séance, telling the medium to point out to the ghost of Bev that I was a teenage girl, for God's sake, and took everything from rush hour traffic to global warming personally.

The class at the Huntington Beach police department went well, too well. It was a foggy day, cold for that part of the world. Dad stood behind the firing line taking pictures, no pressure there. But pressure seems to agree with me, and I shot so well that the instructor broke the rules and allowed me to take my target home as a souvenir. Or what was left of it. I thought Bev would be thrilled; here I was doing what they wanted me to, embracing—and thus giving credibility to—their abiding passion. I was trying to get with the program. I was trying to do my bit to solidify our new Brady Bunch. Dad and I got home during martoonie hour. Bev was at the kitchen counter plucking three cocktail onions out of a jar for Dad's drink. I stood in the middle of the kitchen, smelling of sweat, gunpowder, and Charlie perfume, the web of skin between my thumb and forefinger blistered from the grip on the Colt .45 I'd borrowed from Dad. I unrolled the target.

"Oh," said Bev, handing Dad his drink. "I see you had a good time."

I didn't know much at twenty-two. Since my mother's death, I'd been going through the motions of life, as we Karbos do. From the outside it looked as if everything was fine, even though I was still living behind that infernal piece of Plexiglas, being jettisoned about my business in my personal plastic pneumatic tube. I didn't understand people, couldn't imagine that anything I ever did was cause for another person's adverse reaction. I didn't realize, until I saw Bev grimace and turn back to the counter to screw the lid back on the onion jar, that I'd done exactly the wrong thing; I was a much better shot than she was, and she never forgave me.

The point of all this is that my line of work was both a blessing and a curse when it came time to tend to Dad. Out of necessity, it rolled right on. At the time of Dad's diagnosis I was finishing my motherhood book; writing an anonymous column for *Fast Company*, a trendy business magazine (I was The Spy in the House of Work, a young guy trying to hit pay dirt in the new economy); writing another column for an online magazine called dadmag.com (I was Mrs. Dad, the lone female voice on the site); and under contract to produce four stories a year for a glossy women's sports magazine (where I was currently in hot water for writing about the San Francisco School of Circus Arts flying trapeze school for *Fast Company* instead of bringing it to them first). *Outside* was also trying to decide whether to send me on a diving story to a remote reef in the middle of the Philippine Sea, but was concerned because in nearby Sipadan, off the island of Borneo, a group of divers had been taken hostage by Muslim extremists.

I don't think I mentioned this: I also hate to fly.

12

After he's up and about, the second thing Dad demands I teach him is how to fold a fitted sheet. The first thing was how to do the laundry. I am shocked. Dad, who has six patents to his name, and whose last job before retiring was designing valves, rotors, swing joints, and who knows what else, for complicated commercial irrigation systems used to water golf courses in the Middle East and Japan, cannot run a load of whites.

I'm only a fitted-sheet-folding expert because my mother used to drag me to the depressingly hot and empty Laundromat on Whittier Boulevard every other week, where she paid me a quarter a fitted sheet. She hated folding them too. At home in Portland, I've learned to avoid folding them by taking them straight from the dryer and putting them on the beds. But Dad insists. He wants them as flat and smooth as a flag folded by an overachieving Eagle Scout, so he can put them in the linen closet on the shelf marked "fitted queens" with a piece of masking tape.

He sets a basket full of freshly washed sheets in the middle of the dining room table. I shake one out and tuck my hands into the top corners. The sheets are so old, they're worn through in some spots, and were mended once upon a time by Bev, who ironed a quarter-sized patch over the hole. I see this and am reminded of something I've read somewhere, in which the author remarks that when his father died, it wasn't just the death of a man; a whole way of life went with him. Dad is of the generation that mends sheets long after they should have been replaced; I'm of the generation that buys three-hundred-thread-count sheets online to pamper themselves. Why, I wonder, is my generation in need of pampering and Dad's isn't? Surely human beings haven't changed that much. I put the basket on the floor, lay the sheet out, make sure the corners and the sides form a square, fold the sheet over, smooth it flat, then turn it over again, then over again.

Here is the thing that made Dad great and impossible at the same time, that made living in his disciplined presence so intimidating: Instead of picking another sheet from the laundry basket, he unfolds mine, not wanting to waste a single opportunity to practice.

I'm haunted by the mended spots in the sheets for days. I finally break down and go to J.C. Penney's in Henderson and buy him a brand-new set of plain white, the only kind of sheets a decent person sleeps on, according to DadandBev. When I give them to him, he turns them over in his big hands, perplexed.

"Babe, what are these for?"

"I thought it might feel good to have some nice new sheets."

"I've got plenty of sheets. You shouldn't have spent your money."

"I thought you could use some new ones."

"But the ones I've got are fine."

"I noticed some of the elastic is stretched out. And there were some holes."

"Holes? In our sheets? I didn't see any holes."

"They were mended. They look old. Or oldish. Not new holes."

"Oh, well. You see, I don't need any new sheets."

And, he doesn't. Months down the road, after it's all over, I find the sheets still in their plastic package in the linen closet.

★   ★   ★

Just as I am a member of the three-hundred-thread-count generation, I'm also from the health-care-as-commodity generation. A doctor is to be interviewed, sussed out, and shopped for, as if he were a building contractor. Medicine is not a noble profession, but filled with people who want to make a buck and wrangle a long weekend, just like everyone else. They also tend to be as tight-lipped as the lone witness to a gangland murder. Unless you grill them without mercy for information, you're not going to get any. Most fourth-grade boys have more integrity than most doctors. If you think I'm being cynical, consider a recent essay in *The New Yorker*, where the erudite oncologist and redoubtable sweetie pie Jerome Groopman—the man I want to treat me, should I ever wind up going the way of my parents—admits that doctors as a whole tend to have less interest in patients they don't believe they have a hope of curing.

Dad's first appointment with the oncologist Dr. Florino is at ten A.M. on a hot, windy morning in November. I'm on edge, with a headache in only one quadrant of my head, a sure sign I have a brain tumor, but I don't have time to worry about that now. I've just flown in from Portland on the cheapo, nerve-wracking, crack-of-dawn flight which arrived an hour and a half late because they'd had trouble getting the number-two engine to turn over. I wanted to bolt, but they wouldn't let me off the plane.

On the way to Florino's office, just off Tropicana Avenue in the dowdy shadow of the Strip, Dad and I stop at Mail Boxes Etc., to send some of Bev's nice coats and jackets, circa 1970, to Portland, where I will try to pawn them off on Rachel, explaining that they are vintage. There's a cream-and-olive-green-striped knit poncho with a hood, and a mustard yellow leather vest, with big leather-covered buttons. Dad pats them sadly as he places them in the box, and I remember to mention to the oncologist that this man is not only sick, he's also throttled with grief.

Florino is probably no better or worse than any other doctor, but I'm already leery. On the day of Dad's biopsy, when Daniel and I returned from Paris Las Vegas, Florino had already been in (while Dad was asleep, of course) to drop his card on the metal bedside tray, like some personal injury lawyer. When I called the office to make the appointment—I wanted to find someone who wasn't so eager for Dad's business, but Dad said no, Florino was fine—I was alarmed to hear "Let It Be," the music-box cover version, playing continuously while I waited on hold.

Like Dad's surgeon, the oncologist Florino is five-seven. He has an impressive head of steel-gray hair, a nose that veers off to one side, crooked bottom teeth, a gold chain, and tasseled loafers with lifts. He strides in purposefully, like someone who subscribes to the idea that you only get one chance to make a first impression, and, oddly, I think, addresses me first.

"You smoke? Because that's why your father's in my office. Cigarettes, pure and simple." *Ya think?* He shakes Dad's chart at me for emphasis.

Dad likes doctors even less than I do, but he assumes they're professionals and are therefore to be trusted. They won't tell him how to design a valve, restore a watch, or refurbish a locomotive, and he won't tell them how to treat cancer. He trusts them to the extent that he takes almost no interest in what they propose to do to him. Florino reads Dad's chart aloud. Dad sits at the end of the exam table in one of his dress-up cowboy shirts with the pearl snaps, and listens to what he already knows. I can tell Dad's embarrassed. He doesn't want to be here.

Florino is saying a whole lot of nothing. It occurs to me that being a modern-day oncologist is not unlike being a Hollywood development person: "Yes" means "maybe" and "maybe" means "no," and the answer's almost always "maybe." The days of laying out the hard truth are over. In this new way, there is no bad news. As long as the patient is alive to keep the appointment, there is hope. Telling someone they've only got six months to live is, presumably, too much of a downer. It may encourage negative thinking, and thus compromise the chance for a miraculous recovery. Plus, there's the unwieldy fact that if a patient only has months to live, why would he subject himself to the burning and poisoning that may not prolong his life, but will certainly make what's left of it rife with pain and misery?

Florino offers me a chair, but I remain standing. I'm wearing my black Doc Martens, the ones Katherine calls pilgrim shoes, that make me five-eleven. Until the day my mother died she fretted about my height, worried that it would prevent future marital happiness. To the ghost of my mother I say, I've managed to get married not once, but twice, and men who are threatened by tall women can kiss my ass. I decide Florino is one of them. I want him to say the hard truth. This time, I'm going to hear it.

"Doctor, what is it he has, exactly?"

"It's in his lungs," says Florino. "In the A-P window." A-P stands for aorta-pulmonary. He fishes an overly photocopied drawing of the human chest cavity from a plastic filing tray on the counter, makes a lavish production of extracting his pen from his white coat, and draws me a picture. The mass is long, vinelike, sprouting from outside Dad's left lung, winding its way around his trachea and down around his aorta. This slows me up some, this vine in danger of strangling the blood flow to Dad's heart.

"This is why you couldn't touch it," I say.

"Why Dr. Lagstone couldn't remove it, yes," says Florino.

"What's it called?" I say.

"Adenocarcinoma. Most common type of lung cancer. Ninety percent of the time caused by smoking. There is some good news. This was the only mass. Not a metastasis from another site, as we originally thought. Slow-growing. Probably been in there for three years to five years."

After this wave of hard information hits me I soften toward Florino, feeling a little sheepish about my attitude. Maybe Florino isn't such a bad guy.

The treatment is the usual, even though the tumor itself is inoperable. A three-week course of radiation, with chemotherapy beginning during the second week of radiation. Timing is critical. "It's essential," says Florino, "that the chemo be introduced right after the radiation. This is the preferred treatment, the most effective treatment."

"What do you mean by effective treatment? Effective how?"

"A combination of both radiation and chemotherapy has proven to be the best combination of therapies." Florino speaks as if it were all no more taxing than taking a couple of Advil before bed.

"To do what?"

"In the hopes of reducing the mass, and thus, his discomfort."

"But you can't cure it, can you?"

"We can reduce the mass."

If it strikes you that Dad hardly seems present in this scene, I feel that way myself. He has no questions of his own, isn't interested in taking a look at the drawing of his own chest, doesn't need any more hard information about adenocarcinoma. He waits politely until the appointment is over, like a child waiting for the end of church.

Since the surgery, Dad has gotten in the habit of taking a nap after dinner, which gives me a chance to indulge my new obsession: researching lung cancer on the Internet. For some reason, I feel I have to sneak, as if I'm surfing porn. I know my dad wouldn't approve, wouldn't be interested in what I find, which is certainly a lot of half-baked misinformation. Still, it's better than being in the dark, like I was the last time. I sit at the breakfast bar, at what was Bev's spot and is now my spot. My laptop is open on a brown-and-orange calico place mat, as I research adenocarcinoma. Woodrow is curled up on his bed, twisted up in his rag/bath towel, snoring up a storm. Cancer.com. Lungcanceronline.org. Lungusa.com. I immerse myself in information like a hot bath. I was a biology major in college and understand enough to imagine I'm actually educating myself. I read things like "The better differentiated tumors form orderly glands lined by tall columnar cells with a regular array of nuclei," and feel unaccountably better.

Dad and I fall into our morning routines, slaves to the gravity of habits. They haven't varied much in thirty-something years, even though he is retired and I work for myself. My routine has varied to allow for the introduction of the Internet. At home I get up at seven A.M., drink one and a half cups of coffee with whole milk while checking my e-mail, then take the dog out for his sniff. He sniffs, while I do a half-assed run/walk thing.

At the Palace, Dad is at his battle station by seven-fifteen, elegant in his velour robe, drinking his coffee—three cups, milk, two teaspoons sugar—reading the paper from cover to cover, smoothing each new page by swatting it against his bald head. I lace up my running shoes and head out into the insufferable high-desert heat to run up and down the steep, butt-busting hills. The streets are asphalt, the sidewalks wide and white. Even in November it's hot by eight A.M. It's about two miles down to Hemenway Park, where sometimes the extra-hardy are playing tennis during the only reasonable time of day. Every day I look for the mountain goats, which pick their way down the mountains, looking like ladies in high heels, to feed off the shockingly healthy green park lawn. I look for them, but they're never there. It's all uphill the way back, about two miles straight uphill at an elevation of 2,500 feet. There's almost never anyone outside. Sometimes I meet an elderly woman in a housecoat with a tiny dog panting in the heat at the end of its leash. There are a few empty lots choked with low, sunburned weeds and gravel. As I pass by, I hear scampering, some snake or desert creature. Air conditioners whir like prop planes. We don't perspire much in our family; I would be hard pressed to think of a time when I've seen Dad sweat, even though he walks around in jeans and long-sleeved shirts, like you're supposed to in the desert. On my half-assed walk/run thing, which on these hills at this altitude is a full-blown workout capable of producing a thong-worthy butt in just about any woman, I can feel the sweat run down my sides. It runs into my eyes. Every morning I make the mistake of putting sunscreen on my forehead, and every morning the sweat washes it into my eyes, leaving me with bursting lungs and burning glutes, chugging uphill in the desert heat, eyes stinging. It's very handy, this. I can cry, and even I don't notice it.

13

Daniel calls one night during martoonie hour, which is still called martoonie hour even though Dad drinks orange juice and I drink Diet Pepsi; the whole idea of attempting to duplicate Bev's tremendous martinis is simply too sad to bear. Martoonie hour as we knew it has been retired forever, like a star football player's number. Dad's has lost his taste for alcohol. He goes through a half gallon of Minute Maid Country-Style Orange Juice, No Pulp, a day. And it's got to be No Pulp.

"I don't know what it is about orange juice, babe. I just find it so refreshing."

"It reminds me of being sick. Mom used to make me drink it when I wasn't feeling well, and I always associate it with throwing up."

"There is something barium-enema-like about it."

"You've never had a barium enema," I say.

Dad laughs. "Something new to aspire to! *Salute!*" He raises his glass of juice.

On the phone, Daniel says that Danny and Katherine have between them as assortment of ear infections, sinus infections, and bronchitis. Dad overhears me on my cell phone, pacing up and down the long hallway of the Palace talking about fevers, Dimetapp Cold and Cough, and late homework, and tells me to go home.

"I don't want you hanging around here when your family's sick."

"Dad, you're also my family, and you're also sick."

"Nah, I'm going to get going on the radiation and zap this thing once and for all, so I can go about my business." Dad likes the idea of radiation for the same reason a child might: It's quick, easy, painless, and noninvasive. As medical procedures go, it's tidy.

So, home I go. Even though it means spending fifty bucks to change the return leg of my trip, which Dad also hears me fretting about on the phone to Daniel. When I hang up, Dad tries to give me fifty bucks, which I won't accept.

"Let me help you out," he says.

"Oh my God, put that away," I say, alarmed. What is this about? Dad has never in the history of the world offered me a penny. Money is a touchy subject for us, as it is for just about every other middle-class family on the planet. Dad and I have an old routine that began sometime after my mother died and I was on my own. He'd say, "If you had ten bucks left in your pocket and had a choice between a square meal and a book, you'd buy the book." To which I would reply, "You'd choose the meal, but then you'd hardly eat it anyway." Then he would say, "True, but I'd never be down to my last ten bucks."

Like everyone else I know, I'm always down to my metaphorical last ten bucks. Dad disapproves and always has. I have an IRA and a money market account, and no clue how the latter differs from a regular savings account. I have five thousand dollars in credit-card debt, a shocking fact emblematic of every dumb mistake I've ever made and lazy-ass bad habit I can't manage to kick. It speaks to the fact I have no long-term plan; that I'm on my second marriage, with a man seven years my junior who didn't finish college; that I haven't joined the NRA nor will I ever; that I leave wet towels on the bed and cosmetics around the sink; and that my preparation for Y2K consists of two gallons of bottled water, a dozen Top Ramen, a hundred bucks stashed in a pink ceramic hydrangea in my desk in which

I keep my paper clips, and enough gas in the car at all times to drive to Betty and Jim's, my in-laws, who live forty-five miles away and have accumulated enough cans of Dinty Moore to sink a barge.

Still, it's a point of pride with me not to accept money from DadandBev, now just Dad.

At home, Danny and Katherine are sweet and docile for two days; then they start feeling better and bicker like Fred and Ethel. Rachel is in her experimenting-with-makeup phase and has latched onto some greasy-looking mulberry-colored lipstick that makes her look as if she needs to be intubated. She has also taken to downloading magic spells off the Internet.

I find myself bursting into tears in the most unlikely places. Daniel and I are pressed into going to the Snow Show, a ski and snowboarding trade show, at the local expo center. This is not typically something that would appeal to me, but since Dad's diagnosis, I don't care much how I spend my time when I'm not with him. The Snow Show, with its pervasive order of stale bagged popcorn, salesmen shilling cheap vacations to far-flung resorts no one's ever heard of, acres of booths of jackets and hats, and hourly demonstrations of skis and boards on a giant hill of artificial snow, did not cause me to catch ski fever, or anything remotely like it, although I did donate a dollar to the Mt. Hood Ski Patrol, for which I received a free ice scraper. That night Daniel and I had a huge screaming argument because I caught Danny, he of the ear and sinus infection, using my toothbrush.

Dad's month-long series of radiation treatments begins just before Thanksgiving. At his first appointment with Dr. O'Donnell, the radiologist, the technician examines the X rays and uses a permanent marker to inscribe a small dark blue X just beneath his sternum on Dad's pale, hairless chest. This is where the machine will zap him. X marks his heart. Every morning for a month he will get up and brush his teeth with his electric toothbrush, smooth Vitalis in his hair, Old Spice on his freshly shaven cheeks, put on one of his nice long-sleeved cowboy shirts and a pair of clean jeans, slide his skinny ass into the Explorer and drive a half hour to another squat stucco medical building in the dowdy shadow of the Las Vegas Strip.

Even though I still phone him every afternoon at ten of five, he begins the radiation without telling me. I know he has an appointment scheduled to begin, but he's vague about when. This time I don't blame him for being his usual close-mouthed-to-the-point-of-pathology self, I blame myself. I've made it out that I'm too busy. If the kids haven't appeared in any unwatchable grammar-school pageants or tortured the dog by putting Veronica, Katherine's rat, into her plastic exercise ball—it's the size of a basketball; the rodent scurries along, propelling the ball from room to room; the dog chases it, sniffs it, wags his tail, and in general nearly goes insane—I talk about my work. I can talk endlessly and monotonously about my work. I'm writing a critique of the parenting manual industry for Salon.com. I'm crashing on my monthly "Spy in the House of Work" column; I'm trying to hatch a dotcom love story for the Valentine's Day issue (the day before I need to file the story, I decide on a Romeo and Juliet theme, where the Spy, the poster boy of the new economy, who works eighty-five hours a week for a dotcom, falls helplessly in love with an old-economy girl, who prefers the phone to e-mail, and actually expects the spy to take her out on a date, rather than IM her on a Friday night). I'm also preparing to go to Florida some time after the new year to do a profile of Michelle Akers, the thirty-three-year-old grande dame of the World Cup–winning U.S. Women's National Soccer Team.

Dad's not telling me something the rest of the world might construe as important is nothing new. Just after they were married, DadandBev lived in a condo in Newport Beach, which sounds carefree and glamorous but wasn't. It had gold shag carpeting with large, ominous pet-related stains from previous occupants and not enough windows. There is nothing more depressing than living a mile from the Pacific Ocean in a place without enough windows. It conveys the constant message that life Out There is bright and breezy, but in here, it's a Russian novel. (And not even one of the fat ones portraying a panoramic view of society, but something like *Notes from Underground*, in which the morose narrator never leaves his room.) The couple in the too-close condo next door routinely shouted things like "I cannot take another minute of your crap!," then made caterwauling love in the shower. Dad moved to the Newport Beach condo three months after my mother died, when I was seventeen. It was home only in the sense that no place else was.

Anyway, when I arrived on a Saturday morning, Bev wasn't there. Dad sat at the small dining room table smoking a cigarette and polishing some brass fixtures for a boat he was restoring. The overhead light was on, even though outside the sun was blazing and the sea breezes blowing. When he was finished with the polishing, he and I drove down to the dock on Lido Island where his boat, the *Ballarat Bay*, was moored—the one shown in the black-and-white picture on the paneled guest room wall. Ballarat was a ghost town Dad liked, out in the Mojave Desert. Of course, there was no bay there. There was no water there, period. It was his own private joke, so private, it was only between him and himself.

For the rest of the day, Dad worked on the boat. A large panel on the deck slid back, and he was down there with tools and oil, fooling around with something. I can still see the back of his white T-shirt, his white hair, and the strip of neck in between, darker than the teak on the boat. I watched Dad work on so many projects over the course of my life—vintage cars, power boats, locomotives, pocket watches, antique clocks, drills from gold mines, old airplane engines—that I have as many memories of the back of him as I do the front. On that day, I lay on the transom and worked on my tan and tried to study for some test while he worked.

It was unusual that Bev had not appeared. Usually, while my Dad tinkered, she sat on a faded deck chair and worked on her needlepoint. Then, at five, she made martoonies. The vodka was kept in a bottle Dad had labeled with his label maker, the kind with the narrow plastic tape you imprint with raised white letters. The label maker was one of Dad's favorite gizmos; it stood between him and the chaos of the universe. The bottle was labeled "Old Bilge," another private joke between him and himself. I thought Bev had been at the grocery store, or the library, running errands somewhere, but now hours had passed. Soon, the wind kicked up, and the sailboats were motoring back into the harbor. People who were like my dad, who worked on their boats or sat on their boats but never took their boats out, were firing up their barbecues for dinner. You could smell the lighter fluid. Still no Bev. Driving the mile back to the condo I said, "So where's Bev?"

He said, "In the hospital."

"In the hospital? What happened? Is she okay?"

"She had some surgery."

"*Some* surgery? What surgery? You don't just have some surgery. It's not like dessert. It's not, I'll have some of that pie, please."

"A hysterectomy."

I can't remember how it went after that. Dad shook a Camel from its pack beside him on the seat and pushed in the dashboard lighter with his thumb. The inside of his car was as clean as the day he drove it off the lot, except for the ashtray, filled with identically sized butts, crushed out in the same methodical fashion. I remember that we fell silent. I know I did not ask what happened, why was Bev having a hysterectomy, or was she all right or when was she coming home or should we take her some flowers or candy, a book, something? I could only go so far with what always felt like a cross-examination. I could only badger the witness for so long.

It was like that again with the radiation. Dad, have you seen the new doctor? Has he given you a schedule? What time is your appointment? Is it the same time every day? What about the holidays, how will they work around that? To these questions he says, "I'm on top of it, babe, no need to worry." Or, "I'll let you know as soon as I know."

Then one evening I make my usual call and Martin answers. *Martin?* He's in Boulder City to spend a week with Dad, to move some more of Bev's stuff and scatter her ashes. I'm relieved to know he's there. Martin and Dad have always hit it off. Martin respects Dad's knowledge of machinery and Dad respects Martin's knowledge of desert creatures. In the past, when Martin visited, they'd spend hours hiking around the desert in search of horned toads and curious species of snakes, and in the evening Martin played the banjo. They were both bluegrass aficionados.

"We're going out to a place near the lake, in one of those washes down there, where she loved to go and pick wildflowers," says Martin. I can hear the tears rising in his voice. *Bev loved to pick wildflowers? Who knew?* No one has asked me to attend, for which I'm grateful. I should probably feel excluded but I don't. Now I won't be put in the position of standing there among the creosote and tumbleweeds, in the nose-hair-singeing heat, pretending to mourn the passing of someone I never loved. I thank God for our family's particular brand of dysfunction.

I ask to speak to Dad, but he's taking a nap. Martin says the radiation is exhausting him, even though it's just the third day. I pretend I know all about the commencement of the radiation. We chat for a few minutes about the side effects he's likely to experience: deep fatigue, difficulty swallowing, a constant burning sensation in his chest.

For the next two days no one answers the phone at ten of five. On the third day Dad phones me at noon. When I see his number on the caller ID box, I get that old feeling, my internal organs being squashed by a steamroller. Noon is not the regular time, and no one on earth is more respectful of the regular time than Dad.

"That Liz, she showed up and wanted to take the cherry bedroom set. You don't think I should give her the cherry bedroom set, do you? I'm just afraid she's going to clean me out. I can't live here with pale squares where pictures use to be and dents in the carpet where Beverly's furniture was. Martin tells her to leave it alone, then the next day she doesn't show up for Beverly's ashes. We waited for a goddamned hour and she doesn't show. She doesn't call and she doesn't show up. It's just Martin and me out there. Her own mother, she doesn't even show up."

I'm stunned on many fronts. I can't recall the last time Dad exhibited this much passion. I don't think being worked up like this is good for him; then, maybe it is. Maybe it's better than being catatonic with grief. I tell him not to let go of the cherry bedroom set, or anything else he doesn't want to let go of. I tell him Liz can just deal. I'm thrilled to be asked my opinion, thrilled that the chronically decorous Family Karbo has exhibited a little strife, a little drama, that there's conflict and acting-out and bad behavior. It's a relief.

Dad's first round of chemotherapy is a disaster. Daniel and I take the day off to go skiing on Mt. Hood. We usher the kids out to school at eight A.M., then drive like maniacs up the mountain, stopping only once at the Texaco station in Sandy to pee and buy a Snickers bar to split on the chairlift. We don't stop for lunch, since we have to bomb back down the mountain at one-thirty, to be sure to be home by ten after three, when the kids get home.

When we get home, there's a message on my voice mail from Eleanor, Dr. Florino's nurse. The plan had been to administer a combination of two drugs: navilbene and carboplatin. They ushered my dad into the back of the office, the section with the easy chairs lined up in a row, beauty-shop style. Several minutes after the needles went into his vein and the navilbene began to flow, he clutched the front of his shirt with both hands. To the nurse administering the drugs it looked as if he were having a heart attack. Eleanor called 911 and the paramedics came roaring in with their stretcher and rubber gloves. They wanted to take Dad to the hospital but he wouldn't go. He would not go. They had a portable EKG machine and performed one on the spot. No heart attack.

I picture Dad, terrified and embarrassed by all the fuss, and think what it cost him to sit there in a room full of other patients Making a Scene. In a tone that sounds as if she's describing the tiresome complaints of a hypochondriac, Eleanor says, "Maybe it was an allergic reaction."

I say, "Well, Eleanor, not to put too fine a point on this, but it *is* poison you're pumping into those people. I can't believe anyone tolerates it at all." Once a wisenheimer, always a wisenheimer.

"Or an anxiety attack," she says. "Perhaps his regular physician can give him something for his anxiety."

Fat chance.

When I call Dad, he sounds better than he has since the diagnosis, in part because he's in the middle of what my mother used to call a world-class hissy fit. "I'm done with that!" he cries. "No more of that!"

"Dad, you have to. It's only four sessions."

"Well, you can keep it. It felt as if my lungs were on fire."

"It's the best thing, though. To have both radiation and chemo at the same time. You have four more sessions, then it's over. Reschedule the appointment and I'll come down."

"I've had enough."

"You haven't had any, Dad. This was the first session. You only got the navilbene."

"First and last. I'm not doing it."

What can I say?

On the last day of 1999, we are forced to put the dog down. One of the great shocks of life is that while we're coping with death, or major illness, or some other incident of force majeure, we expect the rest of life to hold still while we get through the crisis. It won't, of course. The hits just keep on coming.

Anubis belonged to Daniel's second wife. He was old when we got him—nine or ten—and when we picked him up at United Airlines cargo in his kitchen-table-size crate, we discovered he had a tumor the size of a tangerine on the inside of his leg. Eight hundred dollars later, he was pronounced healthy for a dog with cancer, and outfitted with one of those Elizabethan collars that looks like a lampshade, which prevented him from tearing out the stitches. It also prevented him from walking around the house with anything resembling ease. Anubis was a big dog and the collar was so wide, he couldn't make it through the door without catching an edge.

Now he is fourteen, and has yet another different kind of cancer, one that was diagnosed a year ago. For the past day or so, he's been listless, not eating, alternately throwing up bright green liquid and leaving thin trails of red-brown diarrhea all over the house. He lies on the sofa without moving for hours on end.

I take to the sofa with a novel, and for hours I lie with him. He curls himself in a corner like a zafu; I prop my feet up on his tawny flank. He sleeps for hours. The night before we take him in, we pop in a videotape, *The Mummy*, and eat what's left of the Christmas cookies Rachel made—sugar cookies spackled with sickly green frosting and chocolate sprinkles. Nubie is so cold. I cover him with a blanket Daniel's mother made for the puppy, Winston. He lies there, his skinny chin propped on the arm of the sofa. He's bloated, his belly as jiggly as a water bed. So sick.

Our appointment at the vet's is on New Year's Eve at noon. It's not an auspicious way to ring out the old millennium. Daniel wonders if it isn't bad luck and won't leave us with a bad memory. I say it doesn't matter what day it is, the dog is suffering. For a second or two, I mourn the old me who would also be concerned about doing something so sad on a day of the year that's so fraught with meaning.

Nubie doesn't seem to care, one way or the other, about going bye-bye in the car. He lies stiffly on the backseat. Daniel has to lift him in and out. In the waiting room, he lies between Daniel's feet on the cold linoleum. He isn't even interested in the cookie I offer him from the apothecary jar sitting on the counter, and when a woman brings in her cat—Nubie! Kitty!— he closes his eyes and sighs. Nubie was famous for treeing all the cats in the neighborhood, something he could do in three leaps, beginning on our front porch and ending at the base of one of the nearby birches or oaks.

We are ostensibly here to see if anything can be done, but I know in my pessimistic Slavic bones there isn't. Daniel holds out hope. A friend who's a vet says it's the men who always think there's a miracle cure; the women know when it's time to say good-bye.

In the exam room they lay a moss-green sheet on the floor. The sheet is only partially for his comfort; they'll also need it to drag him out of the room after he's dead.

Dr. Huff, our vet, a Texas girl with freckles and a crooked front tooth, started out practicing on large animals. She listens to Nubie's heartbeat. She can hardly hear it. She says it's probably congestive heart failure. He's a big, 110-pound dog. He has two types of cancer and lived well beyond his life span. This knowledge does nothing to stave off the sadness I feel pushing up from the center of my chest, from behind my eyes. It doesn't matter. It never matters.

Dr. Huff offers us an alternative: million-dollar high-tech tests normally reserved for people. Ultrasounds and X rays, CAT scans and MRIs. She could drain the fluid from his abdomen. If the million-dollar tests prove that it is, indeed, his heart, and not kidney failure, or one of his two kinds of malignant cancers prevailing, he can be put on million-dollar medication for the rest of what life he has.

Prolonging life. Who can resist? I don't know; either the strong or the weak. Either the person with the compassionate heart, or the person who is tired of the suffering. I don't know which one I am. Daniel would have signed off on the million-dollar tests—anything to prevent us from doing what we had to do there in that small exam room, beneath the cartoon anatomical chart of a mutt (under the arrow that points to the big red cartoon heart it says, "pure gold") and the cold beige linoleum, and the rheumy-eyed dog with his heart barely beating, waiting, just waiting.

I start to weep. Daniel weeps too, the whites of his eyes turning pink like they do.

A dog's death by euthanasia is simplicity itself. It's essentially an overdose of anesthetic. Sodium pentobarbital to be exact. I seem to know the names of everything. The adenocarcinoma and the navilbene and the carbolatin. The sodium pentobarbital. Knowing the names won't make Nubie's death any less sad, but at least I will be sad in the same room with him. I will not be sad all by myself, sitting in the hallway in the dark, with every last door in the house closed and the doors with people behind them, locked.

It's bright pink, the liquid in the syringe that will send Nubie off. His pulse is so low, Dr. Huff can't find a vein. They like to use a vein in the front leg because it's closer to the heart. She's forced to use a tourniquet on a rear leg. I stare at the needle going in. Daniel holds Nubie's tawny face and weeps into his big brown eyes. The eyes just look at him. I stand, since there is no room for me to kneel. I watch his belly heave up and down. Then he sighs. His belly goes still. Gone, gone, wherever it is a dog's soul goes. His eyes remain open, his one ear stuck up at the funny angle that used to make us laugh. Daniel can't smell it, his nose is so stuffed up from crying, but on the way out of the room, we are treated to one last terrific Anubian fart.

Daniel and I drive home and collect the children. We've opted to pay seventy-nine dollars to have the dog cremated, and the children are comforted some by the idea that someday we'll find a good place to scatter Nubie's ashes. They don't understand grief, thank God. They're already saying things they've heard on TV, things people say after they've had plenty of time to heal. Mostly, it's Danny, sitting in the middle of the two girls in the backseat, saying, "Nubie was such a good dog. He was a great watchdog, wasn't he?" Katherine reminds him of the time Anubis pooped on the Christmas presents and ate an entire dozen bagels from Noah's, brown bag included. Danny says, "He was still a good dog. He will be missed." Maybe he just inherited his dad's platitude gene.

We go to a movie to get our mind off things—*Galaxy Quest*, playing at an old theater in our neighborhood, one that serves real butter on the popcorn and has rose-colored serge chairs with ancient springs that rock.

The kids are on their best behavior, something they do when the adults are sad. But *Galaxy Quest* is hilarious. We laugh so hard we can't hear half of it. After the end crawl, when the ushers stride up and down the aisles with their black garbage bags, I ask the guy who seems to be the main usher whether we might watch it again. I tell him we just put our family dog to sleep.

This is an old theater; the head usher is a grown man, a lover of cinema, with acne scars climbing up his cheeks and a thinning head of dust-colored hair. He's lived a little, you can tell. He puts his hand on my shoulder and says, "There's nothing like a good movie, is there?" He knew what I was just figuring out: that you could have a dying father and a dead dog, you could pretty much have misery all around you, but it was still possible to shriek with laughter.

14

The cough begins in early January. Dad is finished with the radiation and he's still feeling lousy. In fact, he's feeling worse than he was before his surgery. His headache is gone, and he can sleep on his side, but now he's perennially exhausted. He complains that his insides still feel fried. It still hurts to swallow. He can no longer drink his beloved no-pulp orange juice. I buy him apple juice, but it's too sweet. According to Dr. O'Donnell, his radiologist, this is an aftereffect of the radiation. *After*effects? How is an aftereffect different from a side effect? I thought aftereffects were something we avoided discussing, since the main aftereffect will be death.

Someone once said we die in the exact way in which we lived. And so it is with Dad's management of his never-ending, innards-ripping cough, a raspy, chugging *ahh-HUH, ahh-HUH, ahh-HUH, ahh-HUH.* It's always the same. Dad buys boxes of white Kleenex bundled in packages of three. The tissues are for one thing and one thing only: to collect the sputum. The cough sounds like retching. It commands his entire attention, as if it were a labor pain. It can be heard all over the triple-wide, this cough, so loud and futile sounding, so mighty I imagine that his lungs are trying to expel the cancer and just might succeed. But they don't. The lungs are dumb. The lungs don't know any better. Indeed, at the end, they'll be the last thing to quit.

Ahh-HUH! Ahh-HUH! Ahh-HUH!

When it seizes him he must sit down and plant both feet flat on the floor, pluck a tissue from the box, then open it into a perfect square.

Ahh-HUH! Ahh-HUH!

He spits into the center of the tissue, then folds the tissue in half, then spits into it again, then folds the tissue in quarters, spits again, again folds the tissue until it's a soggy white one-inch square. Then, between spasms, he drops the tissue into a small plastic wastepaper basket lined with a white plastic bag. When the white plastic bag is filled with the one-inch squares, he knots the top of the bag and leaves it by the back door, to be taken out to the garbage.

Once every few days, during our regular late-afternoon phone call, I ask him about the chemotherapy, about whether he's reconsidered. I tell him about the research I'd done, how the radiation all by itself isn't enough to effect any measurable difference. I find myself slipping into doctor-speak when I get to this part. I hem and haw and can't figure out a way to say what I want to say. It seems rude, hurtful, horrible to say the plain truth. One evening I pussyfoot around no longer. I don't think I could live with myself unless I did everything I could to try to encourage him—hell, *force* is the word I really want to use—to go for the chemo. Part of my frustration is that he can't give me any rational reason why he's against it.

"Have you thought any more about the chemotherapy, Dad? It's only four sessions, and even though it'll be horrible, it's supposed to enhance the radiation."

"I'm through with that stuff. I hate that stuff."

"Only four sessions, Dad. That's not many. And the payoff will be worth it, I think."

"It's just not for me. My chest burned like it was on fire."

"But why? I mean, I know it must be awful, but what makes you draw that conclusion?"

I am irritated, frustrated, and resentful, for a number of reasons:

a) This is like a conversation I might have with fourteen-year-old Rachel, who, like most fourteen-year-olds, never knows why she does the things she does. Her behavior is one glorious mystery. Rachel is smart, a quick study, when she wants to be. She is famous, however, for doing her homework, then forgetting to turn it in. When asked why, she is mystified. She doesn't know why she bothers to do the homework, then not turn it in. She can posit no reason, hazard no guess. She just wants Daniel and me off her back. She doesn't want to think about it. Maybe it's the same with Dad. Except . . .

b) . . . his situation is life and death. He *needs* to think about it. He *must* think about it. If he doesn't want to think about it—it is his prerogative, after all—I wish he'd just come out and say he doesn't want to deal with it, that he'll take the shorter life span over the agony of chemo. I wish he would demonstrate that he's given it some thought, because . . .

c) . . . this is simply not like him. Dad prides himself on knowing how things *work*: cars, boats and trains, quite literally. He is a fan of systems. He subscribes to *Consumer Reports*. He researches things. When I was a child he hammered me to ask questions, get information.

When I was twelve, like every other twelve-year-old girl in America, I wanted a horse. He was not adverse to the idea, but needed to know more. He wondered, How much does a horse cost? Where do you board it and how much does that cost? Is food included? What about shoes? He tossed out some questions over dinner one night, and I dutifully went to the library and looked up the answers. It was the early seventies, and the books I'd found were written sometime during the last Ice Age, but no matter. At dinner the next night, I presented him with the answers to his questions. But then, he had more. "What happens when your horse gets sick and needs a vet? How often should a horse be ridden? What will you do with it when we're down at the beach house in August? Who will take care of it then?" Question upon question upon question.

"You need to get your facts straight, babe."

I never got my facts straight, according to Dad. Meaning I'd never managed to accumulate enough of them, or the ones I'd managed to accumulate weren't the essential ones. It seemed that no matter what I did, he always had more questions. He would be irritated not only because I didn't have the answers, but because I hadn't thought to ask the questions. Sometimes I'm convinced I became a writer to prove to Dad that I *could* get my facts straight.

And now, here he was, facing this very important matter, not only not getting his facts straight, but not bothering to get any facts at all.

Finally one day, out of patience and feeling mean, I say, "Dad, if you don't do this chemotherapy, you'll die."

He said, "From this? Nah. I'll be back in the saddle in no time. As soon as I kick this cough."

Then, one day in late January, he tells me he's going to attempt the chemo again. He will go once a week for a month. When he tells me, it's as if we never had the previous conversations, as if this were a new idea.

I phone Dr. Florino. "Let It Be" still trills along while I'm on hold. Eleanor the nurse comes on. Somehow I get the feeling that Dad and his case are the cancer equivalent of the second-rate writer the literary agent doesn't have time to talk to.

"Eleanor. Karen Karbo here. What's the deal? I was under the impression that the chemo needed to run concurrently with the radiation."

"That's optimal, yes."

"But is there any real point in doing it after the fact? If that was the optimal time to do it, why are we doing it now? Won't it inflict more misery for no real reason?"

"That's a question for the doctor, I'm afraid."

"I'd love to ask the doctor, but I can never seem to get ahold of him."

"He's got patients until the end of the day today . . ." I hear the *tip-tap* of the keyboard. "Can I have him phone you this evening?"

"That would be wonderful."

"Your name again?"

I get off the phone, pop myself some popcorn in a crappy pan with the Teflon flaking off the bottom. This is the best popcorn-popping pan. Cover the bottom with a coating of canola oil and pour in a half cup of JiffyTime white popcorn. Not one burned kernel, but a dozen old maids at the bottom of the pan, which I crack open with my molars. It's two-thirty in the afternoon. This is my lunch. I wolf down the whole bowl with a Diet Pepsi.

I can't do this with my dad; I can't intercede on his behalf with his doctors. The French have a name for a patient's relationship with his doctor: "*un couple malade,*" the marriage between the doctor and the patient. Like all marriages, there's only room for two. If Dad isn't concerned about whether chemo is, at this point, worthwhile, then why should I be? He's both grieving and dying, and I'm the caregiver, that's why. I can talk myself into pretty much either one of these positions, like the top debater on a championship forensics team. The truth is, I'd love to be like the Shirley MacLaine character in *Terms of Endearment.* When her daughter, played by Debra Winger, is dying of cancer and is in pain, Shirley gallops up and down the corridor outside Debra's room shrieking for a nurse to give her pain medication, even though it's not time. I would like to think I would do that for Dad. But I am not his parent, he is mine. My role is a little less clear than that, and it's a cinch to back down, in the name of allowing Dad his autonomy. For in the end, I still have his polite genes. They are a curse in the face of a terminal disease. Florino never calls me back. I never call him back, either.

I'm scheduled to fly to Boulder City for Dad's second attempt at chemo, but receive a last-minute call from the women's sports magazine that soccer grande dame Michelle Akers is expecting me in Orlando for an interview. This is my first assignment since the go-round about the flying trapeze story. Thanks to an hour-long, four-way conference call between me, the editor, the managing editor, and Lydia, my no-nonsense agent, where I explain, like a sheepish teenage vandal to the principal, why I wrote the flying trapeze article for the business magazine instead of bringing it to them first—the business magazine approached me; the trapeze flying was only supposed to be a metaphor for the type of flying-without-a-net hotshot that entrepreneurs are required to be; I honestly didn't think writing about a bunch of trapeze-flying software geeks conflicted with my contractual obligation to the sports magazine to write only for them about women's sports, health, and fitness—I am back in their good graces. They want the Akers profile yesterday and, of course, yesterday is no problem at all.

If one player embodies the whole of women's soccer in America, from the fledgling national team's Bad News Bears beginnings fifteen years ago—when players were paid a whopping ten dollars a day—to the summer of 1999's nationwide crush on the telegenic World Cup champs, it's Michelle Akers. She's played in every Women's World Cup, won an Olympic Gold medal in 1996, and was the first female soccer player to land a paid endorsement. She's also a born-again Christian, a rodeo queen (she owns a horse farm outside Atlanta), and, incredibly, a sufferer of chronic fatigue immune deficiency syndrome. The women's sports magazine is interested in her not for all these interesting reasons, but because the word is that after a fifteen-year career and twelve major surgeries on

148

her knees and shoulder, Akers is going to get cut from the team.

The plan is to hang out with Michelle for three days at her place not far from Orlando, where she conducts soccer clinics for kids as part of her ministry (following the vacation time-share model, kids get an afternoon of free world-class soccer coaching in exchange for listening to Michelle's testimony about how the Lord changed her life), but the night before I leave, I receive an e-mail from her. Am I up for a little side trip to the White House? In two days, President Clinton will be unveiling a $27 million equal-pay initiative for American women, who infamously make seventy-five cents for every dollar made by a man (a statistic that isn't quite accurate, when you adjust for age, experience, and education, but it sounds good), and has invited Michelle to the White House for photo-op purposes, a clever choice, since on that very day, on the opposite side of the country, the Women's National Team is also in contract negotiations with the United States Soccer Federation, in an attempt to gain parity for their own salaries, which, despite their World Cup Championship status, are woefully low compared to the nonranking U.S. Men's Team. Michelle and I will fly up to Washington at the crack of dawn and back to Orlando in the afternoon. I can interview her on the plane. Except I *can't* interview her on the plane, because I'll be holding the plane up using the special method I've developed wherein I squeeze the armrests until my elbows cramp, all the while staring out the window at the wing.

My friend Nancy calls me a blue-collar writer, because I basically take every writing assignment I'm offered and do them all well, or well enough. I struggle with profiles, though, because the only way I know how to get someone to tell me things is to become an instafriend, something people from Southern California tend to be naturally good at. Perhaps it was all those years in a USC sorority. I meet a subject and do everything I possibly can not to behave like a journalist, but rather like a friend, an old roommate. My secret to becoming an instafriend with my female subjects is to bring up the topic of hair problems; no woman on earth, even an Olympic gold medalist, is 100 percent happy with her hair.

The problem is, once I've become my subject's instafriend, I confuse this with being her real friend, and for my real friends I'm a vault; I treat every confidence as if it were top secret. After we compare hair products, we slip into girlfriend talk and we divulge things to each other about our career fears and love lives. But I never include this stuff in the piece, because I'd never betray a friend that way. Sometimes one of my instafriends/profile subjects will remember, in the midst of our second round of margaritas, that I'm interviewing her for a big magazine and ask that something or other be off the record. I'm always tempted to say, "Don't worry! It's ALL off the record."

I pick up Michelle in my rental car at four-thirty on the warm, rainy morning of January 23. I'm on edge; the directions to her house from my hotel were complicated, involving a number of increasingly expensive toll roads that have me scrabbling through the bottom of my purse in the dark for change. I don't know how I'm going to conduct a probing and incisive interview (I forgot to mention that prior to every profile, I vow to try to adopt the mantle of Diane Sawyer or some other respected journalist who would die before resorting to the instafriend method of interviewing; it is never successful) on an airplane, especially when at the first sign of turbulence, I'm going to be squeezing Michelle's hand and burying my head on her powerful, much-operated-upon shoulder.

I'm also upset because I'm betraying Dad in the worst way: It's his seventy-fifth birthday and instead of spending it with him, I'm going to the White House to meet the president. A Democrat.

Michelle is tall but narrow of hip and shoulder. She's elegant in her all-black, meet-the-press pantsuit, which she says is her uniform for such occasions. She has a terrific head of sandy blond curls—the word *leonine* comes to mind—and since Florida is about the most humid place in the country, and humidity causes frizz, the eternal enemy of the curly-headed, I know we'll get along just fine. We chat in the car on the way to the airport about her health, which is touch and go. She was diagnosed with chronic fatigue syndrome in 1992. CFS manifests itself not just as bone-crushing exhaustion, but also as week-long migraine headaches, the inability to concentrate, chronic muscle and joint aches, and, paradoxically, an inability to sleep in a way that's remotely refreshing. It's a life spent feeling as if you're eternally coming down with the flu. To combat it, Michelle monitors her activity level every minute of every day, and maintains a near-heroic dairy-free, gluten-free, sugar-free, caffeine-free, alcohol-free diet.

On the flight to Washington, Michelle studies her notes for the speech she'll make after President Clinton unveils the details of his initiative. She's under a gag order not to talk about her team's contract negotiations, which is of course what all the journalists in attendance want to hear about. Instead, there will be a lot of inspirational blather. I'm happy to have a reason to postpone my probing and incisive Diane Sawyer–style interview until the flight home.

I've never been to Washington, D.C., before. I've heard it's the American version of Paris, my all-time favorite city. Michelle and I are picked up by someone from the White House in a dark blue Lincoln Town Car. The driver even has one of those phone-cord-looking things snaking up the side of his neck and into his ear. I tell Michelle my dad designed the hood ornament and she says, "Ah, you've got an awesome dad too, huh?"

The sky is one gray, cottony cloud. It's cold, but not cold enough to warrant the snow that's predicted later in the day. I'm disoriented, expect to drive past the Capitol building and the Lincoln Memorial, famous landmarks I know from the movies, but we go by some back route that takes us past a large gray bunker, very un-Parisian.

At some obscure entrance to the White House, the guard takes our driver's licenses and gives us red plastic tags to wear around our necks. We've already been checked out by the FBI—I had to call someone in the first lady's office with my social security number before I left Portland—but there's some frowning and rechecking of the computer when the cowboy boots I've worn for the occasion set off the metal detector.

It's sad that life has come to this, but I must go on record as saying that when the press conference began, it was just like being on an episode of *The West Wing*: the podium and the banner with the seal of the United States behind it, the journalists with their cameras, the press secretary doing the introductions. I can compare it to nothing else. President Clinton comes out and talks up a storm. The sound bites don't do him justice.

He chatters for a good forty-five minutes about women and money, about his wife being a working woman, about how men should *want* their wives to make more money, so that then they can kick back and take it easy! He strikes me as both warm and cold, big and friendly and calculating, just as he's been described. His little eyes twinkle. Then Michelle stands up and talks for about five minutes about the struggles of female athletes and I get all teary: That's my instafriend up there! Afterward, Clinton strides out into the audience and shakes the hands of a few of us who've been strategically positioned in the front row. His hand is huge and warm. Before the press conference, one of the pages confided to us that he sometimes wears antiperspirant on his palm. Later, in a room behind the stage, we're offered plastic cups of white wine. *At ten-thirty in the morning?* The president chats with Michelle about how much he loves women's soccer, and wasn't Michelle an amazing warrior during that final World Cup game?

Then, it's a tour of the White House. When you are a guest of the president, or a friend of a guest of the president, a tour of the White House is mandatory. Our tour guide is like every other young woman Michelle and I have come across since we've been here: a gorgeous, tiny thing who weighs less than one hundred pounds, a fine-featured girl with swingy straight hair who whose size-zero black gabardine pants hang loose on her hips. While we're in the China Room, where all the presidential china is displayed—I take a good look at the rather gaudy red-and-gold Reagan china, so I can report back to Dad, not that he'd care—Michelle leans over and whispers, "Have you noticed that we're about a foot taller than all the other girls here?" I laugh. We start wisecracking back and forth in stage whispers: Is it because we're from the West and they just grow girls bigger out there? Is it because you can only get a job here if you sign an affidavit saying your mother refrained from taking prenatal vitamins? And what's with their hair? Do they receive a memo prior to their FBI clearance: "We, in the White House have a strict antifrizz policy. If you suspect your hair might frizz at anytime during your employment, please seek the proper help."

Michelle asks the tour guide what Bill and Hillary do for fun—she uses their first names like that—and the tour guide says they use the Stairmaster. We elbow each other and roll our eyes. I know I'll never be able to write one bad thing about Michelle. (Indeed, after I turn in the third draft, the women's sports magazine kills the piece in favor of running an excerpt from a book on the Women's National Team.)

Later, when I'm back at my hotel in Orlando, I phone my dad and perform a full-blown comedy routine for Dad's amusement, something I haven't done since Bev died. "Dad, I have news! I was at the White House today and I fully understand the whole Monica Lewinsky thing. Every page that works in the White House—and there are hundreds of them!—is weency. They're all bird-boned, swingy-haired, twin-set wearing valedictorians who think a thong is a sandal! Who think a cigar is something you give out after the birth of a child! But Monica, Dad! She's got big hair and a big ass, a lively girl from the West who is no stranger to a Big Mac. Who could resist?" My Dad laughs longer and harder than I've heard him laugh in a long time. It occurs to me that perhaps that's my job after all. Not to argue with his doctors, but to entertain him until the end. I love him for simply laughing, and for not turning this into a political discussion.

Perhaps his good spirits are also due to good news. Dad had an appointment this afternoon with Dr. O'Donnell, who reported that the original mass for which he endured a month's worth of zapping has shrunk. I wonder by how much. Certainly they can measure such things? But Dad doesn't know by how much. He doesn't know how many centimeters it was and how many centimeters it is. He didn't ask to see the pictures himself.

"The doctor said that's it, I'm done. He's done all he's going to do for me." He sounded pleased when he reported this.

"Did he mean, 'We've done all we can do?' or 'Wow, you're cured! We're not going to do anymore because there just isn't any more to be done'?"

"It sure is good to hear your voice, babe." Apparently, he isn't interested in the distinction.

15

Throughout Dad's month of radiation, and the holidays—which he ignores, aside from sending each child a check for fifty dollars—and his disastrous run-in with chemotherapy, he never asks me to come stay with him. He is dead set against my doing anything that resembles caregiving. So we both pretend that I come to see him just to hang out. I make all the arrangements.

In March, Daniel and I drive to Boulder City for a change of pace, and also because I'll be with Dad indefinitely, and need more books and shoes, stuff that resists being easily packed in your carry-ons. More than that, I need a break from flying. I've had it with the tight seats, the wretched food, the anxiety of flying over the Red Rock Mountains and banging straight into the desert thermals over Las Vegas that never fail to bounce the plane all over the place.

But by the time we've reached the middle of godforsaken Nevada, I feel the same way about driving. Unlike a lot of my friends, I do not love a road trip, about which I feel sheepish; Americans of a certain literary stripe are expected to revere the Kerouac-ian philosophy of getting the hell out of whereever you are as a way to improve upon life. But without all the booze and drugs, all you are is someone imprisoned in a car with all your problems. You haven't left them behind; they've simply crowded in next to you like people late for work who squeeze into a slow elevator.

Daniel likes to listen to books on tape, for which I applaud him. Because he's not a curmudgeon with a dad who's dying and making it impossible to care for him, he is lulled by the soothing voice of the British actor who reads *Harry Potter and the Chamber of Secrets*; but I'm irritated. I loved the book when I read it to Katherine and Danny, but now I'm finding it overwritten, now I'm wishing J. K. Rowlings believed as I do in the power and the glory of narrative summary. I try to cover my head with a pillow where the tape is playing. I briefly ponder throwing it out the window, like I did at the age of three, when my mother, Dad, and I moved from Detroit to California. My mother took home movies of all the things I threw out the car window. The entire 8mm movie is taken from my mother's point of view out the back window, one pillow after another bouncing once or twice on the highway behind us as we left it in the dust. I fantasize that my mother howled with laughter at my antics, but after I poured some orange juice down Dad's neck somewhere in the Plains states, I was put on a plane to Burbank, where Luna, my grandmother, met me.

It was better when I was able to read in the car. Now, I snack in the car instead. By the middle of the afternoon I have a fierce case of indigestion from eating too much stale trail mix purchased at various gas stations along the way. Fuel prices have gone up fourteen cents per gallon in the last two weeks, and every time we stop for gas—which we do whenever we get to half a tank, since the gas stations are few and far between in the wasteland of central Nevada—we drive off having spent twenty bucks.

At eight o'clock we stop for dinner at the Station House in Tonopah, a twenty-four-hour casino/hotel/restaurant/mall and antique slot-machine museum (with live entertainment and a dance floor). Tonopah is located at the headwaters of the Extraterrestrial Highway, Route 375, which runs along the northern border of the Nellis Air Force Base, home of the officially denied Area 51. The Station House has a gift shop with a sign in the window: BEANIES AND BABIES. Next to the Beanies, posed on tiny plastic pedestals with their outrageous prices posted on signs above their stuffed heads—for these are collector's items—is a plastic mask of an alien wearing a black hood. Taped to the forehead a little card says: MEMO TO EARTHLINGS: WE HAVE LEARNED AS MUCH AS WE CAN FROM RECTAL PROBES.

Boulder City is still 227 miles away.

Dad is waiting up for us. He answers the back door with the dog tucked under his arm, as usual. I haven't laid eyes on him in two months, and I'm afraid to see the change. My handsome Dad, with that Clint Eastwood thing about him, was haggard then, months ago, at six foot two, one-hundred-thirty-eight pounds. Now he's been through radiation, which caused him on occasion to throw up the Souffer's macaroni and cheese, the only thing that could slide down his radiation-scorched esophagus.

But he's a guy who's lived in the desert for years without sunscreen, without enough water, or fruit, or vegetables, drinking and smoking his head off and not exercising for decades. I didn't realize it until I saw him again, and found him unchanged, that he has always looked as if he had a terminal disease. He has lost more weight. His beige Lee jeans hang down on his hips. I can see his sternum through his white T-shirt. But he's happy, so happy, to see us.

The next night I make fresh enchiladas for dinner, even though there are still an easy dozen in the freezer. I mix the chicken, sliced olives, chili peppers, and salsa in the yellow Pyrex bowl that we used for popcorn when I was growing up. I bake it in one of Bev's baking dishes.

Since Daniel is here, we eat in the dining room—there is only room for two at the Formica breakfast bar. Dad doesn't mind my cooking, but he doesn't want to be waited on. He sets the table; he fetches the fancy paper napkins from a drawer in a buffet in the family room. The buffet is paneled with the same phony wood as every other wall in the Palace. There is a drawer exclusively for napkins: informal paper napkins in peach and aqua to be used for morning coffee and lunch; smaller cocktail napkins; and the larger white napkins for dinner. That napkin drawer! Emblematic of the whole DadandBev ultraorganized domestic thing that harkens back to a time when homemakers with time on their hands took care to have different paper napkins for every occasion—the sort of thing that drove the same women to run to the shelter of mother's little helper, the sort of thing I used to mock with increasingly less derision, until I finally saw it as being sort of sweet in its obsessive ridiculousness. That napkin drawer was the sort of thing that is my undoing now. The sight of my dad, stooped more than I remember him, fishing three fancy white paper napkins from inside their plastic package, makes my heart feel like a big foot being shoved into a shoe three sizes too small.

"I'm no invalid," Dad says, when I tell him to sit down and take it easy.

I serve the enchiladas with refried beans sprinkled with grated cheddar and a green salad. Nothing fancy. Hardly enough for Daniel, really. Dad pulls out my chair for me, then sits down himself. He looks overwhelmed. He turns his plate so the enchilada—I've only given him one—is closest to him, as if heavy lifting were involved. "I sincerely hope you don't expect me to eat all of this," he says.

"Just what you can," I say. This is what I say to the kids when they claim not to be hungry for dinner. I amend it, "Yes, you must eat all of it, or else I'll be highly offended." Better. That at least sounds as if I'm addressing another adult.

"When I was feeling low, and was in bed for those four days, I liked to rub some of that cologne that comes in the green bottle,

I can't recall the name of it, on my chest. It made things not seem so bad."

"You mean the one with the funny shape, with the green and gold label?" *Dad was sick in bed for four days and didn't tell me?*

"No, no, the bottle itself is green."

"It looks like something from around the time of Louis the Sixteenth?" For some reason I'm desperate to know exactly the type of cologne he means. It's part of having all the information, in case I need to buy some for him in the future.

DAD WAS SICK IN BED FOR FOUR DAYS AND DIDN'T TELL ME?

I've talked to him every day on the phone at ten of five in the evening since Bev died, even the days I flew across country and into a later time zone, even the day I visited the White House, even those days when the kids had to be driven to lessons or rehearsals or somewhere in the late afternoon and I was on the road. I phoned every day. Never had he mentioned that he'd been in bed for four of those days. He had never been sick in bed for more than a day in my entire life. I am irritated. I am all he has left now. How can I help him if I don't know? I deserve to know. I am fed up with never, ever knowing.

I tell myself: Let it go, let it go, let it go. But, sick in bed for four days? Sick how? He was tired? He was sick to his stomach? What? Well, let it go. It doesn't make any difference.

"Dad, you were that sick and you didn't tell me?"

He doesn't say anything. He doesn't hear me, or doesn't want to hear me.

"When were you sick in bed, Dad?"

"It was that damn chemotherapy."

"When you had that bad reaction?"

"No, no, another time."

"When? I thought you told me you weren't going to do it? You said you were done. You said the radiation was it. Nothing else. No more. Then you did it anyway?"

Daniel puts his hand on my knee beneath the table and gives it a don't-worry squeeze.

I glare at Daniel, suddenly annoyed. He's wearing a white T-shirt with a line of blue hibiscus marching across the chest and a pair of khaki shorts. He squeezes my knee a little too long, then continues squeezing it while tucking into his enchiladas as though it were a regular night back in Portland. The squeeze is rote. The squeeze is patronizing. The T-shirt and shorts make him look as if he's on vacation, and indeed he is on vacation: no kids here that need feeding, bathing, policing; no puppy to be walked or fed; no laundry to fold. His only job here is to wrangle me and my unruly emotions. I realize part of the reason he's able to behave in such a saintly manner is that he assigned himself to the role of even-tempered helpmate on the day Bev died. And he *has* been even-tempered; he *has* helped. But he can't do the one thing I would love him to do more than anything else: feel the way I do. He's not in the foxhole with my Dad and me after all.

It's well known that part of the difficulty of caring for a parent who's elderly and sick is that the child ends up parenting the parent. I always imagined this meant being forced to treat Dad as if he were a younger child, as if he were my little daughter (see minor chiding over his disinclination to eat his dinner, above); it turns out to be more complicated than that. It turns out, you also wind up treating them like recalcitrant teenagers. *You went to chemotherapy and you didn't tell me? Did you think I'd never find out? Do you think I was born yesterday?*

Halfway through the meal, he has one of his coughing spells. There are so many clocks here, it's nothing to time it. Twelve minutes. For the first few minutes, Daniel and I continue eating, assuming it's going to be over soon. After the next few minutes I say, "Are you okay?" and "Would you like some water?" Then we are silent again.

Ah-HUH. Ah-HUH. Ah-HUH. He bends over his skinny

lap, spitting into his square of Kleenex. "I will need to lie down now for just a minute. I'm sorry I'm being a dud, here."

He's taken exactly one bite of his enchilada. He takes his white plastic wastebasket with him.

Daniel and I look at each other. "I don't know how to do this," I say.

Dad lies down for about fifteen minutes, then returns, still carrying the wastebasket. He insists on doing the dishes, methodically loading the dishwasher, washing all the knives with wooden handles, all the pots and pans by hand. For some reason, he is morally opposed to putting pots and pans in the dishwasher.

Daniel and I adjourn to the guest room to discuss his travel plans. He needs to go home. We've been talking about this off and on all day. Should he drive home and I fly home later (when, later? Days later? Weeks? Months?) Should he fly home, and I drive? I don't like either plan. I didn't want him to go at all. Even though I'm irritated with him at the moment. Not unlike my mother, Daniel, with his good spirits and sometimes aimless chatter and willingness to lie through his teeth and remember Bev fondly (*She really did know how to make a good martini!*), has been a buffer between me and Dad. I try to chat Dad up and josh him and, in general, fill the room with whatever sunniness I can muster, but I am too much like him. Together, we are a pair of tough Polacks: broody, serious, not given to blarney. When it is just the two of us alone together, it is the House of Parallel Play, and we are the Parallel Players. The silence is enough to make you start writing poetry on the walls.

I do not want to stay here.

Daniel and I lie together on the too-soft double bed for a while. I weep on his shoulder. He doesn't own one T-shirt now the shoulder of which isn't stained black with my mascara. You may be able to slug Karen Karbo and she don't even cry, but don't leave her in the desert with a dying dad who refuses to allow her to help.

Daniel strokes my hair and starts in with the optimism. What else is there to do? "You could get some good work done here. It is quiet. Maybe you could look at it as a chance to start a new book? I think it's enough for your dad to just hang out, to just know you're in the house." He reminds me how I'm always saying I yearn to have time to reflect—like retired people do in France—and to write something Big and Important. Perhaps this is a blessing in disguise. I'll have time to begin a new novel, time to read and also be able to spend unlimited time with Dad. It could be okay. Daniel says the same thing he did on the day Dad was diagnosed: he's going to die, but he's not going to die today. I want to pick a fight but I just don't have the energy.

The next morning, on the way back from taking Daniel to the airport, I stop at Barnes & Noble in Henderson, where I treat myself to a ridiculous coffee drink, the kind in a tall plastic cup with a dome over the pile of whipped cream drizzled with chocolate—a Slurpee for grown-ups. I pay for it in cash from my dad and feel decadent, guilty, worried that it is against my credo of never accepting money from him. That morning, as we were leaving, I told him I had some good books for him to read, and he pressed three twenty-dollar bills, folded into thirds, into my hand. It reminded me of a similar gesture he made long ago, one that ranks among the top ten humiliating moments of my teenhood. Sophomore year. Homecoming. My date: Scott Bradley, someone I didn't like, indeed, someone I found just this side of repulsive, but I did it for the team: My two best friends were going with Scott's two best friends, boys they liked. Scott was three inches shorter than I was, with a head of huge black hair, the bangs flipped up over one eye, clammy hands, and breath that occasionally stank. When he came to the door to pick me up, and he shook my father's hand, Dad slipped him a twenty, folded in thirds. Naturally, he told his friends, one of whom teased me about it until we graduated.

With the sixty dollars—part of Bev's large stash—I bought Dad *Into Thin Air*, by Jon Krakauer, about the failed Everest expedition, and *The Perfect Storm*, by Sebastian Junger, about the failed sword-fishing expedition off the coast of Massachusetts, and one of a number of titles about various failed Antarctic expeditions. Dad read anything—my schoolbooks used to disappear from the kitchen table, Dad having wandered off with my history or science book—and I thought other people's disasters might take him out of himself a bit.

Back at the Palace, it's almost noon and Dad is taking a nap. I peek in at him, sleeping on top of the covers with his shoes on, lined up long and lean on one side of the bed, a habit from years of wives sleeping on the other side. He has his hand on his chest, the hand with the nail nub on the end of his middle finger—he had an accident in the machine shop when he was in his twenties—and the gold pinky ring that belonged to his mother. His room is at the end of the long hall, off to the left. There is a small foyer which opens off to the office on the right, and the room on the left. You need to walk several steps into the room to see him lying in bed. You can't just poke your head in, you need to fully enter the room. Months down the road, when he lies dying, taking these few steps into the room will take all my willpower. Even now, as I tiptoe down the hall, I'm relieved to hear him snoring, relieved to know that on this day, at least, I will not find him dead.

I held the common misconception that he would just one day stop breathing and that would be it. He would take one of his naps, his breathing would slow, and he would die. It would be a heart attack, the vine of tumor blooming out of his lung finally strangling his aorta. Or he would break a blood vessel in his head during one of his coughing fits. I didn't know how long a body could hang on, how dying can be imminent for days and days and days.

I go back to the kitchen and eat some jelly beans. Dad has a little red plastic gumball-machine-like dispenser on the counter full of gourmet jelly beans, a gift from one of Martin's daughters. In the cabinet beneath the counter are a few three-pound bags of beans. Dad has a bean or three every night after dinner, turning the small plastic handle to coax the tiny bean to spill out. I just go straight to the bag beneath the counter. There are also about ten pounds of dried apricots down there, part of Bev's Y2K hoard. She collected the strangest stuff for Y2K: the guest room closet is filled to the top with six-packs of Brawny paper towels. In the cabinet beneath the sink in the guest bath there are a dozen huge bottles of hand lotion. When Daniel and I discovered this stuff, we joked that if all the doomsayers of Y2K had been right, and had the world been thrown into chaos and disarray, DadandBev would have smooth hands, regular bowel movements, and spotless kitchen counters. Daniel and I are bad; we have no respect for the dead.

16

The only sound in the Palace is that of the big clock ticking in the living room. Outside, it's nose-hair-singeing hot. All the neighbors sit sealed up in their air-conditioned trailers. The desert creatures are all sleeping in their holes, or under some puny desert shrub. The phone almost never rings. When it does, we cock our heads, as if we've heard something out of the ordinary, an earthquake rumbling, or low-flying choppers. Once, someone calls named George, who lives in Las Vegas and with whom Dad attended Art Center in Pasadena in the 1950s. Dad gets on the phone, plays down his illness, says things are looking up every day. Then they talk about cars.

I hate it here. Despite Daniel's pep talk, I am not using this time to write a Big and Important Novel. Being marooned here in the desert with him reminds me too much of the sad, boring, lonely, excruciating summer spent with him in the Newport Beach condo, in the years just after my mother died, before he married Bev. It's the heat, the silence, the lack of engagement between Dad and me, between Dad and his own life. I'm at sea. I'm lonely. I'm looking for solace that is not forthcoming from Dad—how can he comfort me?

I once had a fantasy that somehow in his decline, our relationship would change. I wanted it to be like the relationship between the mother and daughter in Anna Quindlen's novel *One True Thing*, a book I wouldn't touch for years, since the homemaker mother at the center of the story is dying of cancer and the daughter who comes home to care for her is an overachieving daddy's girl who writes inane stories for glossy magazines, a wisenheimer who disdains her mother's domesticity. When I finally steel myself and crack it, there in the Palace of the Golden Sofa, I see it's pure romance, a fantasia. The mother is dedicated to bonding, to divulging. She even reminisces with the wisenheimer daughter about how difficult it was to give her the birds and the bees speech, how she practiced what she was going to say for weeks.

I launch into a series of intense e-mail relationships with anyone of my acquaintance who has an equal need, for whatever reason, to madly e-mail. These are mostly other writers who claim answering their e-mail helps them warm up for a productive day of serious work. I pitch magazine articles I have no intention of writing, outline a novel. It is to be a female version of *Strangers on a Train* in which two women who meet over a pedicure at a nail salon plan to kill each other's spouses. I have a fantasy of writing it in four weeks I know this is the literary equivalent of having a wedding to attend in a week and believing you can lose twenty pounds between now and then, but I don't care.

After his nap, Dad pads out to the family room for his postnap cough. He hacks away for long minutes at a time. I expect him to keel over from the exertion, but he doesn't (not yet, though one day he will fall off his chair). Eventually, he produces a wad of clear mucus, which he spits into his folded-up tissue. It's impossible to listen to. I can't do anything about it, nor will he invite me in to complain about how there's nothing to be done.

These are the things I cook for him: fettuccini Alfredo, grilled cheese sandwiches, cheese omelets, enchiladas, a thing called Weezer's Cheese Pie, which is a very cheesy quiche. His food preferences are not unlike that of my seven-year-old, whose tastes run almost exclusively to quesadillas and grilled cheese sandwiches. I wonder if at the end of life, as at the beginning, all you really want is a piece of cheese pizza.

Tonight, he wants to take me out to dinner, to give me a break from cooking. He still drives the Explorer in that three-miles-under-the-speed-limit way he has. He still lights up a cigarette while he drives; I know few people who smoke anymore, and no one I know who does, smokes in their car. He still uses the lighter in the dashboard, which I find endearing—until, of course, the car fills up with smoke, and I feel that familiar twirl of nausea and smell the smoke settling into my hair. Then I'm grumpy. But I don't say anything.

We head for the white stucco casino at the top of Railroad Pass on Boulder Highway, its huge electronic sign advertising loose slots and cheap rooms, the only light out here in the desert, except the halogen highway lights, the stars overhead, and the jets on approach to Las Vegas, just over the ridge. Dad has the $4.95 prime rib special and a glass of apple juice. It's different sitting across from him at the table, rather than shoulder to shoulder, as we routinely are at the breakfast bar in the Palace. I feel as if we should attempt some conversation. And since he is dying, I feel as if I should at least ask him some things I want to know, instead of blathering about what's going on with the kids. So I say, "Tell me the first thing that comes to mind about my mother."

He cuts a piece of prime rib, thinks about it. He doesn't think for a minute I am being foolish. He may know what I am doing. Finally, he says, "When we used to come to Las Vegas to gamble, your mother never wanted to sit next to me at the blackjack table."

"No? Why not? She think you were bad luck?"

"She said I embarrassed her. I was losing as fast as she was winning." Then he laughs, delighted at his own memory.

"Tell me something about Bev, er, Beverly." I think, in deference to him, I should give his beloved second wife equal airtime.

"I wish you two would have gotten along better." Dad tucks a forkful of mashed potatoes into his mouth and looks at me gamely while he chews.

"I bore her no ill will, Dad."

This is a lie. I bore her ill will for refusing to forgive me for crying at her wedding, for her resentment that I was a better shot than she was, but the main incident it was impossible to get over was what happened after her daughter Nora's death. Now that I'm a mother myself, I'm able to forgive some of her actions, but not quite all of them. Like color, there are varying shades of forgiveness.

Three months after the misbegotten handgun training class at the Huntington Beach police department, at ten-thirty at night, I received a phone call from Dad. At the time, I was living in the Wilshire District of Los Angeles with my friend Kathy, who was also in her last semester of film school at USC. We were writing a screenplay together based on the life of Luna, my father's mother, dating a cavalcade of losers, and working part time at a movie theater in West L.A. where for two years they'd been showing *Meetings with Remarkable Men*, about the life of the Central Asian philosopher Gurdjieff. We got drunk at film school parties on the weekends and roller-skated on the boardwalk at Venice Beach. Only a few weeks earlier, John Lennon had been shot.

Dad said he had some bad news. Nora, Bev's twenty-seven-year-old daughter, had passed away.

"Oh my God, oh my God. How, Dad? What happened? Was she, oh God, was it a car accident?" I knew Nora had just bought a motorcycle.

"No, no nothing like that."

Silence.

"It wasn't, she wasn't, oh Dad, this is so terrible. She wasn't murdered or anything, was she?" I thought of John Lennon, outside the Dakota.

"No, she wasn't murdered."

It went on like this for several minutes, until I finally coaxed him into telling me she'd slit her wrists in the tub.

DadandBev left that night for Davis, where Nora had been a Ph.D. student in botany at the university. They had to identify the body and begin the horrid process of closing up the apartment, of dealing with the electric company, the phone company, the landlord, of figuring out what to do with all of Nora's stuff. To this day, Nora's suicide, like all suicides, essentially remains a mystery. Three weeks before, she'd spent a week with DadandBev, and she talked about being worried about money, about not doing well in her classes. When DadandBev talked to Nora's professors, they discovered she was getting A's in every class. Now that I'm a mother myself, I understand that taking care of the business of wrapping up your dead child's life is the worst task on earth. There are no exceptions.

Then, however, I was only twenty-two and didn't know a damn thing. Bev's mother, Adele, was a dowager who lived alone in a lovely old California house in La Canada, northwest of Pasadena in the foothills. Adele was in her late eighties and still pruned her own avocado trees. In her seventies, she went back to Cal State, L.A., and completed her college degree. She was a force to be dealt with, and after DadandBev returned from Davis, doing their damnedest to soldier on despite what must have been grief so staggering that it didn't even register as an emotion, but felt like a perpetual full eclipse of the sun, Dad called and ask me to do him a favor.

"Beverly needs to drive up to see her mother and talk to her about recent events and she'd like you to go with her."

"Me? Why me?" *Bev despises me.*

"As a favor to me, babe. She needs someone to go with her."

"But what about Martin? What about Liz?"

"Well, Martin's up in Davis and Liz isn't available."

The drive time from Newport Beach to La Canada is two hours in traffic. I drove a red 1973 Volkswagen bug with no air-conditioning and a large collection of empty Tab cans that rattled impressively on corners. Bev sat on the ripped passenger seat and stared out the windshield. I made the world's most inane conversation. I told her I was so sorry, so incredibly sorry. That I couldn't imagine for a minute what it was like, to which she said, "No, you can't." That shut me up. The entire time DadandBev were married, being in Bev's presence was like being on a job interview, and this was the worst one yet. Finally, I just drove.

Adele was not expecting us. She was small, with wavy blond hair and brown eyes, pretty like her daughter, but she had an ungenerous air about her. She glanced at me and was immediately suspicious.

"What's going on?" she said. "Why are you here?"

The house smelled of furniture polish and loneliness. Adele sat down at the round kitchen table and Bev sat across from her. I was left standing. I wore a white Mexican wedding dress, the kind with embroidery on the yoke and sleeves, all the rage, and a pair of Mexican huaraches. I felt as if I were in my nightgown. I wished I'd put on jeans and boots, something to protect me. My shoes squeaked as I shifted my weight.

"What's going on here?" Adele demanded again. She was frightened.

"Nora's been murdered," said Bev. Her voice was low and flat. No tears. *Murdered?*

Tears squirted from Adele's eyes. "Dear God. It was Liz, wasn't it. It was those diamond stud earrings I gave her. Liz admired them. She wanted a pair of her own." Adele looked up at me, as if I knew something her own daughter didn't.

"Uh," I said. *Huh?* What was going on here? Why didn't anyone tell me Bev and I were driving all the way up here to tell her eighty-something mother a bald-faced lie? I had nothing against bald-faced lies; I was recently a teenage girl, and teenage girls are the world's foremost purveyors of the bald-faced lie, but I could have used a heads-up. (That's what I want on my tombstone: "Here lies Karen Karbo, daughter, wife, mother. All she wanted was a heads-up.")

Bev and I drove home in silence, and Adele went to her grave believing one granddaughter had murdered the other over a pair of earrings.

Now, Dad says, "Beverly sometimes had trouble with you. It would have been nice if you would have tried a little harder."

"Dad, I did try. And you know what? I'm a stepmother now, and I have not one but two stepchildren, both of whom have different mothers they love probably more than me, and it's still part of my job not to hold this against them. Because I'm the adult and they're the children. Just like when you married Bev, she was the adult and I was the child. I was an older child, but I had a dead mother. It was her job to try."

I feel myself getting worked up. I've inherited my mother's quick temper and sharp tongue. I'm on the verge of letting it rip. The slot machines clang, whir, and beep in the casino next door. The simple fact is that Bev was cold and mean. And I'm no longer twenty-two. I know a few things now. I know some of the coldness was really shyness. I know her life was difficult in ways I can't imagine (No, you can't.) and I imagine that every time she looked at me she wished it was me who'd died and not Nora, me or poor Liz. Still and all, still and all.

Still and all, Dad loved her to bits, he misses her, and now he's dying. I've said enough. I see I'll never tell him about the afternoon Bev and I drove to La Canada to lie to Adele about her granddaughter's death. I see Dad will go to his own grave unaware of certain things, and that's how it should be.

17

One morning I go for my run, two miles to Hemenway Park and back, up the long hill. The sweat runs down my arms, my lungs feel as if they're trying to escape from my chest, my face is flushed enough that I think I may have a heart attack and keel over. Then what? No one would find me for hours, since by eight-thirty A.M. they are already sealed inside their trailers. When I drag my sorry ass back home, Dad is dressed in a black cowboy shirt with long sleeves and jeans, ready to go out.

"I need a cell phone," he says.

"Where are you going?"

"To find one."

He says this like someone about to get in the car and drive up and down the street looking for a lost dog.

There is a kiosk in the mall in Henderson, and I suggest we go there. I invite myself along. This is our eternal dynamic. He resists help, and I press myself on him. For years I never did, because it was DadandBev. He didn't need me to do any of these daughterly things. Now he does, but he is dead set against imposing. He doesn't want to disturb me, doesn't want to disrupt my life. It occurs to me that it was Dad, and not my mother, who orchestrated the silence around her illness.

At the mall, the cell phone salesman has a goatee and a pierced ear with a thick silver hoop in it. Otherwise, he is wearing slacks and a blue-and-white-striped button-down shirt. His blond hair is spiked in an eighties style incongruous with the rest of his self-presentation. He's eager not to be there and flips a pen against his palm, eyes flicking around the room as he tells Dad the calling-plan options. It's loud in the mall; besides the music and the general clatter of shoppers, some sort of fashion show is in full swing, with its own blaring music and emcee talking too close to the mike. Dad has trouble hearing. He leans over the counter to hear the spiky-haired salesman, like a cowboy leaning in to order another round from the barkeep. His voice is still faint and scratchy from the radiation. The salesman makes no effort to lean closer to hear Dad; he makes no effort to talk slower or louder.

The curse and the blessing of being fortyish is that you remember very well being the kid with the crappy mall job, itching to get off work. I can imagine him thinking: How many more minutes? Don't look at the clock, time'll go faster . . . I wonder if that cute chick who works at Pacific Sunwear is still on . . . Could book on by there . . . Cool . . . Customers . . . 'Cept this old dude is deaf as a post.

You also see your own father, the eminence who for most of your life you've set your watch by, a man of dignity and manners, even though he feels lousy, even though he can barely stand there, with his elbow on the narrow counter of the kiosk, with all the music and chatter blasting, trying to get a handle on this cell phone thing, and getting treated like shit.

For about fifteen seconds you wish you were the kid, who hasn't an empathetic bone in his body, who is so young he doesn't need one. (Although, you remember, you already had a dead mother at his age and it didn't help you to be any nicer to the elderly and the infirm; you were just as bored by anyone over age twenty-seven as he is.) For about fifteen more seconds, you wish you and your dad could hop into the Way Back Machine, and he would be the old father you knew, the one who would conduct his business while you stood behind him, shifting your weight from one foot to the other, bored to tears at all this grown-up stuff. The kid would stand up straight and call him "sir."

On the one hand, I would dearly love to muscle my way in, get in this guy's face, and ask to see the manager. I'm in the mood to make a scene. This would embarrass this guy, but also Dad, who did not raise his daughter to make a scene. On the other hand, I could muscle my way in, pluck the brochure from Dad's hand, and deal with the guy myself. This would rob Dad of his dignity. He can still talk. He can still make himself understood. On yet another hand, I could do nothing but watch the whole heartbreaking spectacle unfold. Dad, the smartest man I know, hasn't a clue what this guy's going on about, with weekday minutes and weekend minutes and roaming minutes. On the other hand, I could excuse myself to find the ladies' room and not have to watch at all. I have grown so many hands, like a Hindu goddess.

While I'm having my Hindu goddess moment, counting all the possibilities on all of my empty hands, the salesman looks at me. "Do you want him to buy the phone, or rent it for six months?"

He flips the pen against his palm, twirls it between his fingers. He must be an aspiring rock star. He plays drums in some Henderson garage band. He cannot, at this moment, abide his life, and will most likely get blasted out of his mind tonight. I want to say, God, I know, I know.

Dad looks at me. The kiosk is close to the mall's front door and Dad is wearing his photosensitive glasses. I can't see his eyes behind the rims. He's wearing his straw cowboy hat too. His teeth are piano keys in his brown face, still suntanned probably suntanned forever now. From his expression, he may not know what in the hell is going on, but I pretend he just wants my opinion on an important matter.

Since Beverly's trust was disbursed to Martin and Liz, Dad has been fretting about money. Suddenly, he feels poor. Several days earlier he asked me whether I knew any recipes using the canned goods in the pantry, the dozens of cans of Snow's chopped clams and the Spam Bev bought in bulk for Y2K. We've been eating clam linguini for a week. It is another inequity: The Karbo family trust was structured so that if Dad should die first, the money would go to Bev, and then, upon her death, divided three ways between Martin, Liz, and me. Beverly's trust bypassed Dad and went straight to her children. I don't know the details of Dad's finances, but he behaves as if he's battened down the hatches, as if part of his monthly income consists of returning bottles to the market.

As for the cell phone, renting month to month is cheaper, and there's the unspoken fact that in six months Dad might have no use for a cell phone.

Still, I tell him to buy it.

Sometimes in the desert, the weather is cool and windy. The wind gets bad out here. Stoplights are suspended on cables over the street, with oblong vents in the metal framing to prevent the wind from blowing the lights up and over the cable. Dad is freezing all the time now. He weighs about 120. He turns on the heat, wears a sweater while he sits at his battle station. It's cool, but not that cool. I wear shorts and a T-shirt, and wipe the perspiration off the bridge of my nose.

There are days when no amount of madly e-mailing people or running two miles down the hill to Hemenway Park (and two miles straight back up, sweat dripping, knees crackling, half wishing for heart failure so I won't have to drag myself back inside the Palace, with its dark paneled walls and atmosphere of loss) can stem the tide of past and impending sadness.

There used to be good days and bad days; now there are good hours and bad hours.

One night Dad spends nearly an hour bent over in his chair, coughing. His stomach muscles are so sore, he can't hold himself up. He can't lie down, because then he would choke. The sound of his cough is evolving from something that sounds lung-related to something that sounds stomach-related. It sounds like someone who is throwing up liquid.

I sit with him as long as I can, then I have to go lock myself in the bathroom and read a book. My stupid barf-o-phobia kicks in. And he isn't even vomiting, he only sounds as if he is.

I got this tendency to lock myself in the bathroom with a book when the going gets rough straight from Dad. According to family legend, I was reluctant to leave the comfort of my diapers and join the world of well-adjusted commode users. My mother tried giving me a piece of candy corn every time I successfully used my little blue plastic potty chair, but either I didn't like candy corn enough for it to register as reinforcement, or positive reinforcement didn't work on me (a likely explanation; otherwise, how could I have wound up a freelance writer?). The only thing that did work was setting my little chair next to the toilet, and when Dad "went to the library," as we called it in our house, I went to the library. I had my own basket of picture books in there. There we'd sit. He'd read *Captain Horatio Hornblower*, by C. S. Forester, or the recent issue of *American Rifleman*, and I'd peruse *If I Ran the Zoo*.

But now, I can't just run off and lock myself in the bathroom whenever the spirit moves me. If Dad locked himself in his bathroom with a book, and I locked myself in my bathroom with a book, who would take care of him?

Inside the bathroom, I read the wallpaper. It's supposed to evoke the newspaper world of the 1890s; there is a pattern of newspaper clippings offering news of the day interspersed with gents in top hats riding bicycles that were known as bone shakers, the type with a huge wheel in front. I read the headlines in a strip of paper beside the door. Just outside, the tags on Woodrow's collar tinkle. I know he's sitting there staring at the door, waiting for me to come out. I can still hear the coughing.

After a few more headlines, I force myself to turn the knob and come out. Dad is still coughing. He's sitting on the edge of the chair, on his skinny butt, hawking up clear sputum straight into the white plastic wastebasket, bypassing his square of tissue altogether. I think I'm going to have to take him to the hospital, or call the paramedics to have them come and inject him with something to make him stop. Can someone die of a coughing fit?

I put my hand on his shoulder and feel all the bony inside parts. "Dad, Dad is there anything I can do? Anything at all?"

"You really . . . *arrr-UGHH! arr-UGHH!* . . . want to do . . . *arr-UGHH! arr-UGHH! arr-UGHH!* . . . do something for me?"

"Yes! Yes!" I do. Anything. Dad has never before asked me to do anything for him besides join the NRA. He grabs my wrist, encircling it with his long fingers. "Go get me some cigarettes. I can't feel any worse than I do already."

And so begins the part of the story where Dad actually asks for some help, in the form of my procuring the exact thing that's killing him. Every day, until the day he goes to bed and doesn't get back up, I drive up to Albertsons on Boulder Highway and buy a single pack of Marlboro Lights for $3.15, plus tax. I only buy a single pack, because he's not supposed to be smoking at all, and if there's only one pack in the house, he isn't technically smoking. A carton would mean that he was smoking. I should put my hands on my hips and tell him no, I will not participate in making him sicker. On the other hand, why not? Sixty years of smoking has landed him in his current predicament, but not smoking isn't going to cure him. It's closing the barn door after the cow's gotten out. The case can be made that smoking relaxes him, gives him some temporary joy, and makes him feel better.

Still, it makes me feel like a member of Team Kevorkian. Aren't I supposed to provide Dad with a healthy diet consisting of seven hundred vegetables a day, wheat grass juice and smoothies whirred in a blender to the accompaniment of a lecture on thinking yourself well? Or at least make sure he chokes down a can of Dutch chocolate Ensure once in a while and steers clear of the cancer sticks? Isn't that my job?

I take his car keys, the brass bullet on the chain smooth and pleasing in my hand, and roar up Boulder Highway to Albertsons. My father wants cigarettes, and cigarettes he will have.

Now, in the mornings, Dad needs a nap after he reads the paper. He gets up and lets Woodrow out to pee on the gravel berm that runs along the wash. He doesn't bother putting Woodrow on his leash anymore; he's on his own. Dad pours himself a glass of apple juice—his beloved orange juice burns his throat on the way down—smokes a cigarette, opens the paper, coughs to the point of collapse for forty-five minutes, then pads back into his bedroom to lie down.

One day while he's asleep, the phone rings. It's not an electronic ring, but an old-fashioned *brrrrringg!* I hardly know what to do. The phone! The dog stands in the center of the family room, his head cocked. The only one who ever calls is Daniel, looking for me when my cell phone has died, and perky girls selling time-shares, and, once in a blue moon, George, the friend from Art Center.

This time it's Sadie, calling from California. Sadie was my mother's best friend. Sadie and Lou and Joan and Dick all lived in the same stucco apartment building on Murietta Avenue in the San Fernando Valley in the early sixties. Sadie and my mother hung out in the way that women could in the days before moms struggled into panty hose everyday and marched off to work, before anyone had embraced multitasking as a lifestyle. Joan and Sadie would sit around the rectangular pool and do the crossword puzzle or, on rainy days, spend the entire morning gossiping and polishing silver in their bathrobes. Sadie is the repository of memories of me that my mother would have had. She tells me sometimes how I used to have temper tantrums by the swimming pool at the apartment, banging the front of my diving mask against the tile. Sadie, who hadn't yet had her daughters, was worried. Wouldn't I hurt myself? My mother sipped her beer, inked in answers on the crossword puzzle, and ignored me. "She'll get over it," my mother said, and of course, I always did—usually, very close to the time my mother stopped paying attention to me.

Sadie and Lou were the only couple who remained friends with Dad after he married Bev a scant two years after my mother died. The other couples my parents knew drifted away, in part because most of them had been my mother's friends, people who jibed with her raucous spirits, her love of cardplaying, costume parties—my mother hosted a humdinger every year, in which she always came dressed as a devil, in a long black cloak with red satin lining and a pointy collar outlined in black sequins—and a loud good time. My mother played practical jokes on people, took snapshots, bought funny presents, and, when the spirit moved her, cooked up a storm. Bev was an entirely different model of wife. Needless to say, the Karbos no longer hosted costume or cocktail parties. The new Mrs. Karbo thought any card game but bridge was beneath her station, and although she was capable of talking your ear off after a few martinis, there was no loud good time, no practical jokes or gag gifts. The Nutty Mahoneys, who'd relied upon my mother for a good game of pinochle, dancing in the living room, and nonstop marriage counseling, were appalled that Dad could even think of remarrying so quickly, much less, as Aunt Irene once called her, "a stiff like Bev." They drifted away, as did everyone else except Sadie and Lou.

Part of the reason Sadie and Lou kept in touch with Dad was out of love for my mother, and part of the reason was that Sadie had a soft spot in her heart for Dad, who drove her to the emergency room once when her stove accidentally blew up in her face. She'd stuck her head in to pull out a tin of muffins and *blooie!* Gone were her eyebrows and eyelashes. She'd sustained second-degree burns on her cheeks. Sadie said Dad was more concerned for her recovery than my mother, who took domestic accidents in stride. She said that beneath the stoicism and politesse, Dad was a lamb.

Today, on the phone, she says "*Karen . . . it's Sadie.* How are you honey?"

"Oh. Well. You know, terrible. I mean, there are good days and bad days. No, more like bad days and terrible days."

"That's what I thought. Lou and I saw him about a month ago and he did not look good. I call once in a while and he says things like 'I think I've turned a corner, Sade.' I know it can't possibly be true. I can hear it in his voice. He can barely *speak*."

"I know."

"How long does he have? Have they spoken to you about that yet?"

"I don't think they speculate on that sort of thing anymore. I mean, they really don't have a clue. And since they don't, why depress the patient further by giving him bad news they aren't even sure of?"

"That sounds like a cop-out to me."

"I know," I said again. Talking to Sadie was always a little shocking, since she actually said what she thought, unlike in the world of DadandBev, where what was not being said was always louder than what was.

"Are you all right there by yourself? Do you need me to come?"

"No, I'm fine. We're just fine here."

Liar.

Now Dad complains that his shoulder hurts. "Like someone is

180

sticking an ice pick into me," he says. He blames it on the way he is sleeping, which is the way he has always slept, like Sleeping Beauty, flat on his back with his hands folded one over the other, on his chest. Indeed, when he was complaining about the golf ball in his chest, and how he couldn't sleep on his side, my first thought had been *But you've never slept on your side.* He wonders if perhaps the cold snap—mid-seventies at midday—was giving him a touch of arthritis.

Dad has an appointment with Dr. Swifton, his regular doctor, about the pain in his shoulder. I'm confused about the physician division of labor. Is it clear to no one but me that the ache in Dad's shoulder is most likely the spread of the cancer, which means he should go straight to Florino, the oncologist? Why does he need to be seen by Swifton, who will only refer him to Florino, who will refer him to O'Donnell? It took weeks to get these appointments. Doctors and cancer sufferers alike use phrases like "catching it in time" and "if only we'd caught it sooner." Early detection is supposed to be the difference between life and death. But what about after the whole taxing treatment has begun? You've soldiered through the surgery that has failed to get all of the tumor—or in Dad's case, any of it at all—and you're somewhere in midst of feeling sunburned inside by the radiation and dog-sick from the chemo, and suddenly time is like summer when you're nine years old? Suddenly, there's no hurry? Wouldn't a better plan of attack be to work backward? Assume it's the cancer, see the oncologist, let him say, "Nope, just a touch of bursitis," and then head back down the food chain to the regular doctor? Wouldn't a side effect be a lifting of the spirit? A relief?

I ask Dad why he's seeing Swifton instead of Florino and he shrugs. "When I called Swifton's office and told them the problem, the receptionist gave me an appointment." I know he called and said he had a pain in his shoulder, without putting the pain in any context, nothing about the lung cancer, the subsequent treatment.

In Dr. Swifton's over-air-conditioned exam room I sit on the chair and Dad sits on the end of the table, his legs dangling. The paper crackles as he swings his legs. It's the same sound as when my little girl is in the pediatrician's office, waiting for the doctor to give her a shot. Dr. Swifton is tall and bespectacled; he looks like Harold Ramis from his *Ghostbusters* days. He puts a big hand on my dad's shoulder and says, "How *are* you, Richard?" It's the extra-compassionate tone reserved for the suffering and the dying. Since he's not responsible for the success of Dad's treatment, he can afford to be genuine in his inquiry. The other guys, the oncologist and the radiologist who, let's face it, are in the unhappy position of making Dad's life miserable without necessarily prolonging it, bounce in the room and say, "How's it going today!" They are upbeat, and only a spoilsport would say, "Well, sucky, if you must know."

But I am a spoilsport. Dad is always congenial, as if this might be a social visit. When they ask how he is, he says, "Things are looking up!" He says, "Good, good." He seems to have forgotten that the reason he's in the doctor's office in the first place is because he's *not* good, and things are *not* looking up. He's embarrassed to tell his doctor what's wrong.

To Dr. Swifton he says, "I've got a pinched nerve here in my shoulder."

I look at him. This diagnosis was news to me.

"Well, we can't have that, can we?" He says he can shoot the spot with lidocaine. For twenty-four hours or so, it would feel worse, and then it would feel better.

Dad put his hand, ropey and still tanned, on Dr. Swifton's arm. "I knew you could fix me right up."

I stare out through the open slats of the blinds, at some desert tree with a salamander-smooth trunk and dainty, lacelike leaves, and beyond that, the bleached sky that goes on straight on into California. The sixteen-year-old stirs in my chest like the monster from *Alien*. She wants to rise up and roar: *This is not a pinched nerve and this guy is not going to fix you right up. Can't we be honest about what's going on here for five seconds?* At the same time, I understand that Dr. Swifton's offer of a shot to fix things right up is merciful. The truth is here, omnipresent as the air-conditioning. If it weren't, the charade wouldn't be necessary.

The prospect of receiving a definitive cure has cheered my father right up. He gets chatty, talks more than he has in any doctor's appointment he's had thus far. He has a theory about his racking cough. "It's been the orange juice all along. I love that orange juice. I find it so refreshing. I think I was guzzling it. I was drinking too much, maybe as much as a quart a day, and don't you know, I think it was the citric acid that's been irritating my throat and making me cough. I've switched to apple juice and we'll see how that goes. I predict a turnaround."

The corners of Dr. Swifton's mouth lift, a small smile, indulging him. He turns to the cupboard behind the exam table and begins fixing the syringe with the lidocaine. It is so unexotic, the lidocaine, that they have it right there in the room, like Band-Aids and Tylenol.

I start in with the questions, the only thing I know how to do. I've vowed not to try to be a member of the *couple malade*, but I cannot seem to help myself. I read once where the esteemed Oliver Sacks, author and clinical professor of neurology, admitted that every patient needs an advocate, even though doctors don't like them.

What about Dad's cough? Is there anything to be done about it? Is it possible that he could get so bad, he'll collapse with exhaustion? And if he does, what should I do? Is there a cough syrup that might help? What about yoga, or relaxation exercises? Hah. I can imagine Dad performing relaxation exercises. I ask a new question before Dr. Swifton has a chance to answer the last one. Mostly, I am talking because Dad needs to take off his shirt to get his shot in the shoulder.

He unsnaps his beige plaid cowboy shirt, then takes off his white T-shirt underneath. I am afraid to see his chest, pale as the underside of a fish, the bell curve of ribs, the flat, sad areolas. I have not seen much of my father's chest over the years. When we lived in reasonable California, he mowed the lawn in his white T-shirt, even in the record-setting heat of August. At our beach house in Laguna, he spent the days sitting on the deck beneath the patio umbrella, reading a book in his swim trunks and T-shirt. In the evening, he went fishing in front of the house, the foamy surf surging around his skinny ankles, still in his blue swim trunks and white T-shirt. I don't remember him with anything other than a farmer's tan.

I am prepared to see the type of skinny that makes you gasp, but I am not prepared for the small, hard lumps, the size of marbles, erupting from his ribs—two on the left side, on the lowest rib but one, and one on the right. The skin encircling the base of the lumps is dark pink and shiny, the skin stretched taut. I am transfixed by these lumps, which my father never told me about, so transfixed, I miss the opportunity to hold my father's hand while Dr. Swifton injects the lidocaine into a similar marble on his shoulder. My father winces. He said, "I hope this helps, Doc."

There are five marbles on his front. I don't want to see his back. Dr. Swifton glances down while he's giving the injection, down along my father's knuckly white spine, then back up.

I say, "Dr. Swifton, you didn't say. About the cough." I re-ask all the same questions I didn't give him a chance to answer before. I fumble in my purse for a notebook. It's a common delusion I have. If I write down what the doctor says, it transforms it from benign blather to something that might help. I find a pen. On the subject of the cough: Is it the result of the cancer, or is it irritation from the radiation?

"Offhand, I would say it's the emphysema."

"The emphysema? What emphysema? Dad, what emphysema?" I ask.

Dr. Swifton has his back to us, tugging off the latex gloves. He glances over at my father's chart, resting open on the cabinet. "Diagnosed in September '99."

My father snaps up his plaid cowboy shirt carefully, the way he does everything, as if he hadn't gotten dressed a million times before. "I sure hope this does the trick, Dr. Swifton."

After we get home I look up *emphysema* on the Net. It advises quitting smoking. I resolve that I will no longer trot out every morning to get my father a pack of cigarettes. I tell myself that when he wakes up, after he's had his glass of apple juice and forty-five minutes of coughing, and then asks me to go get him some ciggies, I will say no. I will tell him that while smoking may not affect the progress of his cancer, it most certainly affects the overall health of his lungs, in particular the emphysema *he failed to tell me about*. I will do the right thing.

I feel better. I see now that this resolve is not unlike the shot of lidocaine that lifted my father's spirits. I will tell him no more cigarettes, and the walls of his alveoli will begin to mend themselves, and his coughing will ease up.

I buy Dad some Aleve. Since the party line is that inflammation of something or other in my father's shoulder is causing his pain, and since the magical shot of lidocaine was administered to alleviate said inflammation, I think the Aleve can't hurt. Hoisting himself upright in the morning seems to awaken the pain; so when I hear him stirring, I bring in two Aleves—it calms me just to hold the small blue triangles in my palm—and a glass of water, and make him lie still for twenty minutes or so, until they take effect.

My father has always slept naked. He's naked beneath the sheet, pulled up beneath his armpits, his collarbones long and flat, like mine, narrow shelves. My father sleeping naked has always both interested and alarmed me; he is so reserved, so modest, and embodies the opposite of sensuality and lasciviousness. His silent uprightness is the defining trait of his character. But he sleeps in the buff. What does it mean? Is he reluctant to spend the money on pajamas?

The Aleve works. Or else it's the lidocaine taking effect. Or perhaps all my desperate prayers are being acknowledged, if not answered. It's possible that God only checks his e-mail once a week, like a few friends who don't yet "live" on the Net, and the prayers to relieve my father's pain have finally gotten through. I don't bother asking for a cure; I know one is not coming. But a little relief?

Before today I was convinced I would be leaving my family and moving into the Palace, to be with him until he breathed his last, which seemed able to happen at any moment. All day long he's freezing, walking with that creaky, straight-legged, everything-aches walk, hacking his guts out about every ninety minutes. Once, after a coughing fit, he slumped over in his chair, wheezing out, "God damn it all to hell." I thought, this must be the beginning of the beginning of the end.

Then, he rallies. The Aleve, or the lidocaine, or the answered prayers, kicks in, and after eating half a bowl of Rice Krispies and drinking a large glass of apple juice he goes to the post office and the Water Store, where he purchases a new plastic spigot for the water cooler. When he returns he hunkers down and heaves a full bottle of water up on the cistern, eschewing his afternoon nap completely. He even goes outside with a rag and a can of WD-40 and tries to loosen up the tailgate on my Pathfinder, which seems to have rusted shut in the Oregon rain.

He returns to his battle station for a coffee and Marlboro break and worries about why he can't get his cell phone to work properly. He treats it as if it's some kind of new-fangled walkie-talkie. To test it, he goes outside and calls me inside from the driveway. "Dad, you can call the home number from right here, you don't need to go outside." But he does.

I can't imagine how long this can go on, this looking as if he's going to perish within minutes, then a day later, he's out running errands and heaving water bottles. Part of my problem is that I've fallen for the Hollywood view of death. In the movies, dying is slave to the traditional Aristotelian three-act structure; there's no time for endless repetitions of the cycle of hope and despair. And as for deathbed scenes themselves, I suspect they're as rare as a full eclipse. Probably people die when you're out getting a burger, or moving the car to the other side of the street so as to avoid getting a ticket.

The oncologist Florino continues to talk as if my father is merely suffering from a bad case of the flu. I was under the impression it was a momentous decision for Dad to decide to forgo further chemotherapy. By making this choice my father was choosing quality of life over length of life. Dr. Florino had made it clear during Dad's first appointment that the preferred treatment was beginning chemotherapy during the second week of the month-long radiation treatment, that the burn and the poison worked best concurrently. On the day several months before when Dad said, "I'm done with all this treatment," I wept. I don't know what yet another appointment with the oncologist is supposed to accomplish.

When Dr. Florino enters the room he shakes my hand and introduces himself, as if I hadn't been in his office four times before. Fine, he undoubtedly shakes the hand of dozens of stunned family members a day. But then, alarmingly, he also seems to need to brush up on what, exactly, my father's treatment has been to date. "So, you've had some radiation to the chest area," he says, reading the file.

My dad says nothing, as usual. I don't try much to keep a certain tone out of my voice. "Why, yes, that would be the thirty-five-day course of treatment that you prescribed. In November."

Dr. Florino skims the file for another ten seconds, then snaps it closed as if something's just occurred to him. "You know what your problem is?"

Dad sits on the end of the exam table, elbows locked, bony suntanned hands clamped around the edge on either side of him, head hunched between his shoulders, like a cartoon vulture. An expression passes over his face, hope or interest. Or perhaps it's just his exemplary manners: When someone asks a rhetorical question of this nature, it's polite to listen.

"Nourishment."

Nourishment? D'oh! I thought it was lung cancer!

I point out, in a way that I hope is conversational and not adversarial, that even during times of robust health my father has never been a robust eater. I want Dr. Florino to understand that my father has never been a 250-pounder with a lifetime of terrible eating habits to draw from. "He's never been much of an eater. The most he's ever weighed is about one-seventy-five."

Dr. Florino says, "It's important for you to realize that for his height and weight, he's underweight. It's not good to be this underweight. If you're too underweight, what happens is that your body actually begins to digest its own muscle."

I stare at him. I'm wearing my black leather Doc Martens, the ones that make me five-eleven. I think, *Look, dude, you can treat my dad like a child, but you can't treat me like one.* "Dr. Florino. I am a middle-class woman in America in the twenty-first century. I've been on just about every diet known to man, and a few I made up myself. I'm sure I know more about gaining and losing weight that you ever will. Ice cream after dinner will make you fat; dinner eaten before four will help you maintain if not lose weight. At five-nine I should weigh between one-thirty-nine and one-fifty-three. Of course, I've spent my entire life wanting to weigh one-twenty. What are you, about five-seven? You should weigh about one-sixty, give or take. My father is six-two, and has never weighed more than one seventy-five in his entire life. So you can spare me the lecture about weight. I know about weight. I know that he's drastically underweight. But I thought we were here to talk about the progression of his lung cancer. Which, as I recall, is your department. I can take care of his weight. Thank you."

"Buy him some Ensure."

"We have Ensure. He hates it."

"We can't proceed with the chemo until his weight is back up."

"Proceed with the chemo? Would that be the chemo that he's already refused? Isn't that in the chart anywhere? You guys really need to get your act together."

After this, he's nicer. My friend Benson refers to it as the kick-in-the-head phenomenon; some people won't treat you with respect unless you tell them what's what. Dr. Florino and I proceed to chat for a good fifteen minutes about how we might get my father to gain weight. I mention eating a bowl of ice cream at midnight, and Dr. Florino thinks that sounds like an excellent idea.

"Once his weight's back up, we can begin the chemo."

My father, who has been sitting docilely while Dr. Florino and I discuss cuisine, says, "Sure."

The next night, I pick up Daniel at the airport. After many phone conversations, in which I dither over whether I should do the manful thing and drive myself home through the high-desert creepiness of central Nevada—or whether he should come and get me. The pressure to do the manful thing, the stoic thing that causes the least amount of trouble, and not coincidentally is also the least expensive, is high. My father would never make such a fuss; he'll just get in the car and go. However, when I ask his opinion, he says what he's said since my mother died.

"S'up to you, babe." I wimp out. I want my husband to come and drive me home.

I'm not home in Portland two hours and I'm overwhelmed with guilt and worry; what am I doing home when I should be with my father? The Hindu goddess hands present themselves as usual. On the one hand I am happy to be home. I missed the kids and their slamming in and out, the dozens of phone calls, the hubbub. Portland has a real spring; days that dawn with summer sun and end with hail and thunder. On the other hand, my father needs me, even though he will never say so. On the other hand, who am I to decide what it is he needs; isn't he a big boy? He can ask me to stay, instead of encouraging me to go home. On the other hand, he's dying.

I call him at ten of five every day. On the days he's upbeat, I think he's doing it for my benefit. He'll say, "Had a good day. Did a little of this and a little of that, then ran out of bullets at about three." He is short of breath. He always sounds as if he's just run up a flight of stairs. One afternoon when I call, he's watching a documentary on the History Channel about the assassination attempts on Hitler's life.

I'm impossible to please. I was itching to get home, away from the heat of the desert and the Palace—my father has given up on air-conditioning forever, it seems—and back to the rain and the hubbub. Now that I'm here, I'd rather be at the Palace hiding from the sound of my father's coughing in the bathroom, reading the corset ads on the faux-1890s wallpaper.

My life of the spirit consists of praying not infrequently, all the while feeling as if God is perennially watching the Super Bowl while I, his wife, am trying to discuss the nuances of the window dressings I'm planning for the kitchen. I also attend a grand Episcopal cathedral about a half-dozen times a year. The only day I never miss is Ash Wednesday, when I'm always unaccountably cheered by the no-bullshit sentiment

"From ashes you came and to ashes you shall return." The Episcopal church was the church my mother converted to, the church in which I was raised, and from the opening processional to the final blessing, I'm always fighting off a sob-a-thon.

What seems to help more than church are books by Christian brainiacs, a favorite being the *Confessions* by St. Augustine. Now I'm reading Thomas Merton, but he's pissing me off. In *New Seeds of Contemplation*, in a chapter entitled, "The Root of War Is Fear," he says: "Many men have asked God for what they thought was peace and wondered why their prayer was not answered. They could not understand that it actually *was* answered. God left them with what they desired, for their idea of peace was only another form of war." The original edition of *New Seeds* was published in 1961, and the "other" form of war is of course the Cold War.

I read this one evening in the tub, and I'm dumbfounded by this. Is he saying that God will only grant you the secret desires of your heart, even if they're so secret you don't know you have them? You're there praying for one thing, praying to the back of God's head as he perennially watches the Super Bowl, and unbeknownst to you, you're truly praying for something else that you're not conscious of, and it's the subconscious something else that gets answered? In the case of the prayers I've sent up for my father, I'm not asking for his full recovery. I don't believe in those kinds of miracles, but perhaps I should. Perhaps I should be praying for his cancer to go into full remission and for him to live another twenty years in the lonely desert, without Bev. I don't think he wants that, though. I do know he doesn't want to be in so much pain, and so that is what I pray for. That he feel better. That the cough eases, and the pain in his hip and his shoulder abates, that he's able to return to drinking his orange juice and working on one of his projects. Perhaps by failing to pray for his full recovery, I'm in effect praying for all this to be over, and soon. The secret mote of betrayal I've tried to eradicate but have only managed to sweep into a dark corner of my heart, the one that wishes my father would keel over during one of his coughing fits and that would be *it*, because I can't take another day of it and he's miserable and grieving and dying anyway. That's the desire in my heart that God is answering?

18

What keeps Dad alive is the trip he's planned to the Rankin Ranch, a guest ranch nestled in Walker Basin, deep in the Tehachapi Mountains of central California. He invited Daniel and the kids and me to accompany him for a week in late May. DadandBev went to the ranch every fall for nineteen years, put together their portable martoonie kit, and off they'd go. The ranch was a living relic of the nineteenth century, a time in which DadandBev would have been much happier.

The ranch has been in the Rankin family since 1860 or thereabouts. The hay barn on the property was once used as a stopover point by the Wells Fargo Pony Express, and the white clapboard ranch house where they still serve meals was built from a plan published in *Godey's Lady's*, the *Good Housekeeping* of the nineteenth century. Originally a cattle ranch specializing in white-faced Herefords, the operation needed to diversify in order to survive, and opened its doors as a guest ranch about forty years ago. The most amazing thing about the place is its size: You stand at the top of the ridge leading down into Walker Basin, and all that open meadow—the creeks and hills and everything as far as the eye can see—belongs to the Rankins. The ranch is the size of the city of San Francisco.

When my dad sat down at his battle station in the morning, he flipped open his datebook and counted the weeks and days until our visit to the ranch, like any ten-year-old impatiently awaiting Christmas. I was relieved that we had this ahead of us. In anticipation of the trip, he'd bought me a black cowboy hat with a leather stampede strap and an expensive pair of soft leather "chinks" ordered especially from a place in Colorado that specializes in designer cowboy wear. Chinks are a variety of chaps, shin-length with an impressive amount of 1970s-style fringe up the side. I was touched by his generosity. He'd never in his life just bought me presents for no reason. This was the equivalent of blowing his dough on a three-week South Seas cruise, or a trip to Rome, one of those things people who are sick try to do before they get too sick to do anything at all.

Throughout his initial course of radiation and his unhappy relationship with chemotherapy, his mantra was "I don't care what they do, as long as I can get on a horse when it comes time for the ranch." On every good day, when the coughing merely tired him and a forty-five-minute fit did not send him to bed for a two-hour nap, he believed he was turning a corner.

There is so much poetry associated with dying, so many metaphors and turns of phrase that can't possibly be literally true, "reason to live" being only one example. Surely we humans don't need a reason to live, reason being synonymous with desire. We live and our hearts beat dumbly on, whether we can drum up a good reason or not. How else to account for all those sad souls who live on for years in a coma; surely they aren't aware of having a reason to live. Their bodies are machines that keep going like a car engine that keeps running even after the ignition's been switched off. What about the people who tell themselves they have a reason to live, but die anyway? Does this mean their reasons weren't good enough? Does this mean my mother, who was forty-five and had a sixteen-year-old daughter, did not have a good enough reason to go on?

And yet, perhaps all the positive thinkers are right: When you've got a terminal disease, believing that you're turning a corner will keep you alive longer than any professionally administered course of toxins. Returning to the ranch one last time was Dad's reason to live and who's to say it didn't work?

I tell my father I can't wait to go to the ranch, but as with everything else, only part of me can't wait. It might make a difference if I can guess the percentage, but even that varies from day to day. The other part is reluctant to spend a week with him and his cough and the knowledge of his impending death at a place he associates only with the good times he'd shared with his beloved deceased second wife, who despised me, and vice versa.

So the part that doesn't want to go lies. Someone once said you shouldn't be too kind to the dying—it makes them feel less human—but on the subject of the ranch I feel lying is my only option. Denying him his last wish is unthinkable.

Still, the fact that I do not want to go and pretend to him that I do is more proof—as if I needed any—that I am not fit to be the lone daughter of a dying man. Where is the woman who can endlessly attend him with good humor, tolerate his whims and bad moods, reassure him that all will be well, count the weeks and days with him until we'll meet at the ranch? Once on *Six Feet Under*, the television show about a family of undertakers, a bereaved woman nutty with grief asked the one son with the brain condition why people have to die, and his profound answer was: Because it makes life meaningful. Then he went into a sort of oft-heard carpe-diem-style riff on living each day as if it were your last. Why can't I do this? Why do I have no TV wisdom?

As the trip to the ranch approaches I argue about this with Daniel, the eternal purveyor of optimism and platitudes. As it turns out, Daniel isn't going to the ranch; he's already taken more than his allotment of days off at his one-day-a-week UPS job. He could take an unpaid day, but we are desperate for money. One night while stirring a pot of chili, I slapped the wooden spoon down on the stove, clenched my fists, and shouted that I did not want to go to the ranch for the simple fact that I could not stand any more heartbreak. I am staggered by the potential for poignant moments, long-distance-phone-service ads come to life: witnessing my dad's fragility as he attempts to mount a horse; my dad and my daughter riding together for the first and last time; the way the Rankins will look at him, the same way the nurses look at him when he goes to one of his many doctor's appointments and tries to put a good face on the situation.

"Look at it this way, it's an opportunity to spend some quality time with your dad," says Daniel.

"I've been spending quality time with him, week in, week out, for months. What do you think I do when I'm down there but try to actively appreciate him? And it's a strain. He doesn't want to be actively appreciated. You actively appreciate someone for one reason and one reason only: because you know they're not going to be around much longer. I don't want to make a special occasion out of it. It's bad enough as it is."

"You don't have to yell at me, do you?"

"Yes, yes, I *do* have to yell at you. I have to yell at you because you're not dying."

On a Saturday in late May, Dad leaves Boulder City in the Explorer and drives two hundred miles due west to the Rankin Ranch. It's the proverbial hop, skip, and jump compared to our two-day haul from Portland, south on Interstate 5, through the tedious hearts of both states. Ten hours from Portland to Redding, with Rachel, Danny, and Katherine bickering at every bathroom stop over who gets the front seat. Rachel always wins, since she's the oldest and the only one who can run the portable CD player with its funky auto adapter that plugs into the quaint cigarette lighter, as automotively arcane as the glove box. We listen to the Beatles, we listen to the B-52s. Every two hours we rock out to "Love Shack." Rachel, barefoot, with once-colorful ankle bracelets made from a kit I gave her one year for Christmas, sits with her feet on the dashboard, her toes smearing the windshield. She's dyed her hair red.

Danny plays his Gameboy and Katherine colors in a horse coloring book with her markers. I stop too often: for coffee, or to pee from having had too much coffee. I eschew the rest areas paid for by the good taxpayers of both Oregon and California, because it's well known that rest areas are frequented by pedophiles and psycho killers. At rest areas you also can't purchase Nerds, ShockTarts, gummy octopuses, and industrial-size vats of Gatorade in several different Gonzo flavors. At rest stops, you can't try on sunglasses, or beg for a quarter to play the odd video game. But, as Rachel says ad nauseam these days, "It's all good." It is all good; taking care of the kids is a wholesome and worthwhile distraction from taking care of my dad. There's a lot to be said for being sandwiched between two generations after all.

All in all, the kids are good traveling companions. Danny is the nicest one in the family, and even though Katherine has the reputation for being precocious, he's the most reliably quotable child. At our modest freeway-side motel, he's smitten with the basket of stale tortilla chips and runny salsa set out for guests beside the microwave in the lobby, and the small swimming pool with a view of the off-ramp. "They really know how to roll out the red carpet," he says.

The kids are a little unclear why I've taken them out of school two weeks before school is out, to spend a week with Grandad-in-Nevada, whom they barely know, at a guest ranch in California. Rachel and Danny have met him exactly once, at Daniel's and my wedding. Katherine knows him mostly through birthday cards and unusual presents he's sent over the years: a turquoise, red, and white kachina doll that sits on the mantel at home, a Western bridle for a horse she might one day own. They know he is sick, however, and Katherine says, "Between getting to ride horses and seeing us, I'm sure he'll feel much better."

People come back to the ranch year after year, decade after decade, generation after generation, because it never seems to change. Bill Rankin and his wife, Glenda, have been married forever, and their four children look poised to do the same. Glenda is brown-eyed, high-cheekboned, perhaps with some Native American in there somewhere, yet she allows herself to age like a normal person, with some strands of gray and a thickening middle. She is a ranch wife; she doesn't have time for Botox, I'm sure. They are good people with no complicated modern problems, and their gift to their guests is treating them the same way. When I check in with the kids, she shakes hands with all of them. "Your dad sure seems happy to be here, and we're so glad to have him," she says. I appreciate her plain talk, no BS about him looking good, or the awkward impassioned question about how he's *feeling*.

Guests of the ranch stay in a dozen cabins scattered up a hill covered with buckbrush, oak, and California lavender. The cabins are divided into two rooms, with a locking door in between. My father and I share one side and Rachel, Danny, and Katherine share the other. This requires Dad to wear pajamas. Just after dark he retires to the bathroom and comes out wearing a pair of dark maroon cotton pajamas with black piping around the cuffs, very refined. He reports he has gained eight pounds, and says he is getting his voice back, but it sounds the same to me.

At four A.M. I'm awakened by Katherine's muffled shrieks. She's fallen out of bed in the next room and the mattress has rolled off with her, pining her to the cabin floor. Then Danny wakes up and asks for a Band-Aid for a nonexistent blister. Then Rachel sticks her head under the pillow and tells them to shut up and go back to sleep. Then Dad wakes up from his Sleeping Beauty pose, his big tan hands folded over his chest, and blinks, not knowing where he is.

"Kare?" he calls. He sounds old.

"It's okay, Granddad. I just couldn't find shirty." Shirty is Katherine's comfort item, the shred of pink and white T-shirt Katherine pins between her nostril and crooked forefinger when she sucks her thumb. It used to be a full-size T-shirt of mine, which she pinched from the dirty clothes basket when she'd just started walking, and she has carried it around ever since.

"You did not lose shirty. You fell out of bed," says Danny.

"But then I couldn't find shirty. When I fell out, I lost it."

"You guys, go to sleep," says Rachel.

"Shirty?" says Dad. "Who or what is shirty?"

I love this about him; articulate even when it's the middle of the night and he doesn't know where he is.

"It's okay, Granddad, I found it."

"Just a rag," says Danny, "just a thread."

"It is *not*," said Katherine.

"You guys, *go to sleep*."

Dad refolds his hands on top of his chest and closes his eyes. It's still middle-of-the-mountains-black outside. My dad is not used to this sort of everyday bedlam, but he doesn't seem particularly unhappy about it. Maybe the conventional wisdom is true, that having his grandkids around will perk him up a bit. I find myself grateful for the hubbub. It almost feels as if we are a normal, blended Brady Bunch.

Some English queen, or maybe it was Mary Poppins, said, a change is as good as a rest, and she was right. Every day revolves around horseback riding, with one ride in the morning and one in the afternoon, and big meals in between. It's not unlike being on an ocean cruise, only with a lot more acreage. There's a nice swimming pool with a seriously springy diving board shaded by eucalyptus trees, and a tennis court. It's the end of May in central California, and even though we're in the mountains, half a mile high, the sun is already turning the kids' cheeks pink.

The heart-wringing things I'd anticipated and feared start up almost immediately. After a big artery-challenging ranch breakfast of scrambled eggs, pancakes, bacon, toast, a bowed disc of ham, and apple juice, served from a tray by Roberto, a wisecracking kitchen hand who asks, "Tequila, anyone?," we troop out to the corral for the first ride of the week. It's the children's ride, for kids under eleven. They like an adult to accompany the smaller kids, and my dad volunteers.

We assemble in the white-fenced corral while wrangler Dave brings out the horses from the huge red barn. The morning air smells of pine, dust, and manure. Dave wears a red plaid shirt. He's got that dark, leathery cowboy skin, and eyes the same color as lapis lazuli Lake Mead. He's been doing this his whole life and can size up a rider in a minute and pick a horse that shouldn't give him any trouble. The horses here are all big quarter horses on the tail end of their prime. Children become attached to them for their entire lives: Bubba, Popcorn, Flacko—"skinny" in Spanish—Cappuccino, Rusty, Mike. A platform runs along one side of the corral, where the kids stand waiting in a row beneath the sun. Their excited parents lean over the white fence with their video cameras. Inexperienced adult riders also use this platform to mount their horses. Also people who're overweight and out of shape, or wear their jeans too tight, or, one presumes, people suffering from a terminal disease.

Every year my dad is assigned to Leo, a surly gelding who balks at crossing the hundreds of streams that crisscross the property, little babbling things that other horses tromp across without a thought. Leo walks so close to trees and fences, there's no room between his fat sides and the tree trunk for a human leg to pass through, even one as skinny as my dad's. Leo demands a firm hand on the rein and eternal vigilance; thus, he is perfect for someone of my dad's riding ability.

Wrangler Dave remembers that my father rides the cantankerous Leo, and slowly leads him by the reins to where my dad, all outfitted in his plaid cowboy shirt, hat, Lee jeans, suede stovepipe chaps, and boots, stands waiting in the dust in the middle of the corral. His perfect cowboy attire is already breaking my heart. The parents hanging over the fence with their cameras are dressed in regular vacation wear, shorts and T-shirts, and tennis shoes with thick sweat socks scrunched around their ankles. Their children, my dad's fellow riders, wear baggy gym shorts and T-shirts bearing the characters from Cartoon Network, giant sport shoes with the laces stylishly untied.

Dave has the kind of sense found in the personalities of watchful people with few pretensions. He knows my dad is desperately ill, but he isn't about to lead Leo over to the platform, humiliating him in front of a bunch of third graders. My dad stands alone in the middle of the corral, hands on his hips, squinting behind his sunglasses, no big deal, and to the middle of the corral comes Dave leading Leo.

Dad takes the reins from Dave, gets a good grip on the saddle, slips his foot into the stirrup, and slowly hauls himself up, bringing his other skinny leg up and over the cantle, missing it by less than an inch. As I watch, I expect to feel a shade more horrified than I do. What if he falls off halfway up the side of the horse? What if, like Katherine, who is a tall and able horsewoman but just doesn't have the strength to hoist herself up, he needs to resort to the platform? I realize that unless he collapses in the dust at that very instant, we'll somehow muddle through. We always do. But muddling turns out not to be necessary. Dad settles in the saddle and adjusts the reins. He turns the horse around in a few tight circles to show him who's boss, grins at me, and salutes.

I've brought a bunch of books for the week. Every man in my life, from Dad to Daniel, has teased me about my need to travel with no less than four books at any given time. I always take a novel for sport reading (and a backup novel in case I finish the first one), some essays or other nonfiction, usually related to something I'm writing, and a collection of short stories. This week I brought *Tuesdays with Morrie*, a book I avoided before

Dad was sick because I thought it sounded too schmaltzy and knew I would scoff, and didn't want to find myself in my usual curmudgeonly position of scoffing at something not just the rest of the world, but also people I genuinely admire, find Warm, Winning, Wise, and Wonderful. I thought I'd save *Morrie* until I was in one of my rare phases of benevolence, which shows up for a few days in the spring. Now I'm reading it for the reason I imagine most people do: Their own loved ones are moody or withholding or plain old mean, or they're suffering too much to hold forth in a way that's edifying and heartwarming. So we resort to Morrie. He's the dying man of our dreams.

I read the book in the shade of a eucalyptus tree by the pool, watching Danny and Katherine practice cannonballs. Dad shows up, fresh from his nap, and sees the book.

"Why in the hell are you reading that thing?" Dad asks.

"You know about *Tuesdays with Morrie*?"

"Just because I don't go on the Internet doesn't mean I haven't heard of things," he says. "But I don't know what you're getting out of that thing."

"Wisdom of the carpe diem variety," I say.

"I saw that Morrie on TV. He just likes to hear himself talk."

Thursday morning, the day before we leave, my dad tells me we need to have a discussion. Rachel is sunning her pale skin by the pool. Despite being California born and bred, Rachel is not a sun girl or a swimming-suit girl. Before this trip, she's made do with Speedo tank suits, but begged me for something cuter (if ultimately less flattering) and I took her to Nordstrom, where I spent too much on a two-piece in bright tropical-fruit hues. Meanwhile the little kids are sitting at one of the redwood picnic tables on the terrace with their sketch pads, receiving drawing lessons from Ralph, one of the other guests, who is good at drawing horses and cows.

In the cabin Dad unzips his suitcase and draws from one of the pockets a legal-size document from Wells Fargo. He gestures for me to sit on one of the twin beds, and he sits on the other, as if he were a bank manager offering me a seat. The beds are so close together our knees miss touching by only an inch. Dad says it's time to make me cosigner on his bank account. *Oh no*, I think, *oh no*. I obediently take the gold Cross pen he offers me and sign the paper on my knee. While I'm writing, waiting for Dad to make his customary remark about my funky signature, which has always driven him mad with its mix of cursive and printed, capital and lowercase, he says, "Dr. Swifton has said two to four more months."

My tears spill straight onto the paper, the same way as when Lagstone delivered the diagnosis.

"C'mon, babe," he says.

I see this is business. I see he has things to say that are difficult enough without having to cope with comforting me. He tells me where his IRA is, and reminds me of the Karbo family trust. He makes me write down the name of his attorney, who still lives in Whittier. It was the same man he used to settle my mother's affairs twenty-five years earlier. He tells me how to pay his supplemental health insurance, should he be forced to be hospitalized. He asks if I want the dog. He says that if he has time before it gets too bad, he'll board Woodrow at the local kennel.

"Why? What are you talking about? You're not going to be there alone. I'll take care of the dog too. It's twenty-five kibbles in the morning and twenty-five at night."

"Twenty-three kibbles," he says.

I know this is the time to ask. "What do you want me to do with you? Martin could show me where you scattered Bev, sorry, Beverly. Shit, Dad, I really wished you'd told me earlier that she didn't like to be called Bev. Life would have been easier, you know? Do you want to be there? Martin could show me the place."

I snort and splutter, snot dripping out of my nose, hiccupping enough to hyperventilate. Dad sits down beside me on my bed and hugs me, smooths my hair. We Karbos are such a rangy lot. I feel his shoulder blades through the back of his denim shirt. It's reassuring; I've been able to feel them when I hugged him as far back as I can remember, and feel grateful that I still recognize this feeling.

"I'm sorry I've upset you," he says.

"I just, I just, just want to, want to do well by you-ou-ou-ou," I say.

"You have," he says. "I've raised a great daughter. I've had a good long ride. I couldn't have asked for more."

I blow my nose. Dad offers me a stick of Wrigley's spearmint, the white kind, his favorite.

"Let's go down and get us some coffee." On the terrace, on the end of one of the redwood tables, there's a silver coffee urn and a stack of Styrofoam cups. Danny and Katherine have abandoned their drawing lessons and run off somewhere, down to the stables, or over to the creek in the meadow.

Rachel wanders up from the swimming pool on her way back to the cabin to change for her second ride of the day. She stops by our picnic table and slings her sunscreeny arm around my neck, giving me a hug. Rachel had her bad moments when she was in the terrible slough of thirteen, when she was convinced she was a witch. We had some godawful arguments which included my behaving terribly, yelling at her, "Okay, if you're a witch, cast a spell on yourself and ace your algebra test!" But now we're good, or as good as a stepmother and stepdaughter can probably be. People at the small parochial school where she finished middle school see her now from time to time, walking home from school, or at our corner market, and later tell me how much she is coming to resemble me, which secretly pleases us, but still we find it hilarious. You would be hard-pressed to find two people of the same ethnic group who look less alike. Rachel is pale—

transparent, she jokingly calls herself—with gorgeous pale green eyes, like grapes, a pug nose, and straight, dark blond hair. She is shortish and round, with lovely long legs. I'm a good six inches taller, with dark curly reddish-brown hair, angular features, and sallow skin.

Dad says, "You're getting pretty pink there, Rachel." He takes his cowboy hat from his head and plops it down on hers. It's silver gray, rancher style, and made of beaver, not felt, like mine. He's had it for thirty years, at least. He says, "I hereby bequeath you my hat. Now don't lose it."

III

"I don't know what I'm supposed to do."
—Tolstoy on his deathbed

19

Dad has made a mistake. When packing for the ranch he neglected to bring enough Tylenol with codeine—or by now it may already be methadone—to get him through the week, and by Wednesday he begins halving his daily dosage to make it last. The trouble is, half doesn't cut it, and by Friday morning, when it's time to leave, he's is so much pain he winces as the kids, one by one, give him a big hear hug good-bye. I see the wincing. I tell him, "Dad, I don't think you can drive! Dad, let me drive you home" and I'll come back for the kids! *No, the kids can't stay here unsupervised for an entire day. Or, no! The kids and I will all go!*

Dad slides into the Explorer, wincing, face pale and clammy, and roars up the dirt road that leads to a smaller paved road with hairpin curves for nine miles, up and over the pass that leads down to the road that winds through tiny Caliente to the highway that leads to the freeway that leads to Boulder City.

He'll never make it.

But he does. Six hours on the road straight through the scorching Mojave with no painkiller. It was a one-tough-Polack move, if I ever saw one. It gets me thinking I've been wrong all these months, that I should be taking some of this at face value. The doctors don't seem too concerned—yes, well, okay, Dr. Swifton gives Dad only two to four months, but he's just a family doctor, not a specialist—so why am I determined to second guess them? I don't know what's going on. I have no clue. I have half-baked information from the Internet but I have no *hard information*. I don't have his medical file. I don't have his doctors' experience and expertise. Who says I'm not just projecting my bad experience from the last time onto these good doctors? Who says I'm not wishing for the end to hurry up and get here so I can get back to my life? Who says I know anything? The radiologist O'Donnell told Dad at his last appointment that the mass had shrunk. The oncologist Florino plans to resume the chemo after Dad gets his weight up, and didn't Dad report on the first day at the ranch that his weight was up eight pounds? And at the ranch, he ate: French toast, mashed potatoes, a piece of sheet cake with *ice cream*. Thinking this does something amazing, I feel instantly better. The cliché "A weight has been lifted" comes to mind. Indeed, many clichés come to mind. "It's not over until the fat lady sings!" is another one.

I go ahead and make all the travel plans I need to, plans over which I've been dragging my feet. Within the next several weeks I need to go to Venezuela on assignment for *Outside*, then to New York to preside over a panel of writers who are also moms at the Upper West Side Barnes & Noble, part of my tour for the motherhood book, then Seattle next month for another writer-mom panel, then San Francisco for another one. Now, he cannot possibly need me, since I've got all these important work-related plans.

Meanwhile, before the traveling, there's writing, lots of it. So much that the familiar feeling is upon me that I do homework for a living. I have two columns due in two days: one for dadmag.com (about rediscovering the bathroom as a possible location for nooky when you have small children underfoot, who might not appreciate the significance of a closed bedroom door, but will leave you alone in the bathroom), and an installment of the Spy (about the anguish the Spy and other dotcom millionaires feel as they are discriminated by Old Economy types who didn't move fast enough to get on the bandwagon), and a book review due for *The New York Times Book Review*.

Before I leave for Venezuela, I up the ante further on the New York trip: I invite Rachel to come with me. Dad took me to New York for the first time when I was fourteen—business trip, first class, room service, the Empire State Building and Tavern on the Green—and I want to carry on the tradition and do the same for her. I make a reservation at an outrageously priced Midtown hotel, one of the hokey Helmsley ones that shouts "Tourist!" I tell her about the Russian Tea Room and the window shopping on Fifth Avenue. There, now I've got her hopes good and up.

At Dad's appointment on Monday morning, Dr. Swifton tells him that yes, all his new growths are cancerous, which indicates it's growing faster than they'd all anticipated.

I say, "Yes, but Dad, you need to remember that he's a family doctor. His practice consists of prescribing amoxicillin and referring patients to doctors who know a thing or two. And what does he mean by 'all anticipated'? To my knowledge, your doctors have never sat down together and had a powwow, have they?"

"I'm worried because he also upped my methadone prescription. I can't afford to be that foggy. I have too many things left to do," he says.

"And plenty of time to do them, Dad. Plenty of time." I can't imagine what these things are, since everything in his life seems in perfect order.

He asks me whether I think the Johnsons next door would enjoy receiving an order of Omaha Steaks to thank them for all they've done for him. I assure him that yes, yes, they would love it, then rack my brain trying to think what they've done, other than come over on the day Bev died to deliver the news. Perhaps that's enough.

★   ★   ★

The phone rings as Daniel and I are packing the scuba gear. Daniel is coming along because the *Antares Dancer*, the dive boat in Los Roques, is comping both of us, and because I need a guy Friday, and a dive buddy. All the gear is laid out on the kitchen table and he is doing the manly thing, checking all the hoses and gauges for leaks, making sure we have our lights and knives, extra straps and the special liquid for defogging your mask. It's not ten to five but I remain calm, since I know Dad is fine, *fine*. Maybe he's even calling to tell me he's seen Swifton or O'Donnell, and the mass has shrunk even more, or that the marbles on his rib cage are merely cysts or bone spurs. This is much better, letting Dad take charge of his own medical business.

"Hi, babe, how are you?" It's almost his "Dick Karbo here!" superhero voice. Almost. He says that he's signed up for hospice, as recommended by Dr. Swifton. A nurse was just there and did a physical workup.

"She tells me I have the constitution and level of general health of a man twenty years younger. I'm healthy as a horse!"

"See, Dad! There you go. That's great, just great!"

He tells me the nurse will come once a week, and when the time comes, he'll move to the hospice facility. There's genuine relief in his voice. He says that his greatest fear had been that he would decline so quickly that he wouldn't be able to pay his bills, or feed the dog. Now there will be someone else in the loop, someone who's been through this before and knows what she's doing. Someone who can monitor the situation.

I do the most amazing thing here, something I haven't done since Bev died last October. *I stop listening*, just as if I'm the daughter of a healthy man. It feels incredible. Why didn't I think of this before?

20

Outside magazine specializes in out-of-the-way places. They normally wouldn't touch a diving story set in the Caribbean, unless it was some impossible place that no one's ever heard of. Getting to Los Roques, Venezuela, from Portland means taking the red-eye to Atlanta, then a morning flight from Atlanta to Fort Lauderdale (all direct flights from Atlanta to Miami were booked), where we meet a driver to bomb fifty miles south down the expressway to Miami, where we grab a fight to Caracas, then take a prop plane to the tiny archipelago of Los Roques, which means "the rocks," a strange name for a set of islands that are flat and sandy without a serious rock in sight, an archipelago that doesn't appear on most maps of the Caribbean.

I've scored some Xanax from a friend to ease the anxiety of all this horrendous flying. I plan to try and enjoy this trip. The diving is supposed to be nice and easy, much less demanding than Truk Lagoon, where the diving is deep, or Palau, with its fast, tricky currents.

The gargantuan L-1011 from Portland to Atlanta has about twenty-seven people on it, and everyone from about row twenty to the back of the plane has the center three seats to himself. It's so spacious, I feel as if I'm on a space station. I can never sleep on airplanes, since I not only need to be alert, but my eyes need to be wide open, in order to keep the plane in the air, but tonight I manage two half-hour naps, from ten-thirty to eleven and from a quarter past twelve to a quarter to one. *My Dog Skip* plays all through the night. A weirdo in the penultimate row is listening to Nine Inch Nails on his Discman, so loudly I can hear it through his headphones. We land in Atlanta at five-thirty in the morning, two-thirty West Coast time our time. While waiting for our six-twenty flight to Fort Lauderdale, a troupe of Elvis impersonators boards at the next gate, headed to a convention. One Elvis swaggers down the concourse, complete with his own Priscilla in tow decked out in filmy pink baby-doll pajamas. This makes Daniel and me howl. For the first time in a long time, we're having fun.

After we arrive at Caracas International, we find the gate that leads to the thirty-year-old DeHavilland Dash 7 that will take us to Los Roques, and also find there our fellow divers. I'm disappointed to see they're not the colorful collection of nationals I was hoping for. My life is always easier when there's an assortment of folks to profile. I'd heard Italians loved Los Roques, and had never met an Italian scuba diver, couldn't even imagine such a thing, in fact. Perhaps unfairly, I can't imagine an Italian man who could bear to be away from his tasseled leather loafers and *telefonini*—cell phone—for more than an hour. There are no intriguing foreigners among the thirteen of us. We are all Americans, and not just Americans, but mostly Floridians, and not just Floridians, but mostly a species of sad single white guy, and not just sad single white guys, but sad single white guys who are battling a weight problem. I'm not being fair. Only about four of our guys are obese, and one of them is from San Diego, and isn't fat, per se, but he does have an impressive set of love handles. But I don't care, *I don't care!* I'm thrilled to realize I'm still capable of being petty and judgmental and concerned about such a silly journalistic detail.

Diving Los Roques is supposed to be how it was to dive the Caribbean twenty years ago, before most of the reefs were damaged by overfishing, pollution, anchors, and groundings. Of the forty-two islands in the archipelago, only one, Gran Roque, is inhabited. There are small concrete two-toned posadas: yellow and green, yellow and blue, pink and blue, each with its own bright blue water tower. The *Antares Dancer* is moored in the single harbor, a stone's throw from the island's lone disco, whose ceaseless techno beat pounds in our ears all night long.

The next morning at six-thirty, the engines kick on and we power across the Ensenada O Bajo de los Corrals, the huge lagoon at the center of the chain. The bottom is yellow sand, the water, California swimming-pool green. We dive Boca de Cote, a coral garden teeming with hard and soft coral. For days there's not another boat in sight, and no planes fly overhead. There isn't a high premium on what's known in the diving world as "action"—swimming with sharks or catching a great fast current and drift-diving. Between dives, I sit on deck, make notes, and listen to AC/DC or Pat Benatar, the favorite of Franco, one of the dive masters. Franco has long pre-Raphaelite curls, a scorpion tattooed on his shoulder, an impressive collection of black tank tops that started life as short-sleeve T-shirts, and no English, save the Benatar lyrics. As he exchanges air tanks in the tender he sings, "Hey-ll! Hey-ll ees for cheedren!" There is a small video library and one night, in lieu of the usual after-dinner dive, we watch *The Sixth Sense*, in English. Franco starts chortling halfway through, and flipping his curly ponytail over his shoulder. He's not surprised in the least by the surprise ending. How did he figure it out? "Weelis neber change hees close."

I am delighted by Franco, the glass-green waters, the sea turtle sanctuary we visit on one of the tiniest islands, the Venezuelan cuisine that Cookie, our cook, produces in a galley no bigger than a phone booth. I wind up loving each and every one of my chubby fellow divers, who turn out to be erudite, gentlemanly, and a bit shy. They spend their top time reading Paul Bowles and fiddling with their expensive underwater photography equipment. I don't mind the marine-style head that rarely flushes, the shower in our stateroom that runs scalding or freezing, the fact that we have two single beds instead of the double we were promised, or the enormous dead rat we find in the narrow hallway just outside our room one morning. The hallway reeks of diesel and sewage. But I'm delighted by it all, delighted I'm still capable of delight, that all it took was a little *trust* (of Dad's doctors, of Dad, of the benevolence of the universe), a little *faith* (that God was not, in fact, watching the divine equivalent of the Super Bowl while I was trying to get his attention), a little *letting go* (there's some New Agey thinking that goes here, but I'd be hard-pressed to know what it is, since even now I resist all that stuff).

It should have been a clue when, in researching Los Roques, I found a windsurfing company located on Gran Roque, which has no cars, no paved roads, a store or two, a café, the aforementioned disco, three pay phones, and not much else. The wind occasionally howls here. Near the end of the trip it seems as if a hurricane is on the way, rocking the boat, kicking up whitecaps, making conversation on deck nearly impossible.

The fourth dive on the fourth day is at La Guasa, "the pinnacle," located in a channel between two islands. On one side of the channel is the Ensenada o Bajo de los Corrales, on the other side, the Caribbean. To reach the pinnacle, whose coral-encrusted peak ends in twenty feet of water, we pile into a thirty-foot tender that can barely accommodate all of us, our gear, and tanks. The seas are so rocky as we leave the *Antares Dancer* that you need to hang on to the gunwale to stay in the boat. By the time we reach the channel, the tender is slamming into the swells. Up up up! And we are left hanging in the air like Wile E. Coyote, then Down down down the backside and we fall two or three feet back into our seats. My bum carried the bruises from this boat ride for a month.

By this time one of our fellow divers, the San Diegan with

the love handles sitting across from me in the tender, has started "feeding the fish," dive lingo for throwing up. Up came Cookie's big breakfast—scrambled eggs, chorizo, pineapple, and cachapas. Daniel knows all about my emetophobia. He moves to put his hand over my eyes, but the boat lurches and he winds up giving me a knuckle in the eye socket.

By the time we reach the Pinnacle, two more *compadres* are hurling and there's no way out but in. The usual way to enter the water from a boat this small is to sit on a gunwale and roll off backward. I get in position but at that moment the boat tips down, bringing the sea up, tossing me over and into the drink.

The Caribbean is world famous for its gin-clear waters. Visibility in some parts exceeds 150 feet. Today, at La Guasa, it's five feet, give or take. I descend in the murk to the top of the Pinnacle, and search for Daniel. I glimpse what I think are his neon-green flippers and fin off after him. Daniel has a laissez-faire attitude toward being my dive buddy. His general feeling is that as long as he's still in the same ocean, he's doing his bit, which makes me insane. In water with 120-foot visibility this is usually no problem. But now, I can't see my hand in front of me. And it turns out I've sped after someone who turns out not to be Daniel but the seasick San Diegan.

It's too bad he threw up in front of me. I liked him, and now I'll never be able to look him in the eye again. He's a software guy (who actually follows the Spy) and an inventor who's rigged up a waterproof CD player; someone so inclined could take his favorite Wagner or Grateful Dead to depth with him. The problem with his invention is the sound leaks out of the headphones. On this day he is grooving to "Bohemian Rhapsody" and still vomiting.

I madly kick away from him until I don't know where I am. The dive plan calls for descending to eighty feet, then slowly encircling the Pinnacle as we make our way back to the surface. Los Roques is the oldest marine park in the Caribbean, and the fish are huge here, stop light parrot fish as big as retrievers, green moray eels as thick as the trunks of small trees. The only thing I see are tiny jelly fish floating past my mask.

Surge—the back and forth action of the water caused by waves—diminishes the deeper you go. I drop to sixty feet and stay there until my air gauge is in the red. I have no clue where Daniel is. I have no clue where anyone is. As I fin up, I start bobbing up and down. A surface swim would be murder in these seas, but I don't think I have an option. My skills at underwater navigation suck, and there's a distinct possibility that if I try to orient myself underwater, I'll wind up swimming even farther from the boat.

At about forty feet a few black-and-white butterfly fish lurch past, lunging for bits of something pale yellow, which could have been bits of another fish, or . . . no . . . please God . . . scrambled eggs. At thirty-five feet the surge intensifies. I watch my depth gauge: twenty feet, thirty-seven feet, twenty-two feet, twenty-nine feet, seventeen feet, forty feet. Not good, not good. Descending too rapidly is a problem, causing decompression sickness, the bends. I fin in the direction of the fish and the pale yellow bits, which now encircle me like a blizzard. Suddenly, right in front of my nose is the anchor line, covered with small tufts of acid-green seaweed. I grab on, joining the game of crack the whip. There's a diver above me. I can see his blue fins. Just below me I see nothing but clouds of food chunks, and fish wildly snatching at them.

Suddenly, from the depths, I hear the operatic bleating of Freddie Mercury. Oh God, not him. I'm hanging on to the anchor line just above the San Diegan inventor, who's still blowing chow. I'm in line to board the boat, but the closer I get to the surface, the worse the surge gets, pulling the ladder up and out of the water, then bringing it back down with a crash. I've got to time the lulls in the surge. Before mounting the ladder, I need to remove my fins and toss them into the boat.

I've got to grab on to the ladder with both hands and haul my exhausted ass up, plus about thirty extra pounds, if you count the air tank and weights. Then I've got to climb.

I know a guy who chipped a tooth on the gunwale climbing back into the boat in high seas. I know another guy who cracked a shin bone when the ladder plunged back down into the sea while he was hanging on to one of the rungs, trying to get his fin off before starting the climb.

I'm third in line, but I'm not waiting. I start to weep inside my mask. I can't see a damn thing. I won't be responsible for my actions if I don't get away from the swirling food chunks, and the chumming fish, and "Bohemian Rhapsody." And where in God's name is Daniel?

I then do something in full breach of divers' etiquette the world over. I surface, swim up next to the guy next in line, wait until the rail of the ladder rocks down within reach, grab it, and shove the guy out of the way. I know I'll owe him an apology, but if I don't get back in the tender NOW, I know I'll panic, and a panic-stricken diver is a diver on her way to drowning.

Once aboard, I weep. You can slug Karen Karbo and she don't even cry, but rough seas, low visability, and lots of barfing will do the trick. Except, once I was out of my wet suit and had a warm towel around my shoulders, I didn't stop crying. Other divers hauled themselves aboard, got themselves situated, but couldn't decide whether to acknowledge my distress or pretend I wasn't there. "My dad's dying," I blurted out to one fellow who dared to make eye contact. "He's back in Boulder City, Nevada, dying of lung cancer and I'm here on this dive trip having a good time."

His face has the print of his mask on it, and there is a glob of snot nestled in one nostril, but he gives me the kindest of looks. "I wouldn't go that far," he says.

21

We sit in the Caracas airport for seven hours, waiting for our flight to Miami. For some reason our original flight was canceled. We need to show our passport six times to various men with automatic rifles slung over their shoulders. It's tough here. The airport has not had running water for six months; there had been a landslide in a nearby neighborhood—the entire side of a mountain cracked and slid, disrupting the water supply of Venezuela's capital—and the airport hasn't been repiped yet. There is almost nothing to eat in the café—no water also means no refrigeration—and the toilets don't flush in the rest rooms. Old women with buckets full of filthy water and plastic dustpans stand outside your stall and wait until you're done.

This is all good. It matches my mood. I have no doubt that Dad is lying dead in the Palace in Boulder City, and has been for days. The dog Woodrow might be dead too, since he hasn't been fed in who knows how long. How stupid can I be? Have I learned nothing from my mother's death? That bolting just when someone takes a turn for the worse—whether it be back to college for a totally fictional date, or to some weency set of islands in the middle of bum-fuck nowhere—is a terrible idea? The last time I saw my mother, she was in a coma; I would be *lucky* to see Dad in that state. Then I had just turned seventeen; now I am an aged crone with a husband, three kids, and a mortgage. I've apparently learned nothing.

Daniel cannot stand my berating myself in this way. We'll

be in Miami soon enough, and then I can call. To get my mind off it, he suggests a quick tour of downtown Caracas, but Ronald, the captain of the *Antares*, had advised against it. It's not a good time for tourists in Caracas. In the seven days we were at sea the Venezuelan bolivar had plunged from 602 to the dollar to 745. Muggings at knifepoint are not uncommon in broad daylight. Prudently we choose to remain at the airport and have our credit card number stolen instead. (The culprit was a vendor in a curio shop where we shopped for presents for the kids. While paying for the shirts, I left my wallet on the counter to run back to the rack to get a bar of Venezuelan chocolate for my dad. I drove Daniel mad dithering over whether I should get my dad a present; I couldn't bear the idea of buying him a carving of a dugout or a painted plate, only to have it returned to me in a matter of months. Only when the bills showed up for thousands of dollars, all spent in Caracas, did we put two and two together.)

The instant we clear customs in Miami, I flip open my phone and punch in the Boulder City number. If no one answers, I plan to call the neighbors, Elsie and Ron, and ask them to go over and check on Dad. I see now that there are not enough Omaha steaks on earth to compensate for living next door to the father of an idiot such as me. The phone rings and rings. I'm fumbling with the clasp on my purse, prepared to dig for my address book to find Elsie and Ron's number, when Dad picks up.

"Hi, babe, how're you?" I don't for a moment think he's fine—there's a weariness beneath his cheer that's impossible to miss—but he's fine enough to still care about putting up a good front, and this is fine enough for now.

Two days after we return from Venezuela, I fly to Boulder City, my suitcase full of dirty clothes. I've confessed to Dad that I can't afford a rental car, that I need to watch my money, thinking he'll just pick me up, but instead he tells me I'll be met just outside baggage claim by someone named Dave from the rail yard.

Dad says he isn't coming himself because he doesn't want to risk it. Risk what, exactly? As usual I parse the euphemism to myself to no avail. What doesn't he want to risk? The pain that driving will cause him? Driving while under the influence of the methadone? The last time I'd been in a car with him, long before the methadone, we were driving to a western shop in southern Las Vegas to buy me an appropriate hat for the ranch and he veered into the next lane, cutting off a minivan behind us, who then sped up next to me and gave me the finger. I glanced over at Dad; he hadn't seen the minivan, nor had he apparently realized he'd changed lanes.

Alaska Airlines has a policy of giving your seat away if you arrive at the gate less than twenty minutes before they close the doors of the plane. I arrive with fifteen minutes to spare, and discover my seat is gone. I'm relieved to the exact degree that I'm enraged. I thank the agent profusely for booking me on the evening flight, then swear and cry on the way home, telling Daniel I'm going to write an exposé on Alaska Airlines's habit of discriminating against the soon-to-be-bereaved. Now, Dave from the rail yard· won't be able to collect me, and I'll wind up having to spend money renting a car.

At home, I take to the sofa with a novel, then watch *Guys and Dolls* with Rachel and Danny. Rachel pops some popcorn. Danny offers to give me a shoulder rub. I am the luckiest stepmother in the world.

Summer is in full swing here in the pointy tip of southern Nevada, the temperatures creeping into the low 100s every day. Dad must now weigh no more than 120 pounds, with no fat on him that I can see. His ribs are visible through his white T-shirt, as are the tumors that have erupted on them. He sees no reason to use the air-conditioning.

Every time I've visited since he's been sick, I've had to brace myself for further signs of his deterioration. This time, he is thinner still, and there is a portable oxygen machine stationed soldierlike in the dining room beneath Dad's big gilt-framed lithograph of Custer's last stand. When I remark upon the tank, he waves his hand at it. "I tried it once. It smelled like someone's dusty, musty old carpet." And on the fridge, pinned down with four round magnets, dead center, so no one can miss it, his "Do Not Resuscitate" order.

For dinner he asks for clam linguine, in order to start using up the canned goods in the pantry. I make Bev's excellent, simple recipe for old times' sake: garlic sautéed in virgin olive oil, oregano, parsley, coarsely ground pepper, salt, and a can of chopped clams in their juice.

While I'm testing the doneness of the linguine, capturing threads of pasta with a fork, I hear his voice behind me, "I sure am proud of all the things you've accomplished in your life."

I snort, and turn around. "Like what?" My disastrous finances, the eternally fledgling career, my failed first marriage, and this new, complicated second one spring immediately to mind.

"The books. Your children."

"Well—one child. Katherine."

"You took Rachel and Danny on too, when you married Daniel."

Dad is the original feminist. He makes no distinction between Daniel taking me and Katherine on, and me taking Daniel, Rachel, and Danny on. We have all taken each other on. It occurs to me that perhaps he doesn't disapprove of my modern-day Brady Bunch marriage to Daniel at all. After all, he did the same thing, marrying Bev and taking on her three children. They were adults, but the Karbo family trust reflects his feeling that Martin and Liz are his, as surely as am I. For a time I thought it was unjust, but I might just do the same thing, in the interest of fairness, with Katherine, Rachel, and Danny.

In the morning Dad eats half a bowl of Rice Krispies after it has sat in milk and turned to mush. It hurts him to swallow just about everything, including the small white tablet he takes once in the morning and once at night. To this end, he's invented a system straight out of the Karbo Zone: He brings a small glass of water to his battle station, from which he carefully extracts half an eyedropperful of liquid. He drops a pill into the teaspoon and stirs it with his toothpick, which he's whittled to a small, very sharp point. When the white powder dissolves, he slurps it down.

After the cereal, he pushes himself to a standing position using the arms of the chair. I can see a new tumor on the side of his neck. He uses my shoulder to rest on as he shuffles back to his room, where he naps for several hours. I sit next door in the guest room, at the cherry desk beneath all the pictures devoted to depicting DadandBev's brilliant marriage, outlining the novel I know I will never write, the female version of *Strangers on a Train*. There's never a moment I don't have an ear cocked for the sound of his snoring. I am still, this late in the game, so naive. I imagine that he might simply stop breathing and that will be it. I have no idea how tenacious his body is.

After his nap, he shuffles back into the kitchen, down that long hallway, sits back down in the chair using the arms to lower his bony ass onto the cushion, picks up *Hornblower During the Crisis*, lights up a cigarette, and pours himself a bowl full of sunflower seeds. He's making his way through all of Hornblower's adventures. He has long since made it through all the natural-disaster books I've given him. The last time I was here he was reading the one that comes before it in C. S. Forester's humongous series, *Mr. Midshipman Hornblower*.

I remember when I first announced myself an English major at USC—the first major of several—and he suggested I read the Hornblower series, as both he and Bev had been through the series twice and thought storytelling didn't get much better than that. I said I certainly would, all the while knowing my interest in the meteoric career of some naval hero was zip. Instead, I picked up *Howards End*, *A Room with a View*, and *A Passage to India* and inhaled them, one after the other, reading them the way Anthony Trollope was said to write novels: If he finished one during the morning hours he'd set aside to write, he'd place a new sheet of paper beneath his pen and start the next one. For decades Dad and I agreed that Forester/Forster was one of the greatest writers in the English language. There was so little on which we so unanimously and enthusiastically agreed that I hadn't the heart to point out that C. S. Forester and E. M. Forster weren't the same guy.

"Rereading the Hornblower?" I ask.

Dad sticks his thumb in the middle to mark his place and looks fondly at the cover. "He is one hell of a writer, that Forester."

"You know, he isn't the same one who wrote those books I loved when I was in college, *Room with a View* and stuff? That's another writer completely. 'E. M.' And it's 'Forster.' No 'e.'"

"Didn't think it was the same author. I read *A Passage to India* in the army. Didn't seem like the same author at all."

I laugh, punch his arm. I feel his arm bone between my knuckles. It's like punching a broom handle. "Why didn't you TELL me? You let me go on and on all those years about how versatile he was? And remember that lecture I gave you about how someone once said that if you were a genius like Faulkner or Shakespeare you had several voices at your disposal, and if you were just a great writer, you were someone who was able to just find his own voice, and we decided that since C. S. Forester could write both the Hornblower books AND the ones I liked, he must certainly be a genius? Blah blah blah. Why didn't you just tell me if you knew."

Dad reaches out and pats my hand. "You were enjoying yourself so much. I couldn't bear to spoil your fun." Then he asks me if I wouldn't mind going and getting him a pack of cigarettes.

I have made peace with the Kevorkian nature of this errand and am happy to have a valid excuse to get out of the house. At the counter, the checker with the whipped white hair smiles when she sees me. "Marlboro Lights?"

"But of course," I say.

"Things okay? Or as okay as they can be?"

"Yeah, they are, as okay as they can be."

I stop in the grocery section and pick up some pound cake and marble halvah, things Dad used to love.

I remember this as an almost unbearably heart-wrenching time. In my memory, there wasn't a morning when I didn't get up, drink my cup and a half of coffee in the ecru porcelain cups Dad still put out in the center of our place mats every night before he went to bed, check my e-mail, spend forty-five minutes in the already eighty-five degree heat pounding up and down the hills of the neighborhood, sweat dripping in my eyes, fantasizing about keeling over from heatstroke. After my imagined collapse, the fantasy got hazy. Then what would happen? Would someone find me? Take me to the hospital? Or would my guilt at being such a coward overwhelm me, and would I ask them to drop me on the doorstep of the Palace, where I would then need to be tended to by Dad, thus relieving me of a day at least of having to tend to him?

It's telling that in my journal from that week, I mention almost none of this. I record my thoughts on what I need to accomplish on my book, on how I'll handle the revisions on the Los Roques piece. There are endless meditations on, for example, how a coral reef is like an old-growth forest or what it's like to float in a current surrounded by mating Creole wrasses.

I go through e-mail binges, madly double-checking, confirming, and reconfirming minutiae having to do with my upcoming tour for the motherhood book. I make a pest of myself. I am the reason critics of e-mail say that it hasn't made communication easier as much as it's given people more excuses to communicate pointless details that would otherwise be justifiably overlooked.

Subject: biographical information for July motherhood panel.

Subject: one tiny thing I forgot to tell you.

Subject: on related note.

Subject: P.S.

Subject: P.P.S.

Subject: and finally . . .

Today is a big day. At two P.M. Dad's hospice nurse and a social worker are coming for a visit. Even though there is rarely a thing out of place in the Palace, save a pile of newspapers on the breakfast bar, or the neat tower of cigarette butts in my Dad's glass ashtray, and even though Gina, Dad's brand-new house cleaner, has been there within the past week to dust the uncluttered surfaces and run the vacuum, I still tidy up for their visit. The Palace's small dining room is a bulge in the hallway, opposite the living room. It's the brightest spot in the house, with a sliding glass window that opens out onto the carport, and an odd dome-shaped skylight under which sits the small round table. The skylight is made of frosted glass with a slight green tint. I run a dust cloth over the already dust-free dining room table, make sure there are enough chairs for all of us, then I put on a pot of coffee. I sneak on the air-conditioning.

I don't own any decent clothes for hundred-plus weather, and normally I run around in a pair of ancient black Reebok running shorts with a stretched-out elastic waistband that drops them squarely on my hips, and some pitted-out T-shirt. I have jeans and fitted tees packed in my suitcase, and I put these on for the visit. I put on shoes.

Dad's nurse has a name that's too good to be true: Sandra Nightingale. I later joke to Daniel that it must be her *nom de nurse*. Sandra is close to fifty, with auburn hair and blue eyes. Unlike every other person in the pointy tip of southern Nevada (myself included, now that I've been running the hills of the retirement community every morning), she is so pale that she looks as if she works at night, or underground. Her lightly freckled skin is lovely, nearly line-free. Her movements are slow and deliberate. She is thin. She looks as if she might play the harp in her free time. She loves Woodrow and takes him onto her lap the instant she arrives.

My dad is horrified: Lap time for the dog in the middle of the day?

The social worker who accompanies her is Stephanie. She's here to talk about dealing with the insurance, and who Dad can call for help if I'm not here. She looks about Rachel's age, newly arrived from North Dakota, blond and hefty, but not in a bad way. I find it difficult to believe she knows anything about a long, harrowing death. Then again, anyone who glimpsed me tooling around USC on my three-speed bike and espadrilles, trying desperately to pass as a normal sorority girl, would have probably said the same thing of me.

Dad sits down and allows his temperature and blood pressure to be taken. He sits in his white T-shirt and jeans, one leg bone bent over the knee of the other. Sandra asks, "How are your bowel movements?"

"Good, good," he says, nodding. "Can't complain."

"Richard," she says. Her voice is gentle, but she doesn't have time for this nonsense. She tells me that last week there was an "event," one that has made all the difference in their relationship. My father hadn't moved his bowels. It was the methadone.

"I threatened him," she says. "I said, 'If you don't go, I'm going to have to get some Milk of Magnesia. And if that doesn't work, I'm going to have to give you an enema.' His eyes got wide. He was appalled. The Milk of Magnesia didn't work."

"Huh," I say. "What do you know." *Sandra, I can already tell you're an amazingly competent and caring human being but please don't tell me anecdotes about my father's bowel movements.*

"So now we have an understanding." *Oh God. I don't want to know.*

"I keep up with my Milk of Magnesia . . ." says Dad.

" . . . and I don't have to give him an enema," she answers. They are like some musical-comedy duo.

"I'd never had an enema before," says Dad. "Whoo."

I do not want this information. I really do not want this information. We are sitting at the dining room table beneath the frosted, slightly green-tinged skylight. Presumably the glass is a special kind meant to diffuse the heat, but my scalp is roasting. I can feel the pinpricks of sweat. I feel the same way hearing about my father's bowel movements as I did the time when I was in film school and, during one martooni hour—how long ago those now seem—DadandBev reported that they'd seen a movie they'd loved. It was called *Porky's*. Had I heard of it? Had I seen it? They started snickering and snorting . . . remember the shower scene? . . . and the scene with? . . . oh NO! Oh it was so FUNNY! And the scene where . . .

I had to cover my ears and close my eyes. I started singing "Yellow Submarine" in my head—DadandBev, in their cups, chortling over a sex comedy. I was in my twenties. Still, I didn't want to know. And I still don't want to know. Don't want to know anything having to do with my Dad's dick or ass. Not. One. Thing.

This is why children make lousy caregivers. I remembered reading *How We Die* (or parts of it anyway), just after Dad's diagnosis. I'd go to the Boulder City library and sneak peeks of it, read as much as I could take. Then I'd run out the door to the Explorer, where I would sit on the hot upholstery and hyperventilate. The author, Sherman Nuland, said that death with dignity is a nice concept, but utterly unrealistic, that the degradation of our humanity, inch by inch, is part of the dying process itself. It's the people left behind who want their loved ones to be proud, private, and dignified in death, especially if that's how they were in life. How could this possibly be a surprise? We humans never want anyone we love to change. Parents cannot bear to watch their children grow up; spouses have been known to wig out when their partner wants to return to school or loses too much weight. Being with someone who's dying is a species of the same thing.

We need to lose part of what makes us human in order to die. And maybe if we're the one who's dying, we don't mind it so much. Maybe it's somewhat of a relief. Maybe for Dad, discussing his bowel movements in front of me is a relief, a part of the passage, and it's my privilege and agony to watch.

Nah. Never.

After the exam, Dad excuses himself to have a coughing fit in the other room. Stephanie explains how the hospice program works. Once Dad becomes unable to take care of himself, he'll be moved to the facility in Henderson.

"But he won't be by himself," I say. "I'm here. I can always be here. And I know he wants to be at home. He'd rather be at home. I promised when he had the biopsy that I'd never let him go to the hospital again. I know the hospice is different, but you know what I mean. He wants to be here." Stephanie has the kind of benevolent blue eyes that no one could ever describe as flashing. She plays with a small gold ring on her thumb. "O-kay," she says. There's something about the way she says the first syllable that gives me pause. What are her reservations? Doesn't everyone want to die at home? Apparently, everyone does but few people do.

Two nights later there is nothing to do but start a huge argument with Daniel over the phone. While I'm with Dad, Katherine is staying with her own father, and Rachel is at home with Daniel. Danny is in Southern California, spending the summer with his mother. I decide an argument is in order because Daniel is unable to tell me how Danny is spending his days. Both Danny's mother and her husband work full time. Daniel thinks Danny may be going to work with his mother. Or, he may be spending his days at the Boys' and Girls' Club, where everyone over four has to pass through a metal detector. Or, he may be dropped off in the mornings at his stepfather's mother's house. I am lying on the bed in the guest room, an ear peeled for Dad's breathing. He now takes after-dinner naps, then gets up for an hour or two to watch a documentary on the History Channel. I am angry at Daniel for a) playing on the computer while I'm talking— I can hear the faint telltale *tap-tap* in the background—and b) not being concerned where his son is spending his days and c) having two healthy parents. Daniel is long-suffering. I hear the *tap-tap-tap*. He says, "I know. I know."

I rant for a good fifteen minutes. It's a safe emotional amusement-park ride, unlike the one I'm now on with Dad. That morning, after his half bowl of Rice Krispies and morning cigarette, Dad had lain down for his midmorning nap. Not ten minutes later he was hollering for me, "Kare! Kare!" He never calls for me. He would rather die—or, apparently not—than call for me. The adrenaline rolled through me like a big wave in a small channel.

He was lying in his white T-shirt and beige jeans on top of the cream-colored blanket. He never bothered with the bedspread anymore. He looked as if he was trying to pull himself to a sitting position with his abdominal muscles, instead of rolling on his side and raising himself with his arms, the way Sandra has showed him to do. "It's my shoulders, oh God! And I'm too dizzy. I'm dizzy. I'm dizzy." He was bleating now. His eyes were sealed shut with the pain. He tried to reach up and show me, but wound up waving his arm in the air in front of him. I took his arms and put them by his side. I was reminded, suddenly, of the way Katherine's arms waved around days after she was born, like pieces of kelp waving in the current.

I called Sandra. I explained what was happening. Even to my own ears it sounded like nothing to be too concerned about. I talked to her from the other room. I said, "You've got to understand, this is my *dad*. He's never called out for me in my entire life. He's not a calling-out kind of person. He's not the kind of person to call out unless it's really really bad!" I was now also bleating.

Sandra arrived an hour later. In the meantime I gave Dad some more Aleve and told him to stay *put*. We had a mild argument. He wanted to try to get up, but I wouldn't let him. When I heard Sandra's car in the driveway, I went out to greet her, wringing my hands there in my ancient black shorts and pitted-out T-shirt, hopping from one bare foot to the other on the hot pavement. "Is this the end? Is it the beginning of the end? Will it go on for weeks? What?"

By the time we got inside, and Sandra had patted Woodrow's head, and snuck him a little treat from her pocket, Dad was sitting at his spot at the dining room table, waiting for his checkup. "How's by you, Sandra?"

"I'm all right Richard. How's by you?"

"I've got the damnedest pain in my shoulder. Hurts like a son of a gun."

She took his blood pressure. It was 80/60. She put her pale, tapered fingers with their pearly pink nail polish on the big blueish vein on his wrist. His pulse was irregular.

"Your heart's not beating as efficiently as it once was, Richard."

"Huh," said Dad. His head bobbled between his shoulders, his eyes cast down at the surface of the table. It's impossible to tell whether he's trying to digest this news, or he's just being polite.

Sandra called Dr. Swifton on her cell phone, requesting that a prescription for liquid morphine be called in. She told us this would work for the breakthrough pain, but Dad is to continue to take his regular sustained-release morphine every twelve hours. I was still under the impression he had been taking methadone. I realized he'd probably been on morphine since the visit to the ranch. I realized he probably drove six hours through the blazing, boring Mojave while under the influence of a half dosage of morphine. God, how does anyone live through this stuff?

"Is it your professional opinion that he should no longer be alone?" I asked Sandra.

"Yes, it is."

"I see." I felt the tears start to leak and I eased into a sob-a-thon the likes of which I haven't had since Dad's diagnosis. I hiccuped and snorted and wiped my nose with the hem of my T-shirt. Dad said nothing, just reached over and rubbed my arm up and down. Sandra stared at me with neither horror nor a TV movie actress's over-the-top compassion. I felt as if I'd let the team down, crying like this in front of them both.

Why weep at this when other things don't set me off? I've come to the conclusion that it's a sort of relationship vertigo that's got me worn out. Dad and I have been a certain unwavering way with each other for forty years. Before Bev's death, our relationship was evolving on a geologic timetable, so slowly we didn't even notice. Now, it seems, every week it mutates further into something else, something unrecognizable. Today I realized all at once that I've already lost the father I knew. I pressed my knuckles into my eyes. I had a walloping sinus headache.

Sandra left and Dad and I adjourned to our battle stations at the breakfast bar, poised to reengage in the parallel play we resort to out of habit, except that there are things we needed to discuss. It was Wednesday, and I was scheduled to fly home the next day, then on to New York with Rachel on Saturday.

Our two-girls-in-New-York week would be punctuated only by the reason for the trip, the writer moms' panel at the Barnes & Noble on the Upper West Side. Clearly, this would no longer work. It was clear only to me, however.

"But you need to go, babe, it's for your work."

"I can cancel everything Dad, it's not that big of a deal. And you heard what Sandra said."

"You don't want to get a reputation as someone who cancels engagements at the last minute," he said. "You don't want that."

"Dad, I'll be gone a week and you can't be alone for a week. It's impossible. You need me."

"These aren't the sort of values I raised you with, canceling things at the last minute. That's not a good policy."

"It's not a fucking policy, Dad! It's not something I do on a regular basis! But this is an extenuating circumstance, don't you think? Jesus Christ."

This was good. Arguing with your terminally ill parent who is in so much pain, he needs not just one, but two kinds of morphine. I've never sworn in front of my dad in my life. I wanted to say, You're dying, be cooperative, for God's sake. I wanted to say, It'd be nice if you thought about how fucking impossible this is for *me*. But I didn't say these things. This was not the time to have it out. But if not now, when?

"You will disappoint Rachel," he said.

"Rachel is fourteen. She'll have plenty of opportunities to go to New York." The truth is, I agreed with my dad. I was worried about disappointing Rachel. She'd been saving baby-sitting money for this trip, was looking forward to staying in a fancy/cheesy Midtown Helmsley, complete with doorman, room service, and exercise room. "Dad, what do you expect me to do here?" Great. Make it about me. Shit.

"Go up and get me some cigarettes. Would you do that?"

"You shouldn't be smoking," I said.

He ignored me and went back to reading his fucking Hornblower.

I roared out of the driveway in the Explorer. I didn't fasten my seat belt. The notion of canceling my trip clearly pained my dad. The idea was one more unbearable thing on a long list of unbearable things. So I would go. He knew the day I was leaving, but did not know the day I was returning. I would push my flight to Portland from tomorrow, Thursday, to Friday. Rachel and I would go to New York, but we would cut our trip short, flying home the day after my panel of writer moms instead of staying on until Saturday. I would see if I could reroute my trip and fly directly to Las Vegas instead of returning to Portland first.

But who would care for Dad in the meantime? I remembered how Ennie, my mother's older sister, arrived by train from Detroit to tend to my mother. It seemed the natural choice to call her, see if she was available. There was a symmetry to it I liked. But Ennie was no longer the stalwart, capable, humorless sixty-five-year-old dowager she was when she lived with us all those years ago. She was ninety now, and she lived with Aunt Irene and Uncle Dick in a stricken, sun-bleached Southern California suburb. Perhaps I should call the Nutty Mahoneys and see if Aunt Irene could come, though I didn't think Aunt Irene had much of a caregiver streak. She used to smoke her cigarettes, make wisecracks, and play pinochle with my mother. She also taught my cousins and me to make our own tuna sandwiches as soon as we could reach the kitchen counter. She had a fierce temper. Dad, as I recalled, tried to steer clear of her. I couldn't imagine her coming at the drop of a hat, but maybe the idea of coming to my father's aid as he faces death would appeal to her, allow her to prove her usefulness, to prove that in the end, the Mahoneys, despite their nutty shanty Irish ways, would outlive the stuck-up Karbos. Who knows? It would give us a chance to get reacquainted. She could bring me me up to date on

Cindi Su and John. The last I'd heard, Cindi Su had two little daughters on the beauty pageant circuit, and John was a janitor at Disneyland.

At six-thirty, I flipped through Dad's Rolodex looking for Aunt Irene's number. As soon as I located it, I knew I could never make the call. The last time I spoke to her was almost twenty years ago and she was drunk. John's wife, Annette, had had a baby, and Aunt Irene wanted me to come for a viewing. I didn't want to go see the baby. I was nineteen, twenty, and so unhappy, I didn't even know it was unhappiness, I thought it was just life. Aunt Irene was on one extension, Ennie was on the other. They told me I was a disappointment to my mother, that my mother was surely spinning in her grave, that God would punish me for my lack of interest in meeting my new baby cousin. Aunt Irene was shrieking that she would never forgive Dad for remarrying so quickly when I quietly hung up.

Instead I called Martin. Without missing a beat he said, "Oh, my. I've been waiting for this call. I can come Saturday and stay until . . . until I no longer need to stay."

22

The night before I leave, Dad officially begins losing his mind. Brain metastases. I read about them when I was still in my mad research phase, still believing that as long as I possessed information, I could somehow ward off the inevitable, in the days when I still believed knowledge was power instead of just knowledge.

It's the reason lung cancer is one of the worst ways to die. All blood flows through the lungs before traveling to the rest of the body. There, it picks up oxygen and, if you're unlucky, cancer cells, for distribution throughout the body. It's the biological equivalent of an oft-robbed bank branch near a busy freeway on-ramp; robbers knock over the bank and are on the move within minutes; within hours they're spending the money up and down the Interstate. One third of all lung cancer patients develop brain cancer, eventually. Ironically, brain cancer is brutal but contained. It's the only cancer that doesn't metastasize but does its damage from its command post inside the skull.

Dinner is Weezer's Cheese Pie. Again. It's all Dad pretends to eat. I oversteam some carrots, hoping he'll have a little vegetable, even though it doesn't matter. I check my e-mail while he melts his white tablet in a teaspoon, stirring it with his extra-pointy toothpick.

I watch him and decide some joshing is in order. I say, "Dad, how does it feel to be a bona fide drug addict?"

He looks over at me with an expression on his face I've never seen in my entire life. My dad's Clint Eastwood eyes are small and squinty. Their basic look is one of cool appraisal. When he finds something funny, they spark in his brown, angular face. Now, he looks at me as if he's never seen me before. He doesn't say, huh, or what, or say that again. He leans over the arm of his chair toward me, and I lean toward him, and he whispers loudly, as if we are co-conspirators, "I, too, worry about the problem with medical waste."

"Medical waste?"

"I know," he taps the side of his head with his finger. "It's why there are so many plastic bags in the world."

My flight home is at five A.M., Friday morning, the only one I could get. I get up at three-thirty, after my eyes snapped open as usual at three o'clock. I'm nauseated from lack of sleep; the underside of my eyelids feel like emery boards. I pace up and down the long hall drinking coffee, dithering over whether I should wake Dad or not. I shouldn't be leaving. I have no idea whether this new development portends the end, but it can't be good. I zip my suitcase, then stand by his bedroom door listening for his breathing. I don't imagine he's dead, as I have in the past. I know, somehow, that the horror has just begun.

He wakes up with such a start these days, abruptly, his brow deeply furrowed in confusion, as if he has doesn't know where he is. It's the drugs, I imagine. He takes his 10cc of liquid morphine every three hours now without fail.

"Dad?" I call out. Nothing. I step inside the room, beside the California king-size bed. Unlike the guest room, the master bedroom has heavy curtains that block out the orange halogen streetlight. "Dad?" I call louder. I can hear Woodrow's tags jingling as he trots down the hallway toward the room. I'm sure he can't imagine what I'm doing hollering my dad's name in the middle of the night.

For some reason I turn the light on. He's kicked off the

blankets. The flat soles of his big bony feet are together, his knees splayed. I see it all. It's an Auschwitz victim I see, tumors erupting on his ribs, each one visible, his belly as concave as a serving bowl, his penis and dark brown pubic hair seemingly unaffected by the ravages of the disease, his swollen ankles and feet. I gasp, shut the light off. *"Dad!"* I holler, louder now. He starts, the glass of water topples over beside his bed.

"Let me get you your robe," I say. I wind up needing to turn on the light again, anyway. I can't find his robe, which normally lies on the foot of his bed. I find it in the master bathroom, in the bathtub. I bring it to the bedroom, where he is trying to blot up the spilled water on the nightstand with the side of a Kleenex box. It's all wrong.

Once he's safely wrapped in his burgundy velour robe, the crisis is averted. Dad has always looked terrific in a bathrobe, like some forties movie idol. He stands on the back steps of the carport and instructs me to buckle my seat belt, drive safely, and call when I arrive. He salutes as I back out of the driveway. I get the distinct impression he wants me to get the hell out of here so he can die in peace. I drive my little car through the dark, up and over the pass toward the shimmering lights of Las Vegas. For the next few days this will now be Martin's problem. On one Hindu goddess hand I feel guilty, on another I feel justified, on another I feel plain relief, on another, plain exhaustion.

Friday evening Daniel drives me to Powell's bookstore in downtown Portland, where I'm hosting my first panel of writer moms, the kickoff event of the tour for my motherhood book. God, in his peculiar way of doling out of mercy, has seen to it that the event is well attended. Even the cruelest deity wouldn't orchestrate it so an only child leaves her dad on his near-deathbed to appear for a book event attended by the usual appreciative audience of four, three of whom are her best friends. Betsy, the mother of a friend of Danny's, who also cuts my hair, arrives with another friend, both of them with baby daughters on their hips. They have beautiful babies, rosy and blond, who allow their mothers to put them in adorable outfits, with tiny adorable shoes tied to their feet and sweet floppy hats, neither of which Katherine would have tolerated for more than three seconds. Donna, whom I hire once a year to clean out my garden, and who provided the inspiration for the occupation of one of my main characters, arrives with a huge blue vase full of blue and pink sweet peas that fill the car with their wonderful spicy-sweet smell. More important for my eternally fledgling career, strangers are among the friends. Forty or fifty of them, many of whom buy books.

The next morning, the day Rachel and I are scheduled to leave for New York, I lose the dog's poop bag on the way back from our run. My usual route is a three-mile loop around our neighborhood, down Alameda ridge, across busy 42nd Avenue, following the ridge as it loops around and intersects with Fremont. It's a neighborhood of perfect lawns and screen doors made of teak that are architecturally accurate for the era, huge rhododendrons and tulip trees, gardens that routinely show up on the annual garden tour. Winston always poops on the same stretch of parking strip beside the same fine old house on the historic register, and I always pick it up using one of the blue plastic bags *The New York Times* comes in, then leave it beneath the same Japanese andromeda. Then I collect it on my way back. Once, the woman who lives in the house adjacent to the section of parking strip where Winston goes caught me tossing the poop-filled bag beneath her shrub and stood on her porch, threatening to call the police. I assured her that I would swing by and pick up the bag on the way back.

But today, I'm almost home and I realize I don't have the bag. I've left it under the bitchy lady's andromeda. It's drizzling, then raining. The cab is coming to pick up Rachel and me at ten-fifteen. I barely have time to run back and collect the bag. Except, it's not there. I can't seem to remember whether Winston even went in the same spot today, or where, exactly, I left the bag. There's always the chance that the bitchy lady came out and picked it up herself, and now I am really in trouble. I sprint up and down a few blocks, looking for the telltale blue bag tossed beneath a tree, or dropped by the curb, but can't find it. Oh, no. Oh, no.

What am I doing? What in the hell am I doing? Oh, I know. Having a nervous breakdown. Like the word "loser" and the concept of "closure," I've never been sure exactly what a nervous breakdown is. My dictionary defines it as "a severe or incapacitating emotional disorder." Is this it?

I never find the bag.

Rachel and I are both packed, our matching black suitcases on wheels sitting at the front door. She's trying to decide which CDs to take on the airplane with her. I phone Dad and the phone rings and rings. Martin said he'd come Saturday morning and it's Saturday morning. Maybe Martin is there, and Dad is breathing his last while the phone rings and rings. Suddenly, the phone picks up, I hear a brief wisp of breath, then a clatter and room noise. Dad's dropped the receiver. After a long minute he finds the receiver and puts it to his ear. "Hello?" He says it the way you might answer a ringing pay phone, as if you know you'll never in a million years guess who it is.

"Dad, it's me."

"Sorry it took so long for me to answer the phone. I couldn't find it."

"It's right by your bed, Dad. It should be right by your bed. Did you move it?"

"No, it's right here."

"Is Martin there yet?"

"Are you up at Albertsons? Will you get me some cigarettes while you're up there?"

My voice goes up in fear, in exasperation. I ask him about his pills. Sandra told him to keep track of his meds and he'd been doing so on a yellow legal pad with a mechanical pencil, in his small, blocky engineer's printing. "When did you last take your morphine?"

"Well, I . . ." he stops. It isn't the sound of someone thinking. There is nothing remotely resembling cogitation on the other end of the line. He'd done this several times on the night he made the remark about the medical waste problem—just stopped in the middle of what he was doing, like someone straight from *The Man Who Mistook His Wife for a Hat.*

"Dad?"

"Gee, babe, I really wish you were here," he says plaintively. *Goddamn it, why did you force me to go then? Why didn't you ask me to stay? I would have canceled everything, and everyone would have understood. Damn it, damn it all to hell.* I tell him a nurse from the hospice, or me, or Martin, someone will be there soon. I'm supposed to be leaving for the airport in twenty minutes. Rachel sits on the sofa, unalarmed, watching cartoons. I phone Martin and Chrissi's house in Northern California. Martin's only just left and isn't expected to arrive until eight or so in the evening. I tell her about my conversation with Dad, how in the last day or two, he's lost his mind. Chrissi says that Martin is happy I called, is thrilled to be able to help my dad, who he's always loved like a father.

I call the hospice and beg them to send someone out to check on Dad. I have visions of him wandering out of the house buck naked, dissolving pill upon pill in his teaspoon, getting locked in the bathroom. The dispatcher promises she'll send someone, but it won't be Sandra Nightingale. Christ, what if Dad won't let her in? I call Dad back and tell him a hospice nurse will be dropping in to say hi. He wants to know why. Why would she drop in to say hi? I tell him just to let her in. He says he thought I was coming back from Albertsons with his cigarettes. Was there any chance the nurse could bring some cigarettes?

Jesus fucking Christ.

The dispatcher tells me to call back in half an hour. I spend the time stalking around the house in search of my carry-on, last month's issue of *Vanity Fair* in my hand, trying to decide what books to take on the plane and which to pack in the bag I can't find. After twenty minutes I call back; the nurse is still out in the field, i.e., conversing with Dad about the medical waste problem or the plastic bag situation.

I hang up the phone, then try to get a hold of someone to tell me what to do. Rachel is still slouched on the sofa watching TV. I'm grateful she's fourteen, and neither nosy nor anxious. Surely there must be someone, somewhere, who can advise me on what to do in this kind of situation. On how not to screw up. While I was in labor with Katherine, before the epidural, I said to the nurse, "You know, this is really *inhumane.*" I was incensed. I felt as if someone somewhere should have *told* me it would be this way. I'm feeling the same way now. I see that having two parents, who, if you're lucky, die before you is not nearly enough practice. I try my editor in New York (question: Will canceling my New York reading ruin my reputation, so that when my next book comes out, Barnes & Noble won't book me?). I try Betty, my mother-in-law, a nurse practitioner with excellent diagnostic skills whose own father had died and whose mother was suffering from Alzheimer's (question: If I go on this trip and my dad dies while I'm gone, will I feel guilty and horrible for the rest of my life?). But neither of them is home. Daniel is at work and unreachable.

Ten minutes later I call the hospice again. The nurse who visited Dad is already back. After waiting for several minutes, she comes to the phone. "When I got there he was loading the dishwasher," she says. I wonder what in the hell that means.

"It means he's oriented," she says. All I can think of is a confident hiker in the wilderness with a compass.

I impose on this kind nurse in a way Dad would not. I am not a tough Polack but a cheap photocopy. I blather about how I'm supposed to be heading to New York in a matter of minutes, how it's business-related but, more than that, I'm taking my stepdaughter for her first trip to New York, in much the same way my father took me for the first time when I was her age, how my dad insisted I go, how I wouldn't even be here at home in Portland if not for my dad's insisting, and that if I don't go, but show up back on his doorstep in a few hours' time, he'll be incredibly disappointed in me, and that I worry that in his weakened, brain-addled state, being disappointed in me is the last thing he needs.

Finally she says, "If it was my father, I'd get back on the plane and go to him."

Minutes later the yellow cab toots the horn twice from where it idles at the curb. The cabbie is opening the trunk at the same time I open the door and call out from the front porch. "We won't be needing a lift to the airport! Family emergency!"

"Oh yes. No problem, no problem at all." I can tell by his accent that he is Russian, and because he is Russian, I imagine he must understand such a thing. It's also possible he didn't understand a word, and welcomes the opportunity not to have to race to the airport.

Rachel says she understands. She is quiet. The last grandparent she lost was her mother's mother, and she was too small to remember. She hugs me and pats me. She asks if she can bake me some of her special chocolate chip cookies, or ride her bike to the video store to get a movie—maybe some comedies from the eighties? I hug her and pat her. I tell her this: When I'm dying, if you're around and want to take care of me, I'm never going to send you away when I really need you to stay.

For three days I take to the sofa with a novel.

23

Somewhere I read that being with the dying is like visiting a foreign land with interesting and peculiar sights and smells, curious customs, and the sense of never knowing from day to day whether it will be a day of adventure or unremitting tedium. And of course, when you come back from your visit, you are never the same.

I arrive at McCarran International Airport on a Wednesday morning at the end of June. As usual, when I get my rental car, I am stuck behind a couple newly in love who has seemingly never rented a car before, nor have they given a thought to the kind of car they want or how much they want to spend. They gaze at the huge laminated rental-car menu and bicker playfully over what color to choose. I'm fine with this. My idea of the nature of God differs from hour to hour, and at the moment, I don't think he'll allow Dad to die while I'm standing in line behind these knuckleheads.

Ten days earlier I canceled my trip to New York, but on the advice of Betty, my mother-in-law, I stayed put in Portland until the time came when the balance between needing to take to the sofa with a novel and needing to be with Dad tipped in favor of him. She assured me that this tipping would happen on its own, and that as long as Martin was there, I should take advantage of the time, because I'd need my strength and no one knew how long this could go on. Betty said I should send Rachel to stay with them in their manufactured home out in the country, where there are a mess of blackberry bushes to be taken up and tedious documentaries on the History Channel to suffer through (these are also my father-in-law's chief form of amusement).

I spent three days on the sofa reading the Daves: David Sedaris, Dave Eggers, and David Foster Wallace. (I am the only person I know who bought *Infinite Jest* and made it to the end.) I believe I could have gotten my ass to Boulder City a day earlier had I chosen *Notes from Underground* instead, which I reread about once every other year, but I feared Dostoyevsky might have paralyzed me for good. As it was, I woke up in the morning, drank my one and a half cups of coffee, took the dog out for his run, and saw Daniel off to work. The househusband thing wasn't really panning out and we'd compromised on a part-time job with Kozmo.com, the one-hour delivery service, based on one dotcom entrepreneur's hunch that there was money in munchies, that people would pay to have chips, candy, and blue movies brought to them, since they were too lazy to go out and get the stuff themselves.

In New York the "Kozmonauts" rocketed around the streets of Manhattan like bicycle messengers. Rumors were that they were offered drugs and sex for tips. Here in Portland, it was a considerably less glamorous gig. We were a small city with bad weather and a lot of steep, slippery hills lined with houses whose address numbers were sometimes blocked by foliage. Kozmo.com management hadn't yet introduced adult movies— the big mover in other, slicker cities—to the market, so business was slow. The Kozmonauts spent a lot of time huffing and puffing up the hills of gentrifed neighborhoods on their rickety ten-speeds to deliver a single Snickers bar to kids who had access to their parents' credit cards and wanted to see if, like royalty, they could make a grownup bow to their whims. Daniel had several orange T-shirts and was promised an orange scooter to go with it, but the Kozmo service would fail in Portland long before the scooters were purchased.

I don't remember Daniel and me speaking a lot during this time, not out of cold anger but because we'd run out of things to say on the topic of Dad's impending death. We weren't talking much, but we weren't arguing, either. I'd run out of energy to start a fight. When Daniel came home at night he always brought me the overpriced ginger molasses cookies I liked and a movie, which we'd watch sitting on the smelly maroon-and-green sofa, the dog curled up between us. It was always a terrible movie, roundly panned by every critic who'd bothered to review it. Daniel felt about movies the way other people felt about pound puppies; anyone could love a sassy, sleek AKC-pedigreed pooch, but someone needed to adopt those scraggly strays with the bad attitudes, who were only a day away from the needle. The straggly strays were the nearly unwatchable movies Daniel rented, as if in renting them he was sending a cosmic message to the talentless filmmakers not to give up hope. One night, we dropped in at our local bookstore and saw a beautiful pile of my motherhood book with its elegant white cover and pink and orange type. I tried to feel excited and accomplished.

During the day, when I was not lying on the sofa reading a Dave, I was tugging out weeds in the garden, being careful to extract the whole root of each weed, as I'd been trained by Dad. I was already aware of doing things in a way that honored his memory.

I phoned Martin three times a day. Martin is not Clint Eastwood–ish. He is Bob Dylan–ish, as I mentioned, but the young, semimournful Dylan, not the forever-spry Oscar-winning Dylan. By this I mean that Martin doesn't try to put a good spin on things. He's the generation after the Greatest Generation, the one that abandoned the cowboy ethos for telling it like it is. He reported that Dad seems to be deteriorating, hour by hour, keeping mostly to his bed and not speaking much. The last thing he ate was two bites of my Weezer's Cheese

Pie, on the evening Martin arrived. When he did speak it was to ask Martin if he could please go outside and get him a large wheel attached to a stick. Or could Martin please fix the large crack in the ceiling where the moths were coming in. Crazy stuff.

Dad had stopped taking his methadone and morphine, claiming he didn't know where the pain went. Maybe it disappeared through that large crack in the ceiling. Sandra came every day at the appointed hour and said that, one by one, his systems were beginning to shut down. Despite the chaos wrought by cancer, the end is as orderly as a pilot's routine after landing a plane. The kidneys were shutting down, as evidenced by the dark yellow color of his urine. Soon the liver would follow, then the heart. One by one, the systems go.

She offered to send a nurse's aide to give him a sponge bath, but he didn't want one, even though he hadn't showered in four days and it was 106 degrees and he didn't want the air-conditioning on.

I heard about as much as of this I could take, then pretended I had to dash off to breakfast with a magazine editor or have drinks with my agent. Martin still thought I was in New York. I checked the listings at the front of *The New Yorker* to find real museum exhibits that I could pretend to visit in an attempt to soothe my soul. I pretended to see the Paul Klee show at the Met, and the recent print acquisitions by Edward Hopper at the Whitney. I told Martin to please, please, *please* call me on my cell phone if he felt I needed to be there, that I was checking my phone messages hourly and would drop what I was doing, get a cab back to my hotel to pick up my bags, and head straight to JFK to get the next flight out.

Then I hung up and did one of three things: ate a handful of uncooked fusilli, staggered back to the sofa, or dropped to my knees in dramatic prayer. None of the regular praying I was doing while running with the dog or pulling weeds was accomplishing much of anything. I begged God for a good death for my father, but it already seemed a little late for that.

It takes just over an hour to get my rental car. The closer I get to the Palace, the slower and slower I drive. I'm frightened more than sad now. Now, I hope that the God who has a taste for irony has drawn the last breath from my poor dad, and that I will arrive to see Martin and Sandra, the Competent and the Good, on either side of his bed, gazing down beatifically at him. Then, I will be spared. *Coward.*

I apologize to the reader in advance for not being a better heroine. I want to give an unblinking, unflinching account of these events, but I blink, I flinch. I am a blinking, flinching, grief-stricken fool. I squirm, pace, and agonize about all that I should have done for Dad, all that I did and didn't do. I see that Dad, in sparing me an up close and personal view of my mother's decline and death, spared me not just pain, but the sort of self-knowledge no sixteen-year-old should have to obtain, that however much you might love someone, you still are capable of failing them when it counts.

There are good reasons for wanting to avoid someone you love as they lie dying. They will die and go on to whatever awaits them. You, on the other hand, stagger back to your life with your memory permanently altered, and a disturbing image of what's left of the person that overwrites the images that have come before it, like a computer file rewriting the previous one. Seeing someone during those last moments trumps every other prosaic image of them from the past.

There are some old images from the file: Dad, sitting at the dinner table with a martini centered on a coaster in front of him, popping one dry-roasted peanut after the other into his mouth. Here he is standing at his workbench in the garage polishing some bit of some machine with a clean, soft rag. That's him at his battle station in his beige Lee jeans, one long leg folded over the other, smoking cigarette after cigarette, reading a paperback. Perhaps if my trove of mental pictures included him doing something wacky and unusual, like karaoke or skydiving, something out of the ordinary, the sight of him perishing on his king-size bed there in the desert would have some competition, bring some relief.

Dad is lying on one side of the king-size bed when I arrive, his long frame laid out beneath a sheet. It's hot in here, stuffy with the heavy odor of disease, almost like some tropical flower. Martin is dressed in his uniform: black jeans, white tennis shoes, and a short-sleeved plaid shirt. He is not someone whose expression is easily readable, but I feel relief coming off him like steam rising from the pavement after an unexpected storm. He now has a partner in crime. He stands beside the bed as I crawl across the mattress on my knees, still wearing my ridiculously clunky Doc Martens. Dad stares up at the ceiling. He looks hypnotized, but at the same time preoccupied, as if he's doing a difficult math problem in his head. It's an expression I've never seen before. I realize all at once what I missed by spending the past few days on the sofa with the Daves: this receding of his into a new place. It's the difference between seeing someone off on a cruise and standing on the dock waving until the ship pulls away, then continuing to watch until it's no more than a dot of color on the horizon, or dropping them at the dock and speeding off as they stand there with their luggage, trying to hail a porter.

But I'm here now, in the wood-paneled master bedroom in the Palace of the Golden Sofa, with the really ugly quilt I made for my dad after my mother died—rust, gold, black, and olive patches with a Hopi symbol for something I've long forgotten stitched in the center—hanging over the bed as if it were art. I do the only thing I can think of—behave like someone in a movie. I take Dad's left hand and curl it around my own. His skin feels waxy. I call his name, and he cocks his head slightly, as a blind person might. Martin says Dad doesn't seem to have any peripheral vision. Why on earth would that be and why did no one tell me? I'm still asking that dumb question: Why did no one tell me?

"Dad," I say. "I'm here. I love you, Dad."

He wrinkles his brow. I have never seen it this wrinkled, resembling foothills viewed from an airplane. "It's me, Dad, I'm back from New York."

Suddenly, his eyes broadcast his old intelligence. "What's going on in the world, babe?" Just as if this is some normal day.

"Well, Elian Gonzalez went home today."

"Ah, yes. The Cuban boy. What else?"

"It's really hot. A hundred seven or eight today I heard."

"Well, that's the desert for you."

I'm frantic to launch into something meaningful. To ask him about what he has learned in life, or whether he has any great advice for me, and wonder if there's anything else I can say other than that I love him and that he's been the best man I've ever had the pleasure to know, but he interrupts my thoughts.

"Can I ask you something, babe?"

"Yes, yes, anything."

"They're not still playing basketball, are they?"

"Basketball? You mean like the NBA playoffs?" During the time I stayed with him we watched the Trail Blazers play together. He is a car-racing fan, but has never had any interest in team sports, and dislikes the way the endless playoff series preempts all the cop shows he tunes in to on TNT. I begin a dissertation on the Lakers-Indiana final, but his eyes get that distracted, deep-in-thought look again. His consciousness is like a huge ocean-going mammal that surfaces briefly, stunningly, then disappears back into the depths.

"Dad?"

A few minutes or a half hour later, the doorbell trills at the back door and Woodrow, who's been standing at the foot of the bed looking alarmed, charges out the bedroom door and down the hall. That dog's no dummy. He knows it's Sandra, and Sandra has treats in her pocket.

Martin and I sit at the dining room table, waiting. Martin sings Sandra's praises, telling me things I already know—that she's serene, ethereal, knowledgeable, and compassionate, that we're lucky to have her. I note the use of the word "we." On the one hand, I know I will be eternally grateful for Martin's generosity, that he'd dropped everything in his own busy life to come here and be with Dad. On the other hand, I think, how is it a "we" problem when he's been here seventy-two hours and I've been coping with this for eight months with no help? Sandra spends a good twenty minutes with Dad, then comes out with her stethoscope around her neck. His blood pressure is up, she says. He seems to have taken a turn for the better.

"You mean he'll recover?" I say, incredulous.

"No. It means that it won't be within the next eight hours."

"What are we supposed to do? He hasn't had any water in a week. Aren't we supposed to try to give him water?"

Sandra and Martin exchange the briefest of glances. Obviously some bonding has been going on here in the desert while I was rushing off to the Klee exhibit. "This is how your dad wants it," says Sandra. She holds Woodrow on her lap and pets his balding dog head with the tips of her fingers.

"I *know* he's got the 'do not resuscitate' order, but I highly doubt he's got the 'please let me die slowly of dehydration in the desert' order."

"This is part of it," she says.

"How do we know we're not killing him?"

"We're not," says Martin. "This is how it goes, Karen."

I'm suddenly irritated. I detect some condescension. I feel like saying to Martin, You're an expert on snakes, how would you know what it's like at the bitter end of human life? Or, Oh, and when did you join the hospice? Martin is clearly Sandra's favorite, and I don't like it. I ask how long my dad has.

"Probably within the next twenty-four," says Sandra, "though Richard's systems are incredibly strong. They don't want to stop doing their jobs. But sometimes people, even people who are not fully conscious, are waiting for something in order to let go. I thought at first he may have been waiting for you to go, or for Martin to arrive. Strangely enough, if there's a son in the family, many men wait to see them before they die. But perhaps he was waiting for both of you to be here."

Or perhaps he was simply a tough old Polack. For he didn't die within the next twenty-four hours, nor within the next forty-eight, nor the next seventy-two.

24

Martin and I settle in like soldiers waiting for an ambush. In the twenty-three years our parents were married, we've never spent this much time together. For the past decade I've sent DadandBev gift boxes from Starbucks every year for Christmas, an assortment of coffees from around the world. Since DadandBev drank Columbian exclusively—Bev claimed some of those other *foreign* beans were just too *dark*—there are ten pounds each of French roast and Sumatra nestled into the shelves of the freezer door. I've been drinking it for months. Now I no longer have to drink it alone; Martin and I make pot after pot and yak up a storm.

Unlike my father and his mother, Martin likes to talk. We fall into a routine. I'm up at seven A.M., brewing the French roast in my running clothes, which I may have slept in, poised to plunge out the back door and into the nose-hair-singeing heat. Martin's still asleep in the family room. His clothes are tangled up on the floor near his open suitcase and his banjo case. He's brought his banjo because Dad always loved to hear him play. The case remains unopened. Dad hasn't asked for it, and probably never will again.

I've already checked Dad, who is now always asleep at this hour. I stand over his bed, place my hand on his cool, waxy forehead until I feel the tears start up, then I go out running. He hasn't had anything to eat or drink in over a week now. He sleeps with his mouth wide open, his lips retracted over his big teeth. I don't recognize him anymore.

After my run, we sit in the family room with our coffee, having marvelous discussions, the type that make me think about writing a play, where an entire family's history is revealed through a set of conversations between stepsiblings on a death-watch. We compare notes about our parents' obsession with guns, where, when, and how it developed. We reminisce about when they first moved from reasonable California to impossible Boulder City, which Martin adores. I tell him about my first divorce and he tells me about the woman before Chrissi whom he almost married. We talk cooking, politics, music, and books.

Every few hours, like a refrain, we sing our adolescent selves. We roundly hate our parents' devotion to cigarettes, for smoking all those years, even though they knew it would eventually kill them. We're certain they'd be alive today if they'd given up smoking at any point along the way. This is a brand-new experience for me; as an only child I've never had the pleasure of complaining about my parents with anyone who sprang from the same loins. This is the next best thing.

Martin has at his fingertips interesting scientific facts about the effects of smoking on the body's ability to heal itself, and contends that his mother's back problems wouldn't have been nearly as bad were it not for the smoking. We talk about when they met, back at USC. We hunt down the ragged brown scrapbook in the garage and look at the black-and-white snaps of the two of them in the desert. They were beautiful young people.

Sometimes, Martin and I discuss his beloved snakes and lizards, the habitat studies he's participating in, the politics at the research lab he manages, his three spectacular daughters, each one more beautiful and brilliant than the last. We talk about God. He is a scientist to the bottom of his follicles. I tell him I am a believer in Pascal's Wager, that I can't see any harm in believing in God. Back and forth we go. Whenever the conversation hits a snag, one of us gets up to check on Dad.

One of the other things no one told me is how much dying is like giving birth. My daughter Katherine was six days late; after the due date came and went, and the day after that came and went, and the day after that, I gave up believing that I would ever have her. I started to think I would remain permanently pregnant, like someone from a fairy tale with a spell cast upon her. Likewise, the longer Dad survives in this peculiar half-here, half-gone state, the more convinced I become that he is going to live this way forever.

I compulsively check my e-mail, eat jelly beans from Dad's plastic jelly bean dispenser and dried apricots from Bev's large Y2K stash. I take the dog out to pee on the strip of gravel beside the cement wash. I pace, I get us take-out burritos. I pace up and down the hallway while the dog sits with his head cocked, watching. I have work, which I ignore: a Spy due, a column for dadmag.com, book tour business, etc. I've brought my four books to read, but I do not take to the Golden Sofa with a novel. Sometimes, I stare out the big plate-glass window at the quail, the jackrabbits, and the ground squirrels sneaking drinks at the tiny concrete pond. I study the hills behind the wash, looking for bighorn sheep. I never see any. I'm back to biting my nails, a habit I'd kicked not long after my mother's death.

I try to sit in Dad's room, but I seem to have the same sort of ants in my pants that got me put on Ritalin in kindergarten. I simply can't sit here with him. I want my Dad, and this is not him. I put my butt into the gold velvet barrel chair Martin dragged in from the living room and spring out of it again. I go over to the side of his bed, forcing myself to look down at him. I take in his closed eyes with no fluttering beneath their crinkled lids, the tipped-up chin and gaping mouth. Once in a while, I moisten his lips with a cotton swab that Sandra left just for this purpose. Then, I can't stand it another minute. It's like holding my breath under water. I cry, "I love you,

Dad!" and run out of the room. If it's after five o'clock, I raid the liquor cabinet and pour myself some of Dad's crappy J&B on ice. It's so warm that the ice melts almost instantly. Then Martin and I watch *Jeopardy* and even *Wheel of Fortune*. We are in a triple-wide in the middle of the desert in the dead blazing heat of summer, watching *Wheel of Fortune* every night. I don't think I'd ever seen an entire episode of that show until now. It seems to me to be the perfect deathwatch show.

After Sandra leaves on the day I arrive, Dad closes his eyes and sleeps. His sleep is peaceful, but loud. He develops a cartoon snore that could suck the walls of the triple-wide in, then out, then in, then out. He sleeps for ten hours, for twenty. I'm frightened. Martin sits in Dad's room and reads a book in the gold velvet barrel chair.

After Dad's been asleep a full day without waking up, Martin says he thinks he must be in a coma. He hasn't moved in twenty-four hours either. His head is still tipped back and his mouth is wide open, as if he's at the dentist's. His big tan hands are curled over his chest.

I skip my morning run. I skip eating and drinking and breathing in and out. Martin and I wonder what we're supposed to do now. Martin revises his opinion from it *might* be a coma to *what else can it be* but a coma? And since Martin is a scientist and I was a liberal arts major, and since Martin can bear to sit in Dad's room for hours on end without freaking out—and Martin is Sandra's favorite—he must be right. I call Daniel and tell him Dad's slipped into a coma. I also owe the publicist on my motherhood book a call, and tell her that it was good that I canceled my trip to New York because my father has slipped into a coma. I sit at the breakfast bar and play over his final words: "They're not still playing basketball, are they?" I like this as a last sentence. It's complex, mildly exasperating, and witty. I'll take it over some hackneyed summing-up any day.

When Sandra calls to say something's come up and she won't

be there until later in the afternoon, I give her the news. She's quiet for a minute. "It's possible he's just sleeping."

"For twenty-four hours?"

"It's important to know whether he's sleeping or whether it's a coma. If he's only asleep, you need to make sure he continues to get his morphine, otherwise when he wakes up he'll be in a world of pain. You should also try to move him."

I hang up and go in Dad's room, where Martin sits reading. "That was Sandra. She says we need to move him."

"Move him?"

"Roll him over. Or try to. To see if he's really in a coma." She never said this, but I don't want Martin to know I didn't even ask why.

"Ohh-kay." Martin folds over the corner of his book page and sets it on the chair. He's as dubious as I am. He wipes his palms on his thighs. We really have no idea what we're doing. Dad may weigh only 120 pounds—less than that, now—but he is six-two and, once upon a time, possessed of wiry strength. "Did she mention how we were supposed to do this?"

Our idea of moving him is to roll him on his side. Martin puts his hands under Dad's shoulders and I slip my hands beneath his knees and Martin says, "Okay, Dick, we're going to roll you over." As we start to lift him, his eyelids flash open and his brow bunches into tiny pleats and out of his mouth comes a horrible, enraged roar that scares the bejesus out of me. I pull my hands out from under his knees and flap them in front of me. "Oh God, he's mad, he's mad. Look how mad he is."

"We're sorry, Dick. We thought . . . we'll, we're sorry." Now that we've got him up on his side, we think it's best to leave him that way until we get some morphine in him, since, if his enraged bellowing is an indication, he's most definitely in the aforementioned world of pain. Martin reaches for the pillow on the other side of the bed to prop behind Dad's knees.

Lying beneath it is a revolver.

Martin's eyebrows go up, his mouth opens and closes. While Dad's eyes are squinched shut in pain, Martin walks to the other side of the bed and picks up the gun from the mattress. Just as he sticks it in the waist of his jeans, Dad's eyes again flash open. At the dining room table, Martin clicks the gun chamber open and dumps out the bullets.

"Oh God, he saw us take it," I say.

"I'm just glad Sandra didn't discover this. She'd be very upset."

"He's going to be furious, not to mention feel humiliated."

"Do you think he was planning on—"

"—shooting himself? It was for self-defense. He used to talk about having someone else take him out to the desert to shoot him, but I don't think he would. It's too impolite. Plus, it's like quitting. It's against the Tough Polack credo."

And thus commences the longest afternoon of my life. I can't say what happened for sure, but the astonishment and rage Dad felt at being rolled over while he was sound asleep must have enlivened him and moved him into what's called terminal agitation, a term I won't know until much later and will always think sounds like a Charlie Sheen movie. He raises his arms straight out in front of him, like the Frankenstein monster, and shakes his hands mightily. He scoots his skeletal frame around the bed the way Katherine used to scoot herself around her crib when she was an infant. He waves his hands in front of his staring eyes, his long brown fingers curled as if around a baseball. He rotates his wrist madly, as if he's unscrewing a lightbulb in a hurry, as if he's a fussy set designer and his minions have dressed the set all wrong and there's little time to do it right. My urge is to lie down next to him and hold him tight, but I'm simply too horrified. I lock myself in the bathroom and pray for the strength to behave at least as well as people do in movies on the Lifetime channel.

Sandra arrives just before five, with her red hair pulled back in a sleek ponytail, her white nurse's pants clean and without a smudge of dirt or stain that might represent a quick burger scarfed down in the car between appointments or from another confused family dog cuddled on her lap. Sandra herself owns papillons; they're the children of her new marriage, her second or third. She wants to know when Dad last used the bathroom. I tell her it's been days, before I got here.

"If he doesn't urinate soon, I'll have to catheterize him, where we put . . ."

"I know what it is!" I practically shout. "I don't think he'd like that."

"No, I'd prefer not to do that. He's anxious enough."

"He is anxious, isn't he?" I ask. I can hear my own voice rise. I too am anxious.

"Yes," says Sandra.

"More anxious that usual? Is he more anxious than the average person in this situation? I think he didn't plan on this. I think he isn't prepared. I mean, his papers are all in order, and the dog's nails are trimmed and the car is all serviced and he's got Gina the housecleaner coming, but he isn't prepared in his heart, in his soul." I tell Sandra, who has a New Age bent herself, about my pathetic attempt to try to talk to him about his soul, and whether he'd given any thought to the afterlife. It was before we went to the ranch, when I was still under the impression that I could influence the course of the disease or, barring that, alter my dad's personality. I was concerned that he was focusing too much on making sure Bev's closet was cleaned out and the dog had had his shots, and not thinking about what lay ahead, afterlife-wise. I was nervous. My dad wasn't religious. I wasn't about to tell him what he should think, only that maybe it might help, in the name of preparedness, to consider the metaphysical side of what was happening.

The conversation went like this:

Me: Dad, have you, uh, given any thought to, like, your soul?

Dad: What about it?

Me: Uhhhhh . . . how's that Hornblower novel going?

"He always prides himself on being so prepared, all my life it was prepared prepared prepared, and now, *oops!* this is a pretty big thing not to be prepared about, isn't it?"

I indulge in sarcasm even though I know I'm being ridiculous. I know a woman whose mother was a paragon of Catholic virtue, who loved Jesus, Mary, and the pope, who prayed the rosary morning and night, who spent her life performing acts of charity. Her faith never wavered, until she was seventy-hours away from the pearly gates, at which time she wigged out, cussed out God and everyone else for allowing her to reach this juncture, wondered loudly and hysterically about the nature of suffering and where was the good Lord with his world-famous mercy when you needed him, and she died in a state of pure terror. I start to cry. I'm angry at Dad for being anxious, for betraying this weakness. I press my knuckles into my eyes, something a fortyish woman should never do.

Martin says, "There's nothing you could have done, Karen. He is who he is."

"I wasn't talking about *converting* him. I just meant, shouldn't I have pressed him more to give it a little thought? Maybe that way he'd be a little more prepared."

"In my experience, no one ever wants to die and no one is genuinely prepared, in the way we think of it," says Sandra. "You guys are doing very well. Very well. As much as people want to die at home, few people are able to. Usually, the family can't deal with it and winds up calling hospice. Dying isn't as easy as people imagine. Often, the family is too distressed and ill-equipped to deal with the medical issues."

"So you're saying we shouldn't even be *doing* this?"

"I'm saying, most family members have a difficult time."

Jesus, the medical profession and their euphemisms.

"I do have a suggestion," she says, as she punches the numbers in her cell phone. She calls Dr. Swifton for a prescription for more liquid morphine, and Ativan for anxiety. "It might help both you and him to go in and give him permission to go."

The words *go where* pop out before what she's saying registers. "You mean, go in there and tell him it's okay to die?"

"You'd be surprised how comforting it can be to someone in your dad's situation." Sandra tells one of those anecdotes about someone who was on his deathbed for about ten years until his most beloved son told him it was okay to let go, and the dying man breathed his last no more than sixty seconds after the words were out of the beloved son's mouth.

"I don't know. I can't see Dad going for that sort of thing." I tell them about his cowboy ethos, about his feelings over *Tuesdays with Morrie*.

Sandra touches my arm. Her hand is so light, I can hardly feel it. "It won't hurt, and it may allow you to say some things that need to be said."

All right. All right.

I finally summon every last drop of whatever it takes to face the dying—strength is the obvious word, but I don't think that's it—and go to the side of Dad's bed. He's diagonally splayed across it. I sit on the edge near his head and stroke the pleats from his forehead. I tell him I'm here. I'm looking into his staring eyes, and in an instant, he's back. The long involved math problem has been solved and he's able to focus on the world again. He lifts his arms toward me. He's lost the power to uncurl his hands, so he strokes either side of my face with the inside of his wrists.

"Hi, Dad. I just wanted to say that I love you, and you've been the best dad ever and if, you know, if you're sort of sick—well, I know you're sick. D'oh!—I meant, sick and tired, if you're, like, sick and tired of the situation, you can just go. You can leave. Martin and I are good. Well, we're not good. This is actually incredibly difficult. Not that I want to burden you with what's going on with us, that's the last thing I want to do. In fact, we're actually having a pretty good time, in light of what's going on with you and all. It's like having a real brother for the first time in my life, and that's kind of exciting. So anyway, I just wanted to say that you've done your bit here and no one will be upset at all if you just go ahead, you know, and, like, die. It's okay to die."

Suddenly, he's alert. Suddenly, he's glaring at me, not unlike Clint Eastwood in his "Make my day" era. I've startled him in his sleep, taken his gun, and now told him he should stop dragging it out and go ahead and die.

I run out of the room and down the hall, flapping my hands. "Thanks a lot, guys! Thanks a lot. I knew it wouldn't work. I told you, *I told you!* He's mad at me now. My dad hasn't been mad at me like this since I ran away for an hour when I was fourteen. Thanks a lot."

Sandra glances at her tiny gold wristwatch. She rises and removes some adult diapers from her bag.

"What are those? Diapers? I am not changing my dad's diapers. I am not changing my dad's diapers. I have seen his genitalia more in the past few weeks than I've seen them in a lifetime and it's quite enough, thank you." I start to bawl. Martin reaches over and pats my shoulder.

On July 1, the last full day of Dad's life, the washing machine breaks. The tub fills up with water, but it doesn't drain. Martin, who is handy—though not as handy as Dad—believes it may be the washer's belt. We can't find any washing machine repairman in the tiny Boulder City yellow pages, so I go next door to the neighbor up the hill, one of the ladies who brought over potato salad when Bev died. We get the name of the guy she uses. She stands fingering the pocket hem of her housecoat in the middle of her overstuffed living room, wanting the details about Dad, wanting to tell us about being Dad's neighbor and watching him trudge out to the driveway to get the newspaper, month after month after month, in his burgundy velour bathrobe, how he was getting thinner and thinner and thinner. I let her talk for ten minutes, refuse her offer of part of a sheet cake she had left over from some grandniece's baby shower, but allow her to phone the washing machine repairman for me.

While I'm gone, Martin changes Dad's diaper. He gives him liquid morphine with an eyedropper in the inside of his cheek. He daubs his ever-dryer lips with a moistened swab. There is no doubt: Martin is a prince among men.

The repairman shows up in the afternoon. I'm standing at the foot of Dad's bed, fighting the urge to lock myself in the bathroom, as usual. As I've mentioned, Dad is hard of hearing. In the Army Air Corps, at the end of World War II, he was trained to hear things selectively, and for the entire time I knew him, he could never be distracted from the newspaper. As an older man, he was let go from his position as a 911 dispatcher, because he couldn't hear the information accurately. But lo and behold, he hears the repairman at the end of the hall in the utility room, way on the other side of the house, messing with the washing machine. Dad lifts his head just a bit from the pillow, cocks his ear toward the hollow tinny sound of the machine being walked away from the wall, the faint, near-musical sounds of a bolt being loosened, a part being removed and replaced.

"It's the washing machine repairman, Dad. He's come to fix the machine."

Dad lays his head back on the pillow. I imagine I detect a smile in his eyes as they close.

The next morning I awaken at exactly eleven minutes after four, having slept straight through my normal middle-of-the-night insomniac waking at three. I sleep with the door open, and from where I lie on my back on the left side of the bed I glimpse Martin—or someone I believe is Martin; I glimpse a long pale flank—leaving my dad's room. A minute later, according to the red digital clock on the nightstand, Martin passes by my door again, heading back into Dad's room, this time fully clothed. I know it's over. For a strange moment it feels like it used to on Christmas morning when I was small, when something momentous and wondrous had transpired in the dark while the world slept. Another minute passes and Martin appears in my doorway.

"Karen, your father has died."

I'm already dressed in my T-shirt and shorts. I sneak a bra on underneath my T-shirt for no reason other than habit. I am going to do this right. I am going to be brave. I am going to look at all of him. Love at last sight.

My dad is wearing a white T-shirt, the Kirkland brand Costco sells, size medium, purchased for him by Bev before her death, and an adult diaper. His thick wavy white hair, or what's left of it, curls around the side of his head. The top of his head is bald and tan. His eyes are closed—dear Martin has seen to that—but his mouth is cranked wide open, as if in a scream, his lips drawn back from his teeth. His breath smells bad, of teeth and gums rotting. One brown hand is curled up on his chest, the other by his side. Beneath his T-shirt is visible the cliff of his collarbone, the tumors on his ribs. The T-shirt ends near his belly button, where his belly is so sunken, we can see his vertebrae beneath his navel. Sometime just before his last breath, he was still fussing with his diaper, which is pushed down to reveal his huge hips arched up like some exotic southwestern geological feature you might see in a national park. His legs are long and straight, nice looking, even in death, his ankles swollen from the edema, his feet turned out. I was surprised to see his yellow toenails were neatly trimmed. Sandra or Martin, or perhaps a nurse's aide I'd never had the pleasure of meeting, cared for him without fanfare, and undoubtedly against his will.

I stand at the end of the bed and make myself look at

him. I realize all at once why it's been so difficult to look at his ravagement. That body there is mine. The broad bony shoulders. The impressive pelvis and hips. The strong legs and knobby knees. The hands. The feet. All mine, inherited straight from him.

One thing people say turns out to be true: He's gone. Wherever he is, he isn't here, in this room. I never saw my mother's dead body. Martin slips the gold braided ring that belonged to my grandmother off Dad's pinky and passes it to me. I can't think of anything to do, so I lean down and take the uncurled hand and kiss the fingers, now cool, a Slavic gesture of farewell. I put the ring on the ring finger of my right hand. I wear it still.

We call the hospice and they say they'll send a nurse right over to call the time of death. I put on a pot of French roast and take Woodrow out to pee on his strip of yellow gravel. While we are waiting for the nurse, Martin tells me what happened, how he woke up for no reason at ten past four, put on his clothes, went to Dad's room, found him dead, and came to get me.

"You didn't get up and check him once, then go get dressed and check him a second time?"

"It's was so odd. I knew he was gone. I got up and got dressed."

I tell him what a saw, a naked man leaving Dad's room just before I saw him, Martin, pass by in his clothes.

I believe in the unseen and the unknown as much as I don't. Why not? Why wouldn't there be things on earth that will forever defy explanation? Did I see the ghost of my father leaving the battleground of his body, walking down the hall and away into another dimension to be with both his wives? Martin, the scientist, says, "I swear it wasn't me."

The hospice nurse arrives around six A.M. just as the sun is coming up and the Palace is starting to click and groan as the metal expands in the heat. His name is Luis. He wears green scrubs. Woodrow hears the front doorbell ring—a sound he isn't used to, since no one ever uses the front—and leaps around madly, ears flopping as if he's about to take flight. The dog only weighs about fourteen pounds, up from the eleven Dad claimed was his fighting weight. It's the result of my undisciplined dog-feeding habits, of course. The night before Dad died, Martin and I couldn't find Woodrow. He wasn't on his pillow in the family room beneath his bath towel marked RAG. He wasn't at the foot of Dad's bed, staring with unblinking doggie disbelief. We couldn't imagine how he'd gotten out. We went out back and hollered his name up and down the concrete wash that separates the Palace from the craggy orange hills, but found him inside the pantry. His forty-pound bag of Science Diet dog food had tipped over and he was standing inside the bag, choking down kibbles, tags jingling with his mad effort. Everything was going to hell.

I pick him up and tuck him under my right arm as Dad used to do. I let Luis in, and as I go to shake his hand, Woodrow lunges to bite him but winds up biting me instead. Three pearls of blood appear in the fleshy part of my hand just beneath my thumb. Luckily Luis is a nurse. He carries Band-Aids in his breast pocket the way a certain kind of businessman carries a pen.

Luis sits at the dining room table with us to wait for the guy from the crematorium to come and collect the body. We tell him how it was at the end, how half the time we didn't know how Dad was feeling, whether he was in pain, whether he was scared or angry. How we misunderstood each other to the last. How no words of wisdom or pithy phrases were handed in either direction. Luis says death is like that, that it's not a special event like a party.

I take a shower. Martin takes a shower. I make phone calls. Martin makes phone calls. Katherine says, "Oh, Mommy, don't be sad. He got to go to the ranch."

When I talk to Daniel he says, "Oh, Peach"—his silly

nickname for me—then exhales loudly. He tells me he'll search the Internet for the least expensive flight from Portland to Las Vegas. He'll need to use the money I was saving to pay our quarterly taxes to buy a full-price airplane ticket.

Martin and I try to talk about what to do with the stuff, but get nowhere. We pour each other coffee. It's seven-thirty in the morning and we are already exhausted. We talk about Dad's cremation, and I say I think he was already signed up for something through the Neptune Society. He and Bev signed up together. Martin wonders whether there isn't something in Dad's blue safe-deposit box.

I remember this box. It sits on the top shelf of the safe in DadandBev's study. I held it briefly on the night of Dad's surgery back in November. Would anything have been different had I looked inside then?

Martin retrieves the box from the safe and places it on the dining room table. The combination is 000. Inside are all the important documents of Dad's life and some of the secrets, both large and small. There is his birth certificate, in Polish. He weighed eleven pounds at birth. It appears his parents weren't yet married. There are his immigration papers, his passports. Richard is spelled Ryszard. His mother's passport. His marriage certificate to my mother. My birth certificate, on which my name is listed as Baby Karbowski. The legal request for a name change for him, my mother, and me, from Karbowski to Karbo. My mother's death certificate, with her exact cause of death, which I'd never known before. His marriage certificate to Bev. No mention of anything having to do with the Neptune Society, though there is a receipt for a down payment he made on a plot next to my mother at Rose Hills. I think his ashes would be happier commingling in the desert wind with Bev's down by Lake Mead, so I don't give this another thought.

At the bottom of the box is a small yellowing envelope from an outfit called the Detroit Legal News Company dated exactly eight years to the day before I was born, and a year or so before my parents were married. In it is a two-by-two-inch news clipping, a legal notice stating that the Wayne County Probate Court has approved the petition of one Joan Mary Rex that her name be changed to Joan Mary Sharkey.

"Huh?" I read the clipping again. I've never heard of a Joan Mary Rex. Joan Mary Sharkey is my mother. Sharkey was her maiden name, as it was the maiden name of her way-older sisters, Ennie and Dudu.

I don't get it. I do not get it. Martin places the square of paper in his palm, studies it. My mind produces possible explanations. Maybe she, like me, had a couple of marriages. My mother married Dad when she was almost twenty-six; she could have easily been married before that. Maybe one of her way-older sisters wasn't her older sister, but her *mother*. Martin thinks the previous marriage sounds more likely. But why would she change her name before she married Dad? Because Dad didn't know about the marriage? Because my mother didn't tell Dad, the same way Dad didn't tell me? It's my life story: I could have used a heads-up.

25

There have been many recent calamities, but this one looms largest: The damn coffee grinder is missing. This morning, three months and one week after the death of my dad, Sadie, Martin, and I dragged our groggy, exhausted selves straight over from the Best Western knowing we could put on a pot once we got to the Palace of the Golden Sofa, and now there is no coffee grinder. There is the French roast. There is the half-and-half in the fridge, which will be defrosted in a matter of hours and loaded into Martin's U-Haul. Someone must have packed away the grinder by mistake. Martin must have rolled it up in a piece of paper towel and stuck it in a box in the mad rush to get the hell out of here.

We are closing up the house of his mother and my father. Martin is using this occasion to mourn; he is more well adjusted on the grief front than I am, which I attribute to his being part of the Woodstock generation. He picks up every cheap tumbler one of our parents had gotten in a giveaway from a gas station eight hundred years ago and gazes at it. Sometimes he addresses the object, like Hamlet talking to the skull of Yorick. *Mother bought this mug when we were living in Palm Springs. I remember this napkin holder; they got it the year they moved to San Juan Capistrano and were into their gun mania.*

Sad? It's all sad. Horribly, heart-crackingly sad. I try to grieve, but it's like trying to be funny on demand. Mostly, I just wander around in a stupor, but it is a different sort of stupor than the one I experienced when my mother died. Where is that damned coffee grinder? This is the benefit of having an addiction: It puts everything in perspective.

A headache is descending, just over one eyebrow. It's the lack of caffeine. It's the lack of water. You can never drink enough water here in the pointy tip of southern Nevada.

The day before, the eponymous Golden Sofa had been hauled off by grumpy workers from St. Jude's Ranch for Children, just up Boulder Highway. No one else wanted it, neither the Goodwill nor the Salvation Army, nor any of the antique shops I called trying to persuade them that furniture from the seventies was making a comeback in Manhattan and that this sofa was in excellent condition. Every antique shop, without exception, pointed out that Boulder City was not Manhattan and that gold sofas would *never* come back.

The grinder is here somewhere. The bag of French roast is there on the counter, where I'd left it the day before. Maybe the grinder is hiding beneath the flap of one of the boxes waiting to be taped shut, or nestled among the dunes of dish towels and black garbage bags that bloom open on the floor. Perhaps I'd left it atop the six-foot-tall mountain of toilet paper, paper towels, gallons of hand lotion, and pounds of dried apricots – Bev's Y2K hoard – which we'd retrieved from every spare cupboard and closet and which now stood in the center of the living room, like a piece of conceptual art.

I poke around the breakfast bar, between the towers of Tupperware, the industrial-size containers of herbs purchased at Costco, the serving platters, the Crock-Pot, the collections of trivets.

"Okay, losing my sense of humor here. Where's the dang coffee grinder?"

Martin has his head in a cupboard, staring at some plates. He pauses. He pauses for too long. He says, "I bet Liz took it."

"Liz took the coffee grinder?"

"She had given it to our mother, as a gift."

"Liz took the coffee grinder? We're here working our asses off and she needed to take the coffee grinder?"

"For her birthday one year. It had sentimental value."

"Sentimental value? *Sentimental value?*"

Sadie is in the family room, wrapping my father's collection of turn-of-the-nineteenth-century oil lamps in bath towels and packing them away. She knows that coffee or no coffee, we need to keep moving. There is too much stuff and too many feelings.

Two days earlier, Sadie and Lou had come to Boulder City for Dad's ash-scattering, and Sadie stayed on to help dismantle the Palace. If Sadie had not stayed on to help, Martin and I would still be standing in the midst of the half-packed boxes at this very moment, cradling a Ziploc bag full of appliance attachments to an appliance that had long since disappeared and wondering how we found ourselves here.

Sadie pauses. I can feel her ears perk up. Sadie doesn't mind a little drama, and loves to dish afterward, the knowledge of which has perhaps encouraged my temporary insanity. I had one minor fit during my father's illness, not including chewing out his oncologist that one time, but otherwise, I've been a trouper.

I shout at Martin, "Of all the things she had to take, she had to take the fucking coffee grinder that you can go down to Albertsons and buy for like nineteen ninety-five? It's some rare, one-of-a-kind Krups coffee grinder? She's not even *here*. She drives up with her moving van and her movers like she's some fucking Queen of the May and cleans out just about everything that isn't nailed down, as if she's entitled to it, as if she's entitled to my dad's stuff, and she can't leave the one thing we can't do without, the one useful thing in all this crap?"

Martin doesn't deserve this, but he is like my brother now, which means I can now luxuriate in treating him like siblings treat each other the world over. I can display my bad side and know I'll be forgiven. What I'm not quite ready to admit is that Liz probably doesn't deserve it either. However badly she behaved, she too lost her mother, and the man she thought of as her father. Maybe hoarding all their stuff makes her feel as good as getting rid of it does to me.

The previous morning, Sadie and I had snuck out of the Best Western early and gone to breakfast at Jitters, the only coffee place in Boulder City. It sat in a strip mall across from one of two grocery stores in town, between a Cheap Cigarettes and a dry cleaner. Jitters was the cultural hub of Boulder City. There was an Artist of the Month wall—chili peppers and purple mesas in desert dawn watercolors—and every Friday night there was live entertainment. In one corner there was a titty-pink leather sofa and an upright piano of blond wood. We nursed bran muffins and lattes, biding our time until Liz had made her appearance at the Palace, to collect the things she'd inherited from her mother and the things my father had asked to keep until his own death. Or so we thought.

When we got back to the Palace, a Mayflower moving truck was parked in the driveway. A stranger in a black T-shirt with the sleeves cut off hopped out of the back. This was weird. Liz had arranged with Martin to collect the cherry bedroom set that had belonged to their grandmother, the bed frame, dresser, desk, and nightstand with which DadandBev had furnished the guest bedroom. It would have fit in a trailer. This moving van was the size people traditionally hire to move across country. That's because Liz had actually came to collect all the stuff she could: the old VCR and TV and the walnut-veneer entertainment center they sat in; the uncomfortable brown-and-blue-plaid love seat; the wooden TV trays and most of the other tragically out-of-date Summer of Love furnishings—most notably the mile-long Danish modern teak stereo console, on which the preteen me had played *Let It Be* and practiced dance moves on the burnt-orange high-low shag back in Whittier. Liz took the console clock, but Martin got the naval clock that hung over the pantry and chimed twice on the half hour.

It was Martin's idea to put together a party. He invited people from the rail yard and the various museums Dad worked for. He invited Sandra Nightingale. I invited Sadie and Lou. Daniel flew down from Portland. The ticketing agent at Alaska Airlines in Portland recognized him and bumped him up to first class.

I'd thought about inviting my mother's side of the family, the Nutty Mahoneys, but was stopped by some news that made my entire life appear to me like a familiar photograph reprinted backward. Several weeks after I found the news clipping from the *Detroit Legal News* in Dad's safe-deposit box, I asked Sadie's husband, Lou, a retired L.A. County sheriff who now works as a private investigator, to see if he could track down my mother's first husband. I spent a few weeks fantasizing that I had half sibling somewhere, and nieces and nephews galore. I imagined that perhaps I was really part of some large, warm-hearted family who were all nosey parkers and liked to get together on rainy weekend afternoons, the men in the living room watching a football game, the women in the kitchen drinking white wine and bickering, cooking too much of something immensely fattening that made the house smell of sautéed garlic.

Instead, Lou found my mother's original request for her name change, filed with the Wayne County Probate Court. The reason she listed for wanting the change was that Maude Sharkey, the woman I thought was my grandmother, had taken my mother in as a foster child. Before she married, apparently my mother felt the need to legally change her name to conform to that of the people she thought of as her family. Lou also had my mother's birth certificate. She was born in Ann Arbor, Michigan, to a seventeen-year-old girl named Nora Carrigan and a nineteen-year-old boy named Calvin Rex. Calvin, my grandfather, listed his occupation as "Poet/Cab Driver."

Lou handed me these papers when he arrived for the ash-scattering. As a sheriff he's had to cope with thousands of people dumped in the middle of the oddest predicaments of their lives. He didn't say anything as I looked through the papers. Poet/cab driver. There it was. My need to write, my need to *go*. Probably my height, too. The Mahoneys were all weency.

"So, the Mahoneys aren't even my blood?"

"It doesn't look that way," he said.

I laughed. I hoo-hooed and ha-haed and slapped my legs. I said, "No wonder Cindi Su and I looked like we came from different races. We did!" After I stopped laughing I wondered everything: Who were my mother's parents and why did they give her up? How did the Sharkeys get her? Why didn't they formally adopt her? Did this mean I wasn't half Irish? Why did no one tell me? It was another door opening as the door of Dad's life closed.

In any event, I didn't feel up to calling Aunt Irene-who-wasn't-really-my-aunt and asking her and Uncle Dick-who-wasn't-really-my-uncle to explain that Dad, who now *really* wasn't related to them, had died, and that we were having a small get-together to scatter his ashes.

The party turned out half-assed, but that was okay. If there is one thing I've learned it is that sometimes good enough is good enough. You'd think being a mother would have taught me that, but it was being a daughter. People we didn't know showed up, and they didn't know what to say. Martin collected some of the prototypes of stuff Dad had designed over the years and set them out on the sofa console table, including the first mock-up of the Lincoln Continental hood ornament, the cross whose arms bisected the smaller square that framed it, glued to a piece of red velvet. Dad had used it as a paperweight for as long as I could remember. Sadie told a funny story about how my mother used to keep the prototype of the hood ornament on her bedside table to defend us when Dad was out of town on business, imagining she'd stab the intruder with the pointy top of the cross.

Martin and I put out overpriced cheese and crackers we'd bought at Albertsons, deviled eggs, guacamole and chips, the Duncan Hines brownies that I was going to claim I baked from scratch. I wished we had someone to make martoonies, but neither Martin nor I had the determination to either teach ourselves or find someone who could. I wished my mother had been there; she would have put on a fine wake. We settled for beer and Scotch. In lieu of a prepared eulogy we settled for impromptu toasts. The director at one of the museums where Dad spent the better part of his last years, restoring old machinery that looked as if it'd never work again, raised his glass. He said, "The Karbo Zone is now closed. Long live the Karbo Zone." We all said, "Hear, hear!"

I had never been to the place where Bev's ashes were scattered, but Martin knew the way, leading us down the hill toward Lake Mead in a ragtag procession. It was late afternoon, the sun on the brink of setting below Fortification Hill. It was only seventy-five or so, unseasonably cool for this time of year.

We parked in a row by Lake Mead and hiked up a dry wash to an outcropping of Aztec sandstone, the sides striped with desert varnish—the black glaze of manganese oxide and red iron oxide that coats most large rock formations in the high desert. This formation jutted several stories into the white desert sky. It was twisted and sculpted by the wind and the floodwaters that passed through here a billion years ago. The surface was pitted with holes, arches, and cracks, like bone beneath a microscope.

Dad's ashes came in a cardboard box, as had Bev's. DadandBev weren't the sort of people who would want money spent on a fancy urn. I braced myself to do something weird upon opening the box and glimpsing the plastic bag full of ashes – commence weeping, drop the bag, and run off into the desert screaming and flapping my hands — but I was a little past that now. There was a lot of him. He was six foot two, with long bones, broad shoulders and hips. I fed him out onto the desert floor as if I were scattering seeds. You can always hear the wind blow in this part of the desert, even though it doesn't seem windy. Martin, Daniel, and Lou, good men all, sobbed up a storm.

After it was done, I looked up, a habit of prayer that had left me staring at a lot of acoustic-tile ceilings in my day, wondering if God ever got the message. Directly above us, near the top of the formation, was a hole in the rock, through which I could see a patch of fading sky. From where I stood, the hole resembled a heart.

ACKNOWLEDGMENTS

Thanks to my editor, the incomparable Karen Rinaldi, a woman with the courage and energy of ten men, for her commitment and savoir faire, and the smart and generous people of Bloomsbury USA, in particular a few souls who've been eternally available, patient, and tolerant: Lara Carrigan, Amanda Katz, Yelena Gitlin, and Greg Villepique, whose good nature and excellent last name demand special recognition.

I owe a lot to the redoubtable Kim Witherspoon, who year after year makes it her business to believe in me, as well as to David Forrer, also of Witherspoon Associates, who gave me the title and always makes me feel as if I'm the only neurotic writer from whom he receives e-mail.

Danna Schaeffer, Whitney Otto, and Lisa Zeidner are the kind of generous literary friends no woman writer can survive without. Chris Fletcher, Dan Berne, Laura Wood, and Connie McDowell, writers all, deserve an award for graciously suffering more than their fair share of Pepperidge Farm cookies as well as the grumbling that accompanies literary composition.

Cynthia Whitcomb, Diana Abu-Jaber, and Chelsea Cain have generously provided astute editorial comments as well as an impressive array of hors d'oeuvres.

I owe a debt I can never repay to the fine people of the Nathan Adelson Hospice in Las Vegas, Nevada, who took excellent care of my dad and suffered all my foolishness gladly; to Sean and

Terry Barry, honorary Tough Polacks; and to Abby and Harvey Cantor, my true family.

A special thank you to Elissa Schappell, who covered for me once in New York while my dad was sick, and to Dan Newman, whose insight and intelligence never fail to inspire.

And to the classy Jerrod Allen, who makes it all look easy, who knows firsthand what it's like to live with a writer, and who still hasn't run off screaming into the night. Thank you.

A NOTE ON THE AUTHOR

Karen Karbo is the author of three novels, each a *New York Times* Notable Book of the Year, and the nonfiction book *Generation Ex: Tales from the Second Wives Club.* Her writing has appeared in *Vogue, Esquire, Entertainment Weekly,* the *New Republic,* and the *New York Times.* She lives in Portland, Oregon.

A NOTE ON THE TYPE

The text of this book is set in Bembo, the original types for which were cut by Francesco Griffo for the Venetian printer Aldus Manutius, and were first used in 1495 for Cardinal Bembo's *De Aetna*. Claude Garamond (1480–1561) used Bembo as a model, and so it became the front-runner of standard European type for the following two centuries. Its modern form was designed, following the original, for Monotype in 1929 and is widely in use today.